THE MAIN STALK

A Synthesis of Navajo Philosophy

THE
MAIN STALK

A Synthesis of Navajo Philosophy

JOHN R. FARELLA

The University of Arizona Press

TUCSON & LONDON

About the Author

JOHN FARELLA became interested in the Navajo while he was a graduate student in anthropology at Northwestern University. Since that time he has regarded the Southwest as his home but has lived and worked episodically in other parts of the country. In 1986 he returned to Flagstaff, Arizona, where he continues to reside.

THE UNIVERSITY OF ARIZONA PRESS

Third printing 1993
Copyright © 1984
The Arizona Board of Regents
All Rights Reserved

This book was set in 11/13 Linotron Bembo.
Manufactured in the U.S.A.

Library of Congress Cataloging in Publication Data

Farella, John R.
The main stalk.

Bibliography: p.
Includes index.
1. Navajo Indians—Philosophy.   2. Navajo Indians—
Relgion and mythology.   3. Indians of North America—
Southwest, New—Philosophy.   4. Indians of North America—
Southwest, New—Relgion and mythology.   1. Title.
E99.N3F37   1984   191'.08997   84-8803
ISBN 0-8165-0859-3

CONTENTS

[v]

PREFACE

THIS BOOK IS a rather radical departure from the study I initially set out to do. At first, I was going to investigate a fairly limited domain (psychosocial aspects of illness etiology) with a rather rigorous and restrictive methodology. Two things happened. The first was the obviousness of psychosomatics to the Navajos. They knew that all illness had a psychosocial etiology and, further, they found it trivial. I ended up doing the study, but it was not particularly interesting or particularly time-consuming. In addition, it did not seem that there was anything "to discover." And, being a young anthropologist and curious by nature, I wanted to discover something.

The second thing that happened was my growing general awareness of how little I understood about the native view and especially how the pieces fit together. I knew a lot of details, but I had no sense of the whole. At the same time, Navajos insisted that the world view fit together very nicely and that wholeness was an essential characteristic of that world view. The rather rigorous methodology I was using seemed to be of no help in discovering the pattern; in fact, it seemed to be getting in the way. The methodology was too restrictive; it excluded too much.

I then began to read more of the Navajo ethnography in an attempt to make sense out of things. This got me even more confused. For one thing, it seemed to be made up of "bits and pieces" with an attempt on the part of the ethnographer to make sense out of "the data" and put it all together. The Navajos I talked to found these attempts "wrong" or trivial: "Yes, you could look at it that way, if you want to"—which implied that that way of looking at things was not very interesting or very correct.

There were some exceptions to this. Most of them are mentioned in the text. Additionally, at about this time I was given a draft of James McNeley's dissertation (which forms the basis of *Holy Wind in Navajo Philosophy,* published by the University of Arizona Press in 1981). This seemed to be a part of some sort of synthesis of Navajo epistemology. It made sense out of many different pieces by describing one concept.

I had a fairly critical choice to make at this time. To overstate somewhat: I could keep trying harder at what I was doing and keep my restrictive strategy, or I could open up and fairly directly try to make sense out of the whole. This is not a particularly uncommon choice in research of this sort. The restrictive approach guarantees a product and, I think, is becoming more popular in this time when more and more researchers have to justify what they do with grants in terms of guaranteed outcomes. I think this unfortunate; ethnography has usually been a rather wasteful means of discovery, but it is an exceptionally valuable one.

At any rate, I chose to open up the research. My major professor, Oswald Werner, was in Window Rock at the time, so I drove down and talked to him. He was not exactly thrilled by my choice. But, as always, he backed me and, with it, he backed the decision. This is what makes Ossie such a great teacher. He insists on individual choice and responsibility from his students. And, with that, he allows for and respects opinions different from his own. He is very like the Navajos I had as teachers. He and his wife June have been very supportive of me in many ways.

Allen Manning was living on the reservation at this time. He knows a great deal about linguistics, the Navajo language, and Navajo things in general. He was of great help in my investigations, as well as being of help to me in other ways.

My three years of research on the Navajo Reservation (1972–75) were, in part, funded by a National Institute of Mental Health fellowship and a National Science Foundation predoctoral research grant. The Museum of Northern Arizona in Flagstaff allowed me to spend time at their research center and gave me a place to study some of Haile's manuscripts. Katherine Bartlett and Dorothy House were both of great help. Other people have helped with the general ideas: John Schwartzman in particular with the last chapter; Helen Schwartzman overall, and John Engel with the first chapter. Vasilika Zafer was very helpful in typing the final version. My thanks to MacNeal Memorial Hospital for the use of Ms. Zafer and for letting me use other resources. Kenneth Kessell has been very supportive in this endeavor.

I have a personal debt to two women who, in various ways, shared the fieldwork with me. The first is Leanne Hinton. Thank you, Leanne. The second is my daughter, Lisa Farella, who is my link to the future generations that are so important to the Navajo.

My Navajo teachers are mentioned throughout the text although, for a variety of reasons, I have not used the names by which I knew them. Many other Navajos also deserve my gratitude, but again, not by name.

Finally, thanks to my wife Linda for tolerating my less than charming company while I finished this and for being so generally supportive of me.

I am not sure whether or not this monograph will make sense to the reader totally unfamiliar with the Navajo ethnography. If assistance is needed, the relevant concordance headings in Gladys Reichard's book *Navaho Religion* may be helpful.

I also expect that most readers will find my use of Navajo words bothersome or annoying. At one level, my sole intent in this work is to "teach" the reader the meaning of these terms, and, I know of no other way to do it. Brief translations are certainly not the answer. Nor are temporizing definitions, as for example when a writer says, "I will translate X to mean Y, but the reader should keep in mind that it doesn't really mean Y," or, ". . . that it means Y only in a very limited sense." When I read something like this, I certainly do not edit every time I see the word, and I really don't think anyone else does.

I hope that the reader gets three things out of what follows. First, I would hope that he would come to know something about

Navajo philosophy. Second, I would hope that he would come to think that Navajos have some pretty good ideas, rather than just viewing these concepts as one views exhibits in a case. And third, I would hope that the reader will accept the possibility that other peoples in general may have something in the way of philosophy and ideas to teach him.

JOHN R. FARELLA

THE MAIN STALK

A Synthesis of Navajo Philosophy

CHAPTER 1

NAVAJO RELIGION

THE NAVAJOS ARE PROBABLY the most studied group of people in the world. There are hundreds of volumes devoted exclusively to their religion. Included are books on all of the major ceremonials. Some of these are in English; some are published in both Navajo and English. There are published behavioral analyses on everything from what happens in a ceremony to relatively minor aspects of ritual technology. In addition, there are hundreds of thousands of pages of unpublished manuscripts, thousands of hours of audiotapes, films, and photographs, as well as many artifacts in museums and in private collections.

The two major architects of this ethnography are Father Berard Haile and Gladys Reichard. Reichard's work emphasized the rather formal presentation of the religion. She was especially interested in the ceremonials and focused her attention on subtleties of ritual symbolism. With this information as a data base, she extrapolated a more general statement on the Navajo philosophical system. In contemporary studies, Victor Turner's approach is similar to Reichard's.

Haile was a Franciscan Father who spent over fifty years on the Navajo Reservation. His approach was rather different from Reichard's. I think he would have seen himself as something of a Boasian empiricist. He was primarily, if not totally, an ethnographer, and he is the ethnographer *par excellence*. His work is very detailed. He elicited stories ("sacred texts") which he would first transcribe in Navajo, then translate literally and finally do a "free" translation.

When there was a cultural or linguistic question or point to be made, he would include a footnote. These footnotes are an ethnography in themselves. Haile's production is immense; the total runs to hundreds of thousands of pages. Some of his work is published, but most of his texts are used as the basis for other people's works.

With (or perhaps, because of) the volume, detail, and intricacy of this ethnography, there is a void. There seems to be little sense of central or key symbols and, with that, an absence of how it all fits together. One has the sense of standing too close to a pointillist painting.

The emphasis on detail and concommitant absence of synthesis are not just features of the ethnography of Navajo religion, but are characteristic of the way non-Western, non-"major" religions have been viewed in general. This stance derives from two basic presuppositions inherent in how we have viewed the philosophy of others. We have, first of all, presumed these religions or philosophical systems to be of a different order of reality than what we call "truth"* and instead viewed them as systems of belief or even as superstition. The second basic issue is related. It concerns the question of the level of abstraction in an ethnography. That is, are we to take what natives say literally or metaphorically? Related to this is the level at which the native intends his statement to apply. Ultimately, these are both questions about what is to be contained in an ethnography.

TRUTH AND BELIEF

As observers who make commentaries on what we see in the world, we usually distinguish between ourselves and our object of study. As Von Foerster (1970) has pointed out, this is rather more difficult when it is man observing man than it is when men are observing

---

*In the West this is usually derived from science.

atoms. This level of self-reflection necessarily limits what we can know in the study of man.

A rather different sort of self-reference question is asked in epistemology. Stated simply, a statement about knowledge must be true for itself since the statement itself is knowledge. The simplest example is the statement, "All statements are relative." If I accept the truth of the statement, I must take the claim itself as relative; if it is taken to be true it would mean, "It is relative that 'All statements are relative.'" If we deny the statement or if we state "Some statements are absolute," we do not have a similar self-reference problem.

When we have studied the religion or world view of others, we have operated on the assumption that the religion is of a different and lesser order of knowledge than the level of analysis we are employing to study it. If, for example, we set out to study the "beliefs" of another people, we are presupposing that the object of study is not factual. Since belief is of a lesser order of knowledge than is fact, the statement "This is what the Navajos believe" presupposes, first, that these people are very likely mistaken and, second, that I as an outside observer can in some sense distinguish what is "fact" from what is questionable.

In this regard we can look at one of the better "definitions" or formulations of what a religion *is:*

> A system of symbols which acts to establish powerful, pervasive and long lasting moods and motivations in men by formulating conceptions of a general order of existence and clothing these conceptions with such an aura of factuality that the moods and motivations seem uniquely realistic. (Geertz 1973:90)

I take this to be a statement that is not all that provocative and one that most of us who look at the religion of others would generally accept. We may have a few quibbles, but nothing of major consequence.

The latter part of the definition, " . . . clothing these conceptions with such an aura of factuality that the moods and motivations seem uniquely realistic," has two implications. The first is obvious: the statements in a religion are not true (or for that matter false), but they seem true (to the believers) and are therefore, I should think, unquestioned. The second point is that the definition is presumed (by Geertz) to be of a different sort, or on a different level, than that part of "reality" to which it refers. One can call it analysis, a definition, interpretation,* or whatever. The definition of religion is assumed not to be a religious statement.

The validity of this assumption, however, is far from obvious. Geertz is more likely saying what a religion seems to him to be. But in stating it, he states it so as to "seem" to the reader to be "uniquely realistic." So it may be that we have a self-reference problem here. If so, we have the same difficulty that we have with "All statements are relative." Geertz's definition makes no sense when applied to itself. Finally, note that the epistemology of others is always labeled by outsiders as world view, religion, or belief.

The only arena in Western society to which Geertz's statement applies is the domain of science. That is, science seems "uniquely realistic" to us; and it is perhaps the only world view that does so at a societal level. But Geertz, in the broadest sense, is speaking as a scientist. Is he, therefore, speaking religiously or scientifically or, for that matter, are these areas different?

One could argue that the stance of skepticism that I am applying to Geertz's statement is characteristically analytical or interpretative; or, in other words, that the skepticism is itself of a higher logical type than the statement itself is. But to this statement we can readily apply the self-reference test. This would amount to nothing more than the absolute acceptance of skepticism as a part of, say, our religion of analysis or of science or whatever. It makes no sense to argue for such absolute acceptance, for I would need to be skeptical of such a statement.

We can go on with this *ad infinitum*. The process is the same each time. An epistemological claim must, of necessity, be true for itself, as the domain that the statement is claiming to describe includes the statement. A statement of or about philosophy, world view, epistemology, or religion is almost by definition a statement that ex-

---

*The title of the book from which the quote comes is *The Interpretation of Culture*.

cludes nothing. It may be (it seems certain to me) that we cannot make a statement of a higher logical type than the religion we are claiming to describe. In the language of anthropology, there may be no such thing as an ethnologic statement; there may be only ethnography. Further, the ethnography becomes a part of the philosophy it claims to describe.[1] It is more exegesis.

I currently teach physicians and medical students. On occasion I talk to them as if what they regard as knowledge (i.e., disease concepts, the efficacy of medical and surgical treatment) were beliefs. For example, I may say something like, "You believe that there is such a thing as disease." With some exceptions, this approach upsets them.

The scientist, the Western epistemologist, and the Navajo philosopher are all saying, "This is the way the universe is"; they are presenting facts and truth, not opinions or beliefs. If we want to do an ethnography of "Navajo Religion," we of necessity fail if we at the outset only attempt to catalog "beliefs."

Facts or truth are debated, accepted, denied, or modified. They require active participation in the form of judgment on the part of the observer. Beliefs, on the other hand, can be passively collected, but, in doing so, the entire basis of the philosophy (that is, that it is empirical and true) is denied. It is the difference between knowledge as artifact and knowledge as interaction.

If we begin by treating native statements as philosophy or fact rather than belief, we initially create something of a dilemma. For in reading through the literature we find that most of the Navajo statements are unbelievable. They talk about spirits, a variety of gods, monsters, and many other things that we as Westerners trained in a materialistic and scientific epistemology would have difficulty accepting.

This problem presents itself only when we give up on labeling native philosophy as "belief"* and, with that labeling, remove it from the critical realm *a priori*. What we have in the literature on Navajo religion are statements that have been taken very literally.

---

*In the field of anthropology, this stance is associated with and the foundation of cultural relativism.

The level of analysis is very akin to the fundamentalist Christians in our own society, who place great emphasis on "literal" meaning in the Bible.

But, of course, there are other approaches. Some Christians would take the Bible as a metaphorical statement. The references to Satan, for example, can be viewed as a story of an angel who fell from grace and who is physically present in our world or they can be viewed as a metaphorical description of good versus evil.

Natives have been assumed to be fundamentalists. Along with this has gone the assumption that they are cognitively operating at a very literal level. Metaphor, or interpretation, has been the job of the ethnographer and, I think, presumed to be either an entirely different sort of thing than what the native does, or a different level of abstraction than how the native conceptualizes.[2]

I have a favorite Navajo example of this. Naayéé' is a rather important concept in Navajo philosophy. In English it is always translated as "monster." Further, many of the beings labeled naayéé' in the stories seem very like monsters. The most common and most correct translation would be something like "anything that gets in the way of one's life." This would include things like depression, poverty, physical illness, worry, or a bad marital relationship. The "monsters" for some native practitioners are merely the objectification of these relatively intangible entities so as to make them manageable or exorcisable. This is not to imply that there are not fundamentalist Navajos. It is to say that the "metaphorical" interpretation of the term (although it is really an interpretation of the gloss) is perfectly appropriate in the Navajo context. Furthermore, as already noted, it is the most common usage.

This is an important example, but it is by no means an isolated one. The question, of course, is why has this not been noted? It is not because the knowledge is esoteric or especially secret. On the contrary, it is the most obvious and superficial explanation available.

What has happened is that the basic premise underlying our research on the religion of others—that we must "respect" their *beliefs*—has produced unquestioned literal interpretations that can be treated only as if they were beliefs, for from our perspective, they cannot be fact. It creates the native in the image that we presupposed that he would fit.

This emphasis on a literal or concrete level of analysis has a much more troublesome side effect. The questions that philosophy or religion struggles with are important ones. People question birth and death, good and evil, joy and sorrow—in short, the meaning of it all. An emphasis on detail produces reports of ideas that are really not very interesting philosophically, although they are of interest to those who care about pantheons of exotic gods or the itemizing of a religion as another datum for cross-cultural comparisons.

I accept some sort of qualitative measure of, or even evolutionary basis for, epistemology. At a minimum this means that some ideas are better than others. Further, the questions that matter to human beings are shared. We need not just catalog and keep separate the philosophies of peoples *x, y,* and *z;* we can question these people on the same issues and see who has the most interesting answer.

The essential point is that we have disqualified much of what others have to offer by taking it too literally. We have treated Navajo philosophy as if its adherents were all fundamentalists. Much of what is offered is less concrete and more in the realm of metaphor.

Beginning with a fact- rather than a belief-based premise in evaluating philosophy forces us to examine different levels of meaning in an attempt to make sense out of what is being said. Treating something as belief can result in a rather passive acceptance and recording of anything that is reported. Examining something as fact requires an active participation in understanding and discovering meaning. To reiterate a previous point: it treats knowledge as interactional rather than artifactual.

LEVELS OF KNOWLEDGE

Related to this is the conception of knowledge as hierarchical and differentiated according to degree or level of abstraction. On a continuum, this view would have concrete ideas at one extreme and synthetic or abstract concepts at the other. Ethnographies have generally focused on very limited aspects of this spectrum. Specifically, they have looked at the very concrete, and they have described ritual.

The "concrete" end of the continuum used to be referred to as "taboo" knowledge by anthropologists. For the native with this perspective, mastery of the environment is limited to an awareness of things that are safe and things that are dangerous—that is, things to approach and things to avoid. Such knowledge is always incomplete. A world view based solely on concrete knowledge is too uneconomical to be effective. There are simply too many details to remember, and consequently one must "violate" one or more of the rules fairly frequently. The emotions that are a part of this way of looking at things are fear and, especially and predominantly, anxiety. Reichard (1970:80) comments on the first of these characteristics, the lack of economy:

> If a person knew and heeded them all [the restrictive taboos] he could exist only as a hidebound ascetic, hardly free to do much required by his daily life, or most of his time would be occupied in removing the harmful effects of broken taboos.

One of Reichard's informants also touches on the uncertainty inherent in such a view:

> Causes and mistakes you know about are not bad because you know what to do about them [this anticipates my second "level" of knowledge], but those you don't know—they are the ones that are dangerous. (Reichard 1970:82–83)

The world views that Westerners label "psychotic" seem often to be based on the premise that there is only taboo knowledge. At the level of a culture, there are always a certain number of people who behave on basic premises of taboo in certain areas of their lives. One example is the way that middle-class parents instruct and supervise their children in avoiding the evil things called "germs."

Fortunately, it is rather more difficult to find an entire society that has only taboos. Perhaps the closest example is found in Margaret Mead's (1952) description of the so-called "Antler People." In this group of Plains Indians, medicine bundles were traditionally an important element in their control over nature. At the time when Mead visited them, however, there was no one left who knew how to safely (that is, ritually) open the bundle. At the same time, a bundle was much too dangerous to destroy and, here again, there was no one left who knew how to safely let the bundle and its contents go back to nature. Therefore, the people who had inherited them lived in constant fear of making a mistake or of doing something with, or relative to, the bundle that would bring them harm. The once powerful and useful bundle had become only extremely dangerous.

Some ethnographic descriptions of the Navajo describe only the taboo level of knowledge, or even imply that this is the only level of awareness in Navajo world view. Newcomb (1940) is the most obvious example of this. But the more respected Kluckhohn and Leighton (1962) also generally limit their description of the Navajo to normative statements about behavior. The more theoretical statements are provided by the ethnographers.

The second "type" of knowledge emphasized in Navajo ethnography is ritual. From this perspective, the world is not seen as given, but as subject to alteration or manipulation. More specifically, ritual can "correct" mistakes, or anticipate and immunize against them. The ritual expert is a "fixer," both in the literal and colloquial sense of the term. Ritual offers fairly active control of one's environment as contrasted with the fairly passive control that taboos offer.

The three examples of ritual practitioners in our society that come most readily to mind are engineers, lawyers, and physicians of the clinical sort.* Notice that they practice in a setting where the larger context is not limited solely to ritual knowledge. That is, the society includes a higher level of synthesis, call it theoretical, as well. In a society where the more synthetic knowledge is lacking and where ritual knowledge is the highest level of synthesis, some

---

*I am obviously not limiting myself to what anthropologists traditionally label "ritual."

very strange things happen. Generally speaking, in such societies correct ritualistic behavior becomes crucial. It is in this context that ritual becomes compulsive. This statement is true both in that the participants behave compulsively and in that they are operating on the assumption that the "right," in the sense of correct, set of behaviors (especially verbal behaviors) or magic will compel[3] the "forces" to operate as they are directed.

This type of behavior is seen especially clearly when the ritual does not work. Since there is no theory to fall back on, one assumes that a mistake has been made. (One could, of course, also assume that the ritual did not work or that the situation could not be controlled, but I take it as a given that human beings assume that they have the potential to control.) To correct the mistake or to attempt remedy, one can only pay more and more attention to detail, try to do it better and better, in the ultimate sense of making finer and finer distinctions.* The context is one in which there is too much meaning (that is, there is no basis for deciding what is important), and the behavioral strategies we label obsessive-compulsive and the world view we label paranoid are appropriate adaptations to such a setting.

As noted previously, the Navajo ethnography is exceptionally rich in descriptions of ritual. The implicit assumption was that ritual was the most synthetic or abstract knowledge that the Navajo had to offer. Theoretical statements were either not made, as with Haile, or provided by the ethnographer, as with Reichard. What is ironic is that, although this view was incorrect when the studies were made, it is more and more becoming the case. Today, there is increasing concern being voiced by natives that the ceremonies are being "done wrong." Further, when such an accusation is made, the most usual defense is by reference to authority; that is, "That is correct because it was taught to me this way by so and so." Similarly, medicine men are beginning to sit on "advisory" boards that decide correctness in the ritual. Finally, it is becoming more common for medicine men to practice a ceremony without knowing the

---

*In science, this is, of course, the "pure" empiricist's dilemma.

"story"* it is based on. Haile mentioned this fifty years ago, but it is becoming quite common today.

The clearest example or indicator of the level and degree of ignorance is found in witchcraft accusations. In brief, if one is ignorant, he will very likely (for a variety of reasons) label that which he does not understand as "evil." The level and frequency of such imputations today are unbelievable. A perverse sort of feedback occurs with such an increase. With rampant labeling of statements as "witchcraft," knowledgeable people are more and more reluctant to talk about certain things. Coupled with this reluctance to teach, the level of ignorance increases and with it the negative labeling, and so on. In short, there is a deviation-amplifying process which accelerates the process of loss of synthetic knowledge.

When ritual is a society's most synthetic knowledge about the universe, things very quickly become rigid, behavior becomes compulsive, and thought becomes stagnant. People cease creating and dealing with questions and instead become obsessed with correctness—or more accurately, with not making a mistake. Ethnographic descriptions have assumed this state as having existed in Navajo society since the 1930s, but it was not that way. Today it is very nearly the case.

The third and final segment of the knowledge continuum is the "synthetic" type or level of knowledge. Of course, all knowledge is by definition synthetic. The continuum I am describing is divided in terms of level or degree of synthesis or abstraction. At a certain point on this continuum we have the beginnings of knowledge I would label as synthetic. Others have referred to it as theoretical, meta-theoretical, or paradigmatic. There is also a point on this imaginary continuum where the knowledge or the statements become so general that they are vacuous. An example would be, "All living things are alive," a statement that is both true and synthetic but that most certainly contains no new information. Thus, the objective is general statements about knowledge, but not statements that are so general they become meaningless. Within any domain

---

*A primary locus of "synthetic knowledge" is the story.

there can be many synthetic statements (hence the weakness of labeling synthetic a "type" of knowledge); there need not be a single theory to tie everything together (although ultimately that would be preferable).

An example of a highly synthetic statement in Western society is the Second Law of Thermodynamics. It claims to describe a universal (in the literal sense) process, and this general statement has been applied to a variety of domains. A second example, although one that may be vacuous in the sense of being tautological, is Darwinian evolution and its varied applications.

The synthetic level of knowledge allows more choices and, more importantly, provides a basis for selecting among choices. Choice is a problem when there is only taboo. It is especially troublesome when there is only ritual. If something goes wrong and needs to be corrected in the ritual, there is no basis on which to decide among various solutions that are possibly corrective. Similarly, if someone is accused of performing a ritual wrong, there is synthetic information or theory to fall back on and argue the matter. It is not necessary to rely only on authority.

When culture is "lost," as the anthropologists like to put it, or when it erodes, it is the synthetic knowledge or the meaning that goes first. Without this knowledge, nothing else in the culture, especially the ritual, can make any sense.

What is ironic for anthropology in general and the Navajo ethnographic material in particular is that this synthetic knowledge has rarely, if ever, been studied. Navajo philosophy provides the perfect opportunity for such a study in part because of the excellence and volume of the previous work, especially Haile's texts.

THE SYNTHETIC PREMISE

Access to cultural synthesis is through a people's key or central symbols, the concepts that unify.

> If a world view is to make sense out of experience, and give it form, direction and purpose, it cannot be fragmentary or in-

coherent. It must be more than the sum of its parts. It must be a unified whole which has a central hub and theme where everything comes together. Rather than an admixture of diversified themes, world views *tend* to develop central, unifying themes. (Witherspoon 1974:46)

Others have referred to these central or unifying themes as core symbols (Schneider:1968), dominant symbols (Turner:1967), and key symbols (Ortner:1970, 1971). Evans-Pritchard (1951:80) has summarized it rather nicely (as quoted in Witherspoon 1974:46–47):

Every field worker knows, the most difficult task in social anthropological field work is to determine the meaning of a few key words, upon an understanding of which the whole success of the investigation depends.

The task of field work, then, is to seek these key concepts, and the task of ethnography is to explain one's understanding of them. With this understanding goes the understanding of the whole of the culture. The alternative is to treat world view encyclopedically or anecdotally, leaving us with a list of detail without unifying theme.

The overtly ethnographic task not only poses the question of the identification and definition of these concepts but also raises the issue of the locus of this knowledge. That is, who in the society knows these concepts, and how and to whom are they transmitted?

It has generally been assumed that there are specialists who know relatively more than do the other "members of the tribe." For American Indians, these specialists are generally thought to be the "medicine men." But, as noted previously, the Navajo medicine men need not have synthetic knowledge. My primary teachers were not ritual specialists at the time I knew them, and, as it turned out, a part of their wisdom was in this choice not to practice. They gave several reasons for this, the most common one being social. If they intervened in such matters they were necessarily going to incur negative social feelings, including jealousy about the knowledge and the wealth it brought them, anger for accusing some people of wrongdoing and of not curing others, accusations of being a "witch," and so on.

But, another reason given was more impressive to me, and in a sense it subsumed the social rationale. There was a genuine reluctance

to intervene in something which could never be completely understood. To alter the process or the structure at one point produces
"effects" elsewhere that can only partly be anticipated. Thus, the
essence of the stance of wisdom for these men was to realize their
ignorance and to learn to accept the inevitability of most of what
happens. To be wise is to do nothing—but to have actively chosen
this passivity.

Some of my teachers had been ritual practitioners prior to my
knowing them, but they ceased to practice as they grew older. All
had at some point been ritually active in their own and in their
family's lives, but in approaching old age they confined themselves
more and more to the "minor" everyday ritual acts that are primarily celebrations of existence—the use of corn pollen, the spreading of corn meal in the morning and in the evenings, and the smok-
ing of mountain tobacco. All these men could abstract generality
and significance from the details that were (usually) ritually
bounded.

The key concept in Navajo world view and the one I talked to
these men about is są'a naghái bik'e hózhǫ.* Witherspoon (1974:47)
makes this comment on its importance, especially in everyday
usages:

> In Navajo those key words are found in the phrase Są'a naghái
> bik'e hózhǫ, or in its shorter version as simply hózhǫ. Kuckhohn
> (1968:686) identified hózhǫ as the central idea in Navajo religious
> thinking. But it is not something that occurs only in ritual song
> and prayer, it is referred to frequently in everyday speech. A Nava-
> jo uses this concept to express his happiness, his health, the beauty
> of his land, and the harmony of his relations with others. It is used
> in reminding people to be careful and deliberate, and when he says
> good-bye to someone leaving, he will say hózhǫǫgó nanináa doo
> "may you walk or go about according to hózhǫ.

Reichard (1970:45) makes a similar observation:

> Consideration of the nature of the universe, the world, and man,
> and the nature of time and space, creation, growth, motion, order,

---

*In parts of the text I will abbreviate this as SNBH.

control, and the life cycle includes all these and other Navajo concepts expressed in terms quite impossible to translate into English. The synthesis of all the beliefs detailed above and of those concerning the attitudes and experiences of man is expressed sạ'a naghái, usually followed by bik'e hózhǫ́.

So, as Reichard points out, an understanding of sạ'a naghái bik'e hózhǫ́ is an understanding of the whole. In fact, in a very literal sense, sạ'a naghái bik'e hózhǫ́ is the whole. This understanding was the goal of my research, and the goal of this exposition is to convey my knowledge of this concept.

Although, (as Witherspoon noted) SNBH has everyday usages, it is also (and primarily) highly esoteric.

The difficulty with studying these esoteric aspects of the concept is that most Navajos do not understand them very well, or they are reluctant to talk about them. Haile (1968:31) comments on this attitude for Navajo esoterica generally, utilizing sạ'a naghái bik'e hózhǫ́ as an example:

> There are, moreover, certain subjects which are surrounded with more or less secrecy. To the singer this knowledge is his life or "breath," part of his inner self or soul, which he carefully guards in the firm conviction that, the moment he imparts it to others, his usefulness in life is spent. Pleading and tempting offers are useless, the usual reply being that "when old age is upon me and death is approaching, I will tell." As a case in point may be instanced the two words sạ'a naghái and bik'e hózhǫ́, the true meaning of which is known probably to few living singers. But the person and legends connected with these two names are not divulged by those who know even at a price which to us would seem prohibitive.

In this work I am attempting to explain, insofar as I know it, sạ'a naghái bik'e hózhǫ́. And by explaining this, I will be making a synthetic statement about Navajo philosophy.

A part of this understanding necessarily must include an understanding of the end of the current Navajo way of life. Philosophy and religion in general, and Navajo philosophy in particular, struggle with existential questions. And the Navajos are especially concerned to create meaning out of birth and death. In fact, ultimately that is what SNBH and the world view are all about. Along with this, however, there are many things that we would view as inanimate that the Navajo conceptualize as "living, breathing things," including, importantly, a language and a way of life.

So everything that follows about living beings and about animation, the crux of Navajo philosophy, is self-referential. It refers to the stories (which are "animate"), the language and the way of life. The discussions of beginnings and endings refer not just to human beings but to the culture as well. In Bateson's terms it is all a metalogue.

This fragment from my fieldwork describes it very abstractly:

Before, the beginning, the world was without sound and without movement. It was as if there was a perfectly still body of water. And then a stone was thrown into the middle of this pool and ripples started to move out from the center. At a certain point (now past) the ripples started to turn back around and move back toward this center. Time has turned back around. Soon it will be still again.

Traditionally, after a man died he was left on the ground (in a house that was then abandoned) or he was buried. His body then decomposed and, to oversimplify, his molecules were recycled. His memory, his thoughts, and his descendants arc the part that lives on. To put a man into a coffin or to put chemicals into his body to preserve it is viewed with disgust. It interrupts and violates this cycle. Ours is perhaps the only society that has so massively attempted to inhibit or even stop process. That is what technology is, the attempt to deny process.

This points up the dilemma in this work and in much of anthropological research. Ethnography can be a part of this technology. Very often, if not usually, ethnographers set out to preserve some bit of culture that was about to be lost or to die. The act of "preservation" was accomplished in some manner by recording the object of study. Usually this was in the form of writing, but tape-recording, still cameras, and video cameras were also used.

We have also used museums to preserve and display artifacts that had something to do with culture. These are the acts of a society that believes in material culture to the extent that ideas are thought of as things* that can exist outside men's minds and outside a society that holds and practices them.

The Navajos are not especially good at material culture, nor are they in the linguistic habit of describing their world concretely. Archaeologists and linguists who have studied them will tell you that. They are good at ideas, however. A primary theme in their stories is the acquisition and loss of knowledge, the point being that all things that come into existence last for only so long and then cease to exist. The acquiring of wisdom as one ages has to do with the acceptance of this process. Thus, our attempts at preservation deny the basis of the world view that we are supposedly preserving.

A part of my task in understanding what was taught has to do with finding meaning and accepting change in the ideas I came to value. It is again a point of self-reference; the essential notion in the teachings is the acceptance of process. A part of this knowledge is that the context which bounds it must change, and with it the teachings themselves. A part of understanding this concept includes seeing it as a part of that teaching and accepting it. It is, of course, paradoxical. If you accept the philosophy, you must accept that the present ideas will no longer exist. If you care about it to the point that you want to preserve the details of the philosophy, you deny the teaching.

This work is, in part, the result of three years of fieldwork on the Navajo Reservation. During that time, and following the fieldwork, I read all the Haile texts that I could locate. I thus had five primary teachers, four Navajo men and Haile. I chose, for the most part, to use Haile's materials in the references in this work. There are several reasons for this. The first is the quality of his work and his attention to detail. His knowledge of the Navajo language and his resultant texts and translations cannot be matched. Second, the essence of my work is to offer a new synthesis or a new way of putting things together. If it has any validity, it should apply and add new meaning to previous material. Finally, I always have doubts

---

*The caricature of this viewpoint was, of course, Kroeber's Ishi, who spent the last years of his life in a museum on the University of California campus in Berkeley.

about "new" material that argues that the old ethnography was "wrong." What I found instead was that Haile's texts were impressively correct.

I relied especially heavily on Father Berard's work on hózhǫ́ǫ́ji (the most usual translation being "Blessingway"). This rite is the backbone of Navajo philosophy, and Father Berard's text and commentary on it are one of the supports of my work.

Navajos commonly conceptualize and refer to their philosophical and ceremonial system as a corn plant. The junctures where the plant branches are the branching off of the major ceremonials. The "roots" extend into the underworld and, of course, refer to the pre-emergence stories. The main stalk is, on the one hand, a reference to hózhǫ́ǫ́ji, and, on the other hand (but really the same thing), a reference to the essence or the synthetic core of the philosophy.

For those readers unfamiliar with the literature on Navajo religion, it should be noted that there are several ways in which this work does not agree with other views. Perhaps the most important of these is on the nature of good and evil in the Navajo universe. I argue essentially that this is an inelegant way of viewing it. Others have basically taken a dualistic premise. This argument is covered more fully in Chapter 2 and later in the book. The crucial point to my way of thinking is not which is correct but that these are the sorts of questions a philosophy allows and provides a framework for debating.

In what follows, I discuss four general subjects. In the next chapter I discuss diyin dine'é. In a way these are the Navajo "gods"; in a more important sense, they are not. Following this, I discuss Navajo creation, or more accurately, creations. These two chapters serve both as an introduction to the reader unfamiliar with the Navajos and as a correction for what I regard as previous misstatements made on the subject of Navajo religion. The fourth chapter is on ałkéé naa'aashii. Again this is a very abstract notion, an essential part of an understanding of this philosophy. In some ways the concept is more esoteric than są'a naghái bik'e hózhǫ́. It is seldom mentioned in ritual and is commonly associated with "witchcraft" in these times of relative ignorance. Thus, people are very reluctant to talk about it. Then, we will discuss są'a naghái bik'e hózhǫ́, although in a way, this is the topic of the entire monograph. For, diyin dine'é, creations, and ałkéé naa'aashii are all subsumed by this concept.

The final chapter elaborates the issue of change in Navajo epistemology. This is crucial to understanding these ideas and parallels the process my teachers must have gone through. As noted, the question is how to find meaning in the loss of something that is highly valued. The answer is that the world view rests on the acceptance of process; it predicts and accepts loss and change.

CHAPTER 2

DIYIN DINE'É:
GODS AND MEN

A GOOD PLACE TO BEGIN this discussion is with the Navajo concept diyin. To arrive at an understanding of this idea, the native studies the actions and the statements of diyin dine'é or diyinii.* These are recounted in the stories and they are experienced directly, because the Wind, the Thunder, the Sun, the Rain—in short, the class of entities we label natural phenomena—are all diyinii. It is tempting to overlook the experiential, for it seems rather mundane when contrasted with the drama of Navajo stories and ceremonies, or when compared with the more dramatic experiential states of possession and hallucination experienced by other peoples. But, this firsthand experience of diyinii exists, and it is ominipresent, not just occasional. It is the experience of being a part of something larger and grander than oneself, the direct experience of oneness, something quite profound if not conspicuous.

The stories describe the most elemental human acts, and they cover those that are the most intense and the most remembered.

---

*The terms diyinii and diyin dine'é are not identical, but I use them as synonyms here primarily to have an economical, nonrepetitious means of reference. The usual translation label for these phrases is "Holy People." Although I do not consider this gloss accurate, I mention it here because it will appear in quotations.

Breathing, giving birth, death, defecation, the raising and consumption of food, these and almost everything else that a human being thinks, says, or does, are, in a sense, "sacred" acts. The stories describe experience, and in that sense they create it; but the stories are also contingent on experience. There is no faith here; if a person listens to the stories, thinks about them, and relates them to his own life, he will necessarily perceive that they are true. Having learned this, he will experience more; having experienced more, he will understand the stories better, and so on.

Grey Mustache describes this process to the children of the People:

> Children, I want you to know how I think. I'm very old, Grandchildren, Children, and what I have to offer you is getting scarce. The old people's knowledge is that by which one looks up and sees the world after the sun has risen. By means of knowledge, one makes one's way through the day from the time the first light is seen in the East until the darkness rises and finally the world becomes dark. At that time, one can no longer see.
>
> And so it is that when one doesn't know the traditions one has nothing to light one's way. It is as though one lived with a covering on one's eyes, as if one lived being deaf and blind. Yet when one knows the traditions, one has vision to see as far as Black Mountain and beyond, to see all the way to where the land meets the ocean. It's as though one's vision becomes as good as that. I long for you to realize what it is that your ancestors had, and how it is that some of us old people still live our lives.
>
> If you would only come to know our words and would take the time to think them over, you would come to know that they were true and valuable. These teachings are of a kind that you would someday want to use in teaching your own children. But hardly any of you will listen to us anymore, even though there are now so many of you. And so it is up to those few of you who do want to learn. You will never be alone. You'll learn one thing after another and the old people will help you. Then, the more you learn, the more you'll be able to tie things together and to understand.
>
> And so it is up to those of you who are really interested to listen and to make sense for yourselves of what we say. Then you will come to be respected and sought after for advice . . . people will think of you as a living sparking fire.
>
> And then here's another thing. Others will speak of the dead in the past tense, but you knowledgeable ones will say "So and so

says this," even though the teller is dead. Though the person had died, the knowledge has been passed on and is alive. . . .*

The everydayness and the constancy of a world view or a religion is something that is very difficult for us as Westerners to appreciate, as we are inclined to see a strong separation between gods and men. It is not surprising, therefore, that analyses of Navajo religion have often claimed such a separation. It is true that diyin dine'é, at a certain point in time, did "leave" the earth-surface people, at which point they warned them:

> This past day and this night alone you have again seen Holy People. From this day on until the end of days you shall not see them again (in person), that is final! (Wyman 1970:324–25)

But, they went on to say:

> . . . Although you apparently can see the wind (now), you will only hear its voice (in the future). You will see a holy one when you see a white feather (of an eagle), when you see a bluebird, a yellowbird, a big blackbird. . . . And when white corn, yellow corn, blue corn, variegated corn, and plants move (grow?) this way, you will be seeing a holy one. . . . And too, every day, every night, every dawn, every year your mother (Changing Woman) will be instructing you (in person). Arise, go to sleep, eat, drink, defecate, urinate, by means of all these she will be instructing you! (Wyman 1970: 324–25)

In addition to this spatial proximity, there is an emotional and genealogical closeness between diyinii and earth-surface dine'é. Through the clan organization, the Navajo descend directly from diyinii (Reichard 1970: 58–59). In addition, the emotional states of diyin dine'é are described in very human-like terms (perhaps the converse of this statement should be emphasized). These "gods" are not aloof and without emotion. They are described as feeling things like worry, jealousy, desire, anger, fear, and joy.

But, the class of the ones that are diyin is not even that discrete. The boundary between gods and men is flexible and ever changing.

---

*This statement was elicited and translated by Allen Manning and Frank Harvey.

The typical chantway story describes how an individual comes into association with diyin dine'é, from whom he learns things of importance. He then returns, usually to his family, and recounts to them what he has learned. He then permanently leaves the company of men (it is perhaps more accurate to say that he gives up permanently his human form) and returns to, as well as permanently becoming, diyinii. Reichard (1970: 55–56) describes this process:

> Many chant myths follow a certain pattern: a youth, for one reason or another, cuts himself adrift from his family, enters upon a series of adventures, experiences terrifying enough to break the hardiest, which make him for some time an associate of deity. Eventually he leaves the earth to join the gods, whereupon he himself becomes divine. Many legends end with the disappearance of the hero; none tells which god he became or what his permanent human-deific position is. It is generally understood that Monster Slayer and Child-of-the-water are the War Gods, having been transformed from earthly beings. . . .

It is the possession of knowledge that makes one (to use Reichard's term) "divine." Rather than "divineness" existing as an inseparable attribute of a being, it is acquired, and it is a quality or ability that one may choose to use or not to use. In contrast, other students of Navajo religion have emphasized the superhuman powers of diyinii:

> In Navajo conception two world of forces oppose each other, as it were. One world of forces may be comprised in the generic term of diyin dine'é, which we render holy people, or supernaturals, in the sense of being superhuman, or endowed with a power which excels the human. . . . (Haile 1943: 65)

These powers are used to argue for a strong boundary or separation between the sacred and the profane (Kluckhohn and Leighton 1962: 180).

First and foremost of these "supernatural" features is the creative ability of diyinii. Further, everything that exists has, for the Navajo, been created. This includes emotions, animate beings, natural phenomena, knowledge, language, places, states (like birth and death), everything. But, acts of creation do not just happen; they are achieved ritually, and the successful creative ritual performance depends on acquiring a large body of rather precise knowledge. Often the stories describe how a particular "god" goes about gathering information regarding a certain type of creation from several other diyin dine'é, each of whom knows only a particular part of what is needed.

This creative process is, in fact, continually replicated today—not just by the gods but more commonly by men. It consists simply of the acquisition and the ritual exercise of knowledge. This is especially true for hózhǫ́ǫ́jí which is, for the Navajo and for diyinii, *the* creation ritual. The stories describe this process as well as instruct people today in how to bring it about. This in itself is a metalogue, for the "people" who are described as participants in the stories are themselves receiving instruction. That is, the stories which are instruction have as their primary theme diyinii themselves being instructed. These two facts—knowledge being acquired through personal instruction (or personal experience) and the necessity of ritually exercising what is learned for it to have effect (or power)—are features of the Navajo universe generally. That is, they are atemporal and not reflective of a sacred/profane distinction.

A second feature that is given as characteristic of diyinii is their sensory superiority or excellence. They are often talked about as being able to see "great distances," a statement that refers to temporal as well as spatial distance. Similarly, they are often informed of the future by nítch'i biyázhí (a possible gloss is "little wind" or "child wind") who is near or at their ears. In short, they can hear "great distances." But the ability to "see" the future and to see great distances is held by stargazers and users of datura. Both of these activities are forms of what Westerners call "divination," and they are in use by Navajos today. Here again rituals are associated with these practices, and the future may be perceived in this manner only if the rites are properly implemented. Traditionally, Navajos also had the ability to divine by "listening." This practice is not in use so much, if at all, today; but a form of "listening" may accompany datura divination. Finally, one may also hear things "on" or "through" the wind or see things in dreams. Events such as these are happening constantly; in fact, too much is happening. Ritual is a means of bringing the things into focus, of distilling the events that matter. But, in order to understand even the everyday experience of perception, one must be instructed.

A third characteristic of diyinii that appears frequently in the stories is their mode of movement. It is described as álílee bigááł, where bigááł is usually glossed as "moving power," or a being's characteristic way of moving. It is an indispensable part of a life form. One can, for example, refer to the characteristic way in which a bear moves or the way a particular man, John Nez, moves. Álílee is usually glossed as "supernatural," but this does not help much. One can also say álílee naaghá, which refers to a particular act of movement; that is, "he moved or walked here and there in an álílee manner." The movement of diyin dine'é is often described in the stories as álílee. They move by means of Rainbow, Thunder, the Wind, Sunrays, and many other things. Their movements from one place to another is extremely rapid: "You just think of the place and you are there."* In addition, they are often invisible, and one can hear them (or sense them in other ways) only by ritually making one's own senses more excellent. Often in a story, people look away for a moment and, upon returning their glance, they suddenly see someone standing there; they turn away again and, when they look back, the person is gone. This occurrence is always taken as evidence that they have just looked at someone who was diyin, or "a great one."

In certain instances, however, human beings can move this way as well. Today a skinwalker's† or werewolf's movements can be described as álílee; they move quickly and cannot be seen or heard. Warriors and hunters may learn to move this way, and, of course, such knowledge is greatly valued. Moreover, this way of moving is

---

*Several men said it in just this way.

†"Skinwalker" is the most usual gloss that a Navajo bilingual will give to yeenaaldłooshii. These are were-animals, humans that take on animal form. Most commonly, lay people associate them with witchcraft. The skinwalker is capable of great speed, invisibility, and various other powers. See Kluckhohn (1944).

assumed in other situations. Hóchx̨ǫ́ǫ́jí prayers describe the movement of the singer and patient into and out of the underworld. Corporeally, of course, they remain wherever the ceremony is taking place, and this is perceived and agreed upon by all. But, a part of the person has made the journey described in the prayer. Similarly, in dreams the body remains where it is sleeping, but a part of the person has traveled elsewhere. On that part's return, the experiences that have occurred spatiotemporally remote from the body are remembered. If the wandering part of the person does not return, the person dies.

These creative, sensory, and motor abilities and processes are all viewed as "natural." They exist but in an uncontrolled state. In attaining knowledge one learns what they are and how to control them. A dream, for example, can be a very frightening experience, but it is less so if one knows what has happened and, further, if one knows that there are people who are capable of "controlling" the dream in various ways.

In these examples, then, I have tried to demonstrate that the "supernatural" or "superhuman" powers of diyinii are contingent on knowledge that is available not only to diyinii but also to man. Power presupposes knowledge and does not exist as an inseparable attribute of a being, as in the case of the Christian God. The question that we must now ask is whether or not this statement is more generally true. That is, is diyin an attribute primarily of a class of beings who are rather rigidly bounded in space and time, or does it refer to a process of becoming through learning that is available to all "thinking" beings?

The statement of Grey Mustache quoted above reflects the importance he placed on learning the stories. He would always describe his life, and the life process in general, in terms of the progressive acquisition of knowledge. As one came to know more, one became more and more like diyinii. At death, one who knew the stories would die without leaving a ch'į́įdii (a term usually glossed as "ghost"). After death, such a man would be talked about in the present tense and referred to by name or by the term of address used while he was still alive. Other writers (e.g. Haile, Wyman, Reichard) have talked in a similar way about the "coveted death by old age," but the primary characteristic of such a death is knowledge. It is true that the possession of knowledge and longevity are strongly related, but a hypothetical question about the death at a young age of one who knows the stories is acceptable, although such an occurrence is improbable. Even a (relatively) young man (as any person who has knowledge) dies without leaving a ch'įįdii, and he becomes diyinii. The interpretation of how this happens varies, but there is agreement on the fact itself. In a more general sense, it seems as if there is a constant transference of the life stuff of diyin dine'é (especially "Dawn" dine'é and the Sun and the Moon) and earth-surface dine'é.

This symbiosis pervades (if it is, in fact, not the essence of) other aspects of this relationship as well. The Navajos obviously need their gods, for they are the source of anything that men value. But, these gods also very badly need the Navajos. The Corn provides the best example of this, and it is the example that a Navajo will most commonly use. Corn is, first of all, diyinii. Other diyinii, notably the Sun, various water phenomena, and the Earth contribute to its growth. But, Corn is, of course, the essential domestic plant; there is no wild form. Unless it is cultivated, it cannot survive. Man, of course, does this and in return he is fed; but the corn meal and corn pollen are also the food of diyinii, and these are returned to diyinii in the form of offerings. This food provides sustenance both to diyinii and to the earth-surface beings. With such sustenance the Navajos reproduce and grow in population, and there are more people to grow more corn. Similarly, the beings that are on the diyin side also increase, and thus there is more Water, and the Sun becomes more powerful.

Thus, the system is closed but geometrically increasing as long as both sides participate. But, it also has the potential for geometric decrease if both sides do not work together. Finally since the system is closed, there can be no outside help. Things are bad on the earth's surface today because the people have not maintained their half of the bargain. There is drought, almost no corn, and a paucity of grazing. Similarly, people will say that diyinii are "hurting" because they are receiving no offerings. The total system is decaying.

As already noted, the view expressed here is not shared by all students of Navajo religion. The primary alternative theory is advanced by Haile and, following him, Witherspoon. Their attempt was to discover and state how the Navajos view the world. Within rather important limits they succeed. My argument, quite simply, is that there is another, I think, better way to look at it.

THE DUALISTS

Diyin dine'é is usually translated "holy people."[1] This gloss nicely summarized the two predominant features of Haile's and Witherspoon's theory of Navajo religion. They, first, regard the quality diyin to be an attribute "inherent" (Witherspoon n.d.: 15) in a certain class or set of beings. "Inherent supernatural quality," of course, is part of the definition of "holy." In the preceding section, I argued that diyin was instead a concept of becoming and of process rather than of inherency.

The second feature of the term "holy" and the thing that Haile and Witherspoon emphasize most strongly in their statements is the idea of "goodness or moral sanctity." Their description of Navajo world view is almost pure Manicheism.* Everything in the universe, including but not limited to knowledge, people, gods, behavior, ritual, thought, and language, are divided into the good and the evil.

Hózhǫ́ is taken by the dualists as the metaterm for good or for goodness. The word is comprised of the stem -zhǫ́ and the prefix ho-. The stem refers to things like beauty, excellence, and quality.[2] It refers to the essence, or to the essential feature, of that which we regard as aesthetically positive. The dualists, in addition, assign (or claim) a moral quality for the concept. As Wyman (1970: 7) puts it:

---

*A religious system during the third and fifth century A.D. that represented Satan and God as co-eternal.

the Navajo term includes everything that a Navajo thinks is good—that is, good as opposed to evil, favorable to man as opposed to unfavorable or doubtful. It expresses for the Navajo such concepts as the words beauty, perfection, harmony, goodness, normality, success, well-being, blessedness, order, ideal, do for us. . . .

The prefix ho-, according to Witherspoon, refers to environment in a total sense—to the world or the universe as a whole. Hózhǫ́ then can be said to refer to ". . . the positive or ideal environment. It is beauty, harmony, good, happiness, and everything that is positive. . . ." (Witherspoon 1974: 54).

The name of the ceremony hózhǫ́ǫ́jí obviously comes from hózhǫ́. Usually, this is translated "Blessingway," although I think it best to forget such translations. This is the main Navajo rite; the mainstem from which all other ceremonies branch out. It is the "main stalk." One cannot overestimate its centrality in Navajo thought. It is for the Navajo synonomous with the continuation of their way of life.

According to Witherspoon, hózhǫ́ is also associated with and descriptive of Culture. It describes the imposition (today through the ceremonies) of the form and order that is Culture on the original disordered and even chaotic state of nature. The result and the goal are again goodness, beauty, and harmony. Hózhǫ́ǫ́jí was and is the primary means of reimposing or reinforcing this quality on the worlds of the People. It functions by attracting the power and goodness of "benevolent holy people" (Witherspoon n.d.: 14–28). The source of this quality is the entities (or perhaps they are a single entity) sạ'a naghái bik'e hózhǫ́.

The "benevolent holy people" of the dualists are primarily represented by Changing Woman and/or White Shell Woman, Earth Woman (a strong association and, in some contexts, identity exists between Changing Woman and the Earth) and the beings that are labeled "Talking" and "Calling Gods" in English. Witherspoon (n.d.: 16–17) describes this benevolence as it applies to these beings and hózhǫ́ǫ́jí:

> Songs of Blessingway illustrate the pattern of identifying with and incorporating the good of benevolent Holy People. Earth Woman

is a Holy Person who is incapable of doing harm to anyone. She is only capable of blessing, aiding, and sustaining; and, as such, is the very essence of benevolence.

Hóchx̨ǫ is the metaterm for evil in the minds of the dualists. Here again we have the prefix ho-, now paired with the stem -chx̨ǫ. They gloss this as ". . . the ugly, unhappy, and disharmonious environment" and note that "It is not considered to be a part of the natural cycle of the universe, and comes about only as the result of evil intentions and evil deeds" (Witherspoon 1974: 54). This seems to contradict Witherspoon's association of hóchx̨ǫ with the disordered and chaotic state of nature that existed prior to the imposition of knowledge and form (Culture). So, on the one hand, he states that evil can only be created and is not part of the natural order of things, and, on the other hand, he states that it is descriptive of the primal state.

The general emphasis in this paradigm, however, is on the former: the creation of hóchx̨ǫ through the evil deeds of witches or by coming into contact with that which is dangerous or báhádzid (Witherspoon 1974: 56). Its ultimate source is said to be ánít'įįjí są'a nagháí and ánít'įįjí bik'e hózhǫ́, the ánít'įįjí being glossed as "witchcraft way" (Witherspoon n.d.: 19; Haile 1943: 75). The "Satanic" deities in this view are First Man (especially) and his associates who, at a minimum, include First Woman and the primal Coyote.

The dualists claim that the good/evil axis is the primary division of the universe. Spatiotemporally, evil is associated with and derives from the underworlds, the time prior to the emergence of the People onto the surface of this world. This was the time when First Man was chief and when there were evil deeds and actions. In addition to being the source of "evil," this is the ultimate locus for that type of knowledge and power. Witches today continue to draw on it as the source. Good, on the other hand, is associated with the earth's surface. Here Changing Woman predominates and here resides the "good" knowledge and the practitioners of the good way.

Today, in the world of men and in the universe in general, there is, according to the dualists, a fairly constant struggle between good and evil. In this conflict, good is seen as usually being victorious, as order is imposed on disorder and culture subsumes chaotic nature:

[33]

> In the battle between the forces of disorder and evil and those of order and good, the good side has the advantage. This is based on the idea that through ritual knowledge and circumspect behavior one can acquire an immunity from evil, but there is no immunity from the ritual control and compulsion of good. There are no evil forces that cannot be transformed or exorcised. (Witherspoon n.d.: 20)

The prototype of this "struggle," especially for Haile, was found in the conflict between First Man and his associates, on the one hand, and Changing Woman and Talking God, on the other, over the control or ownership of Blessingway. Father Berard, in fact, preferred Slim Curley's* version of the story primarily because it allowed for less interference by the "evil" First Man group with the "good" Blessingway.

In the remaining sections of this chapter, I will examine the three elements that form the basis of this argument—the character of First Man, the character of Changing Woman, and the nature of their "struggle over the control of hózhǫ́íjí." The theme that connects this chapter and the work in general is that the dualistic way of looking at the Navajo universe (and the universe in general) just does not work. But this connective device is not the overriding theme of this work. The topic of good versus evil is just not very important in Navajo theoreticians' discussions of the nature of things. In short, the dualists divide things the wrong way.

The locus of the axis (and the dualists are quite correct in this) is between hózhǫ́ and hóchxǫ́. The division is as abstract a one as can be made. As Witherspoon noted, the ho- prefix refers to total environment, but not so much to the external, so-called objective world as to the subjective, egocentric universe. Thus, when one has an hóchxǫ́ǫ́jí type of ceremony, the primary intent is to bring about a gestalt shift for one who is, for example, chronically depressed. It must be remembered that our thought/action, mind/body distinctions are not very strong for the Navajo. Thought is a type of action

---

*The two versions of hózhǫǫjí or Blessingway that I cite most frequently are Haile's Version I, given to him by "Slim Curley" and Haile's Version 2, given to him by Frank Mitchell. Very often throughout this work I refer to the texts by version and/or by author.

that begins the behavior that we regard as more tangible. Everything that exists, both tangible and intangible, began with thought. Everything that will or can come into being will begin in the same way. If the mind can be changed, the world changes. But this way of putting it is incorrect in that it implies diachronicity or causality, whereas in Navajo co-occurrence and synchronicity are intended.

The hózhǫ́/hóchxǫ́ axis bisects the universe of the People aesthetically. But, whereas we are inclined to limit the realm of beauty (and ugliness), in Navajo it is all-pervasive. Anything at all can potentially be described as nizhóní—a pair of moccasins, a rug, a child, the sheep, the day, an idea, a person's appearance, the sky, the stars, a way of speaking, a language are just a few examples. Up until about one hundred years ago, Navajos greeted each other in terms of the -zhǫ́ stem; many older people adhere to this today, rather than using the more common and more recent -t'ééh stem (as in yá'át'ééh). Nichxóní is its opposite, and, again, it can apply to anything.

As these concepts are much more abstract than our notion of morality and of rightness and wrongness, it makes no sense to attempt to reduce them in such a manner. In fact, I'm really not sure how morality does relate to these ideas. For example, an elegant solution to a moral dilemma could (and probably would) be described as nizhóní. Similarly, many of the acts that we regard as immoral could be labeled nichxóní. But, this is not the way to look at it. Thus, if a Navajo kills an enemy in war, the death and the blood are certainly nichxóní but the act is not immoral. In addition, the heroism displayed and the booty captured are nizhóní. I am not trying to say here that Navajos are amoral; I am arguing that our simplistic dualistic notions are not the way to describe their (or, in my opinion, any) ethical system. To reduce the aesthetic to a rather graceless morality destroys the elegance of the universe the People created.

The example of the warrior points up a very important feature of hózhǫ́/hóchxǫ́—namely, that they are a part of the same whole. They exist together, or neither one exists. At one level this is a tautology. One cannot define beauty unless there is ugliness to contrast it with. And here resides the basis for the ultimate failure of any dualistic position that attempts to maintain one side, whether it be the good or the beautiful, and do away with the other, in this case the evil or the ugly. You do away with one side of a contrasting set, and you of necessity eliminate its opposite.* In brief, the Navajo creation can be described in terms of the creation of wholes that are pairings of opposites or of complements. These pairings should not be regarded as tangible and as temporally fixed, however; it is better to look at hózhǫ́/hóchxǫ́ as temporary, although cyclically reappearing, points in an ongoing process.

The creator of all of this is First Man, and the essential feature of his creation is that he did what was necessary to bring about conditions on the earth's surface as they are today. The appropriate way to look at and understand his actions (and the way Navajo thinkers look at it) is teleologically. He created the conditions that are described as hóchxǫ́ because he had to. Without them, there would not have been the conditions described as hózhǫ́. The only alternative was a world of indifference, without either the qualities we value or the qualities we dislike. In short, it would have been a bore.

Similarly, since both were created and since the ritual today continues creating them, they are both reducible to, or a product of, "Culture." We could also, of course, say that they are both "Nature." But, this is simply an imprecise way of saying that the nature/culture dichotomy is not very much a part of Navajo thinking.† A Navajo simply does not separate himself that strongly from the things we label "natural"; he is more of an ecologist, not in the sense that he keeps things clean but in the sense that he regards himself as a part of something larger, rather than as having a separate existence. This is a part of the lack of separation (or the lack of a strong separation) between the People and their gods that we noted earlier.

At one level, then, hózhǫ́ and hóchxǫ́ describe points in a process that is continual or ongoing. It is better to say that they are

---

*There is a better way to look at this concept, which will be presented in Chapter 4.

†There is, however, a raw/cooked or a wild/domestic distinction, but it is not a part of or reducible to nature/culture. More on this later.

descriptive of the process that is the universe. To view this only in terms of conflict, as the dualists do, is to deny the essential characteristic of what is taking place. Struggles and conflicts do occur, but they are not based on anything so lofty as a battle between good and evil or Satan wrestling with God. The conflicts occur between men, or between deities that are much like men, or between deities and men. Forces can be utilized in these conflicts. Some of them are relatively safe and, therefore, rather "weak." Some of them are very powerful and, therefore, very dangerous or báhádzid. But, all diyinii are potentially báhádzid (diyin báhádzidii). Power and danger form another whole; there can be no utilization of power without incurring risk.

From this practical aspect, it is more accurate to look at diyinii in terms of a power continuum. All power for the Navajo and for diyin dine'é is, as already noted, based on knowledge. In curing, for example, the singer calls on the aid of a relatively powerful being to rid the patient of a relatively weak one that is causing his problem. Thus, for instance, the Red Ant, or the chief of the ants, is called on in wóláchíi'jí to aid the patient and the singer in getting rid of or pacifying other ant dine'é. If the harmful being is relatively unimportant, the curing alliance can be relatively safe. But the cures that call on various yé'ii, or ii'ni' łigai (White Thunder), or on the animals (and other beings) that hibernate must be used with great caution; a mistake in these instances can bring disaster not only to the patient and his family but often to the singer, and sometimes even to the People as a whole.

To oversimplify: it is a question of amount of risk relative to payoff. Misfortune is the result of a mistake or of inadequate knowledge. Employing ritual knowledge to harm others, for example, is probably the most dangerous thing that one can do. The reason is that, in order for it to be effective, one has to call on very unusual and very powerful forces, while one's opponent will always be able to call on relatively safe beings for protection. Such a conflict, of course, has to escalate. People will always say that a "witch" who is identified is finished; he will die soon after he is discovered in the act. The reason for this again is quite simple. The essence of this type of knowledge is secrecy; if one is discovered, it is an absolute indicator that the practitioner made a mistake or that his knowledge was inadequate.

An essential characteristic of the dualist position is that good must ultimately be victorious over evil and that "There are no evil forces that cannot be transformed or exorcised" (Witherspoon n.d.: 20). Stated somewhat differently: if this view is correct, there should be nothing which is incurable, that is, no evil force which cannot be overcome by good. If the continuum view is more correct, there should be at least one problem or illness that cannot be ritually resolved. There is a part of hózhǫ́ǫjí that is referred to as ná'iiską́. It is used to remedy non-observance of the four-day period of sexual abstinence that is necessary after any ceremony. But, a person who does not observe the abstinence period after ná'iiską́ is finished. There is nothing more that can be done. Whatever forces are operating here, they have to be at the top or at the end of the power continuum. The name of this particular force is są'a naghái bik'e hózhǫ́. It is the essential force or power in the universe; all others derive from it. For the dualists, it is the source of good—in fact, it is simply the source. There is no other way to look at it. If we adopt the dualist position, we end by saying that the ultimate good or the source of good in the universe is (within the context of ná'iiską́) the ultimate evil.

There is one final point to be made about power. The danger or safety of a force is heavily dependent on context. One cannot make a list of Navajo gods from the most to the least powerful. For example, beings called Talking and Calling Gods in English are relatively safe, their ritual context being, primarily, hózhǫ́ǫjí. In other contexts, however, they appear as yé'ii, and they are quite powerful and quite dangerous. The names by which one calls them are different in each case, and, with this, their function for man alters. The same can be said for all forces and for all deities and for all beings, including man. They are too complex to be regarded as embodiments of abstracted qualitative essences. In the end, this simplifies our task of understanding them, for we can draw on ourselves and our own motives and feelings as we begin to enter their realm. These "gods" are not all that different from ourselves.

Let us now turn to a more detailed examination of two of these gods—First Man and Changing Woman.

FIRST MAN

As already noted, the dualists regard First Man as the embodiment of evil. Father Berard, the originator of this view, comments on this and other features of the primal man and his associates:

> The supernaturals known as átsé hastiin* 'first man' and átsé asdzáá [*sic*] 'first woman,' are . . . 'the very first to come into being' in the underworlds, and were born of earth and sky. But this statement is qualified again to mean that 'first man' is supposed to have originated in the sky, and is identified with azee' doit'íní [*sic*] 'invisible medicine,' or ánít'į (colloquially: nt'į) doit'íní 'invisible witchcraft.' His sister is also his wife: átsé asdzáá 'first woman,' who originated on earth, and is identified with azee' olch'íshii 'noisy medicine,' and . . . 'she got to be gray witchcraft.' In explanation d.n. [Haile's informant] adds: 'while witches can travel in wolves and coyotes without making much noise, the azee' olch'íshii 'noisy medicine' is so-called because it makes a noise like a mouse and is connected with witchcraft.'
>
> . . . With first man and first woman he (d.n.) associates three others: átsé hashké 'first scolder,' commonly known as mą'ii 'roamer,' the coyote, átsé ashkii 'first boy' and átsé at'ééd 'first girl.' In origin legends, especially, first scolder often functions as informant and messenger of first man, and reports the results of his witchery to him. Of first girl and boy it is said that: 'she took standing position in the earth, while the other (first boy) stands (continuously) in the (dark) sky' . . . First boy and girl are, apparently, not the children of first man and woman, but originated independently of them. The children of first man and woman are

---

*When I quote Navajo words or texts, I have, throughout this work, adopted the convention of putting the transcription into modern symbols while not altering the phonetic opinions of the ethnographer. When the transcription is strikingly bad I use a [*sic*]. But mostly I simply accurately quote. This choice may not be the best one, but it is the one I have made.

known as: ánít'ịịjí sạ'ah naghái bik'eh hózhóón 'witchcraft-way long life, happiness.' Other informants mention additional associates of first man, as many as nine all told. Even then first woman is always mentioned as sister and wife of first man, though no children are, as a rule, born to them. Some of his associates receive various assignments from first man, and they and better inclined supernaturals eventually leave him, because he and his wife prefer witchcraft and malevolent practices. They are now located at some point between the east and north cardinal points. Witchcraft prayers and songs mention . . . 'dark wind' first, then 'blue wind,' . . . 'yellow wind,' and 'white wind' which, as said, represents an improper sequence of color mention. Supernaturals endowed with wind souls of this color sequence betray their wickedness in their actions, just as supernaturals endowed with souls of the proper color sequence show their benevolence in acts of kindness. (Haile 1943: 75–76)

Other stories do not always have the primal couple as "the first to come into being." O'Bryan (1956: 1), for example, has the prototypical cardinal light phenomena as the first in existence; they, having the attribute of gender, "give birth to" First Man and First Woman, along with the Corn.

In the above, ánít'ị is glossed "witchcraft" or "witchcraft medicine." It has two forms today on the earth's surface. One is the flesh and other material from a corpse; the second is sexual fluid. These can be used to hurt others, and, in that sense, it is correct to call them "witchcraft medicine"; further, the primary association of the concept ánít'ị is with this usage. But, as we shall see shortly, there are other usages. Finally, the ones labeled First Boy and First Girl in the above are rather important personages, although they do not usually go by these names. First Boy and First Girl are, in fact, not "names" in either the Navajo or the Western sense; they are instead indicative of these beings' relationship to the primal couple.

Reichard's view of the primal pair is rather more balanced and, I think, more correct than that of Haile. In her opinion, the pair do both good and evil acts toward man. Their reasons for acting as they do and their character are summarized thusly:

There always seems to be some undesignated cause of dissatisfaction that keeps the First Pair in a bad temper regarding man. Perhaps they are only fumbling. They have an inkling about what is good and some desire to bring it about, but because of ignorance, the mixed character of such knowledge as they have, and the absence of harmony, they move back and forth between good and evil in a kind of experiment with the cosmos. For these reasons they belong to the class of undependable deities. (Reichard 1970: 437)

Although more balanced, this view still reduces to the concepts that Haile uses. Here they are said to do both good and evil; the question is why? The answer is: their knowledge is incomplete; they are fumbling; they are ignorant. It follows from this description that their behavior is often "experimental," in the sense that they cannot know the outcome before they begin to do something.

In part this view comes from a superficial analysis of First Man as he appears in the stories. The picture is of a being who, on the one hand, seems to be the creator or at least the primary creator, and yet who, on the other hand, often achieves his creations or brings about current conditions "accidentally." This perspective rests on a very literal interpretation of a few of the stories. No Navajo thinker I encountered looked at First Man even remotely in that way.

My teachers instead defined First Man as omniscient; as part of this, he is seen as having purposefully created events on the earth's surface today. In short, he is the creator and he wanted to create *just* what he created. There were no accidents or mistakes or fumbling; he knew the effect of his actions before he carried them out. Good and evil are not terms that describe the intent of his creation, although they may, for human beings, describe the outcome. He created "packages" or sets of entities that were necessary to the Navajos, even if embodying both "good" and "evil."

Further, the assumption of omniscience means that First Man is related to all of creation. If he appears unrelated, one must assume that he was acting secretly and that there was a reason for his secretiveness. If he appears to make a mistake, there must be a reason for his attempting to create this impression. The thinker's task, then, is often to discover the reason behind First Man's actions in light of current events on the earth's surface.

My purpose here is twofold. First, I want to demonstrate this omniscience or, rather, to give examples of it. This will be attempted in this section and throughout this chapter. Second, in a later chapter on ałkéé naa'aashii, I try to explain the nature and the purpose of some of the "wholes" that he created.

The first example concerns the kidnapping of téhołtsódii* biyáázhí, an incident which appears in all versions of the emergence story. The young (either one or two) of téhołtsódii were stolen by Coyote who hid them under his arm or his coat. Apparently, none of the other beings around at this time knew that he had done this. Téhołtsódii in an effort to find her young, and perhaps intending revenge, flooded diyin dine'é. The flood drove them out of the lower worlds and finally out onto the earth's surface. Here the stolen young were discovered and thrown back into the water at the emergence place; at which point the water stopped rising. In most versions of this story, particularly the published ones, it appears as if Coyote is acting on his own and of his own volition and, further, that the other diyinii are in total ignorance of what is going on.

However, Coyote is almost always someone else's agent. This circumstance is the main reason for his being regarded as a fool. He is always working for someone else and not watching out for himself. In the stories of this time, hc is usually the agent of the primal couple. Additionally, since this event is so major, one would have to assume their involvement. There are two published descriptions of the incident that make this involvement somewhat explicit. The first of these is O'Bryan's version. The events described begin in the third world just after the sexes† are reunited:

> The people moved to different parts of the land. Some time passed; then First Woman bccame troubled by the monotony of life. She made a plan. She went to átse' hashké, the Coyote called First Angry‡, and giving him the rainbow, she said: "I have suf-

---

*Usually this is translated as water monster or water buffalo; perhaps water sniffer is better.

†This important incident is described in Chapter 4.

‡Usually this is glossed "First Scolder" instead of First Angry. Coyote, of course, had other important names as well.

fered greatly in the past. I have suffered from want of meat and corn and clothing. Many of my maidens have died. I have suffered many things. Take the rainbow and go to the place where the rivers cross. Bring me the two pretty children of Tqo holt sodi [*sic*], the Water Buffalo, a boy and a girl."

The Coyote agreed to do this. He walked over the rainbow. He entered the home of the Water Buffalo and stole the two children; and these he hid in his big skin coat with the white fur lining. And when he returned, he refused to take off his coat, but pulled it around himself and looked very wise. (O'Bryan 1956: 8)

Diyinii then moved up until they finally reach the surface of this world; at this point, Coyote shows them what he had and relinquishes one of the young. They also make offerings to the "Water Buffalo."

Goddard's version is similar, but First Woman's involvement is made explicit by Coyote only after they are on the earth's surface and after he is found out and criticized by other diyinii. At this point Coyote says:

"It is true I did that but not of my own initiative. With you, First Woman, as my leader, I did it. Your leadership was altogether unfortunate. You told me you wanted to win. By your direction I took the young of toholsodi [*sic*]." (Goddard 1933:136)

All that is going on here is not clear. These versions seem to take as their primary theme either a competition between First Man and First Woman, or a desire for movement and security on her part, or both. In this sense they are both extensions of the separation of the sexes incident. The versions told to me have a rather different emphasis, however. The primary purpose of the taking of the children is to bring diyin dine'é to the surface of this world. First Man especially and, to a lesser extent, First Woman foresee the ultimate necessity of this. Then they employ Coyote as the agent for the kidnapping.

Another "goal" or necessity that seems to be realized by means of the kidnapping is associated with the flood that follows the return of one of the young of the "Water Buffalo":

The Turquoise Boy took a basket and filled it with turquoise. On top of the turquoise he placed the blue pollen, tha'di' thee dotlig [*sic*], from the blue flowers, and the yellow pollen from the corn; and on top of these he placed the pollen from the water flags, tquel aga'di din [*sic*]; and again on top of these he placed the crystal which is river pollen. This basket he gave to the Coyote who put it between the horns of the Water Buffalo. The Coyote said that with this sacred offering he would give the male child back. He said that the male child would be known as the Black Cloud or Male Rain, and that he would bring the thunder and lightning. The female child he would keep. She would be known as the Blue, Yellow, and White Clouds, or Female Rain. She would be the gentle rain that would moisten the earth and help them to live. So he kept the female child, and he placed the male child on the sacred basket between the horns of the Water Buffalo. And the Water Buffalo disappeared, and the waters with her. (O'Bryan 1956: 10)

Other statements are often made with regard to this incident, the crux of them being that téhołtsódii was angry because her baby was stolen and, as part of this anger, would send thunder and lightning in the future. But this would also include rain, and part of the movement to the earth's surface involved the need for rain.

One final point with regard to the wisdom and necessity of moving out of the underworlds. Some of the chantway stories, particularly Red Antway, describe how the beings living in one underworld become overcrowded, with the result that they kill each other through witchcraft. The movement to this world was a movement to attain enough space to allow people to live in peace. Unfortunately, this world is not big enough (despite the fact it is the largest available), especially now that it is being reduced. And, exactly what occurred in the underworlds because of overcrowding is happening today.

The method of leadership that First Man employs here seems rather indirect, even convoluted. Stated in the form of a question we might ask, "Why not tell the others that they have to move for their own good, rather than do it secretly and with all the underhandedness?" There are several answers. The first one is that democracy does not work very well in crisis situations. But, among Navajos, democracy works especially badly. There are very broad individual differences of opinion that make clear, decisive action rather improbable. Especially would this be so in the case at hand, where it is necessary to move people from a relatively comfortable and secure state to one that is unknown and therefore uncertain. A leader often simply does things without letting others in on it, keeping his involvement secret so as not to incur the displeasure of his followers. He leads by his knowledge of, and ability to create, the future and keeps the secret that distinguishes him from and elevates him above other men.

A second example of First Man's involvement where he appears to be uninvolved occurs in the discussions of diyin dine'é about death. Accounts differ, but the basic theme of the story is First Man seemingly divining for eternal life, with Coyote interfering and causing death to be part of the state of man and thereby incurring the anger of the other diyinii. The following is atypical only in that it makes First Man's involvement explicit:

> Meanwhile Coyote was running around here, they say. 'We shall dwell (here) without dieing' [sic] said First Man. "Ho! Why should there be no dieing" [sic] Coyote asked. One of those scraping poles, which had been used down below, some had grabbed for themselves. At once First Man picked up one of these. Again Coyote spoke: "If there be no dieing, there should be no births as well. Let the number of people remain as their number is now!" he said. At once he threw this pole mentioned into the water saying: "If this does not float up again, it is settled that there will be dieing." In a (very) short time that pole came up to the surface. Coyote, (however) quickly picked up one of those river boulders, which were formerly used for pounding things (and) were called kéł'áni. At once he spun this at the edge of the water and threw it with great force down into where that pole had floated out again. "Should this float up again it is settled, there shall be no dieing" said Coyote. That water only closed up over it for good. "Accordingly as this wood returned floating to the surface, so too, consciousness will return (at times)" said Coyote. "While according to this kéł'áni thrown into the water (once) it shall be: Once dead always dead!" said Coyote. *(But) this he had done according to the mind of First Man himself lacking courage to say that there shall be dieing. So he commissioned Coyote to do it, and from now on you may be sure it is according to his own mind, if as days pass on (it is said that) one thing and another is taking place according to Coyote.*[3] (Haile 1932: 49–50; emphasis added)

This is very clear. Death exists as part of the birth/death whole. For the Navajo, increase is the essence of life and of livelihood. As is clear from the above, there can be population increase only if there is death. But for those who will be the first generation to die, this decision will not be popular or spontaneous. So it is accomplished through the meddling, or interference, or mistakes of Coyote. In other versions it seems as if he acts on his own, but it is quite clear here that First Man is responsible.

In these two examples[4] then, First Man is generally mentioned as not being involved or as being only indirectly involved.

But, although Western analysts, like Haile and Reichard, have chosen to emphasize such examples, they are in fact very unusual and quite atypical. First Man's direction and involvement is usually made quite explicit and, in fact, emphasized. Immediately after the emergence,* the primal couple were discussing something in whispers. First Boy and First Girl asked what it was they talked about. In answering, First Man and First Woman's central involvement in creation is first mentioned on the earth's surface:

> "It is not an unwise thing we plan," said First Man. "We plan for the time which is to come, how we shall live, and how the people will live upon the earth. It is nothing but that my child. . . ."[5] (O'Bryan 1956: 14)

At this same time they build a hogan and in the process they sing the "Chief Hogan Song" which summarizes and celebrates the knowledge of their chief and of the chiefs that will exist in the future. First Man begins by announcing what lies ahead for them:

> "All these things (that exist) will have inner forms," but added nothing more. Then they first of all put the surroundings of the hogan in nice shape, its interior too was nicely prepared before they seated themselves there. "Those songs with which you originated back there, all of these without exception, you will sing, you will plead with them," they were told. "This you will somehow decide for yourselves," he told them. (Wyman 1970: 112)

---

*From the underworlds onto the earth's surface.

This placement of the inner forms, or, more precisely, animation by such placement, is the purpose of hózhǫ́ǫ́jí and the theme of
the rest of the story. One of the first things animated is the hogan.
Further, this animation takes place according to or by means of
"Those songs with which you (the ones that accompanied the primal couple to the earth's surface) originated back there. . . ." Thus,
the songs of hózhǫ́ǫ́jí, the ritual for creation on the earth's surface,
originated in the underworld. Finally, he tells them that they will
have to decide on the use of the ritual for themselves. This is the
essence of Navajo ethics: diyin dine'é, and in this case First Man,
provide instruction, but the individual decides its use.

The story continues with the other diyinii beginning to praise
First Man's knowledge:

> "This much is clear that from the beginning of time this leading
> chief of ours had full knowledge of things, no doubt about it,"
> they said. (Wyman 1970: 112)

This "full knowledge" is, on the literal level, the mastery of
house construction. More importantly, in the building and animation of this "first" hogan, a model for (and summary of) later creation was constructed. Similarly, when Navajos build today, they
are re-creating that which was brought into being in the beginning,
just as those who have built homes all along have continually re-
created and reanimated all that is of value. Throughout this work, as
I recount this story through textual materials, it is important to
keep the more general meaning constantly in mind. I hesitate to
state something so obvious but think it necessary to do so, because
these materials have been taken so concretely in the past.

The story continues:

> "And these (main poles) of the hogan along the east, the south,
> west, north, four in number, will be the important ones," was
> said. "And the one in the east is going to be picked up first, the
> south one next, the west one is between the others, the north one
> being the last in line. And on the east side two stones are placed
> for its pole, by which that side may be recognized," was said. And
> this person who directs it will speak of it as it goes along. So it was
> decided. Right along these points the line of the song runs. . . .
> (Wyman 1970: 112–13)

Just as the main poles of the hogan are raised, so will the supports for the Navajo world and the Navajo way of life be placed. Those beings of the four directions will include the mountains which support the Sky, the roof of this world, and they will include the light phenomena of the cardinal directions who are the immediate "energy source" for animate beings on the earth's surface. Without them there would be no animation (giving birth) or reanimation (as in the ceremonies). In short, they are the main poles for, or the supports of, the Navajo way of life.

The "Chief Hogan Song" continues by describing what will be placed on this basic structure that is the "place home" for a family as well as the dwelling place of all beings on the earth's surface:

> Of origins I have full knowledge.
> Of earth's origin I have full knowledge.
> Of plant origins I have full knowledge.
> Of various fabrics' origins I have full knowledge.
> Now of long life's, now of happiness's origin I have full
> knowledge. . . .
>
> (Wyman 1970: 112–13)

Mentioned here are some of the components of the hogan and of the Earth. These are also things that will be created or "placed" later in hózhǫ́ǫ́jí and which are continually being re-created and placed today by means of this same ritual. All are są'a naghái bik'e hózhǫ́. And, it is their chief, First Man, whose knowledge is being referred to at this time. Today the song still has him as a referent as well as referring to the singer's knowledge, which necessarily includes a knowledge of First Man's creation of the universe.

The song continues:

> Of Mountain Woman's origin I have full knowledge.
> Of Rain Mountain's origin I have full knowledge.
> Of various jewels' origin I have full knowledge.
> Now of long life's, now of happiness's origin I have full
> knowledge.
> Of Water Woman's origin I have full knowledge.
> Of collected water's origin I have full knowledge.
> Now of long life's, now of happiness's origin I have full
> knowledge.

Of Corn Woman's origin I have full knowledge.
Of pollen's origin I have full knowledge.
Now of long life's, now of happiness's origin I have full
    knowledge.

(Wyman 1970: 113)

The above describes, in outline form, what will be brought into being by means of hózhǫ́ǫ́jí. This song continues by elaborating on this knowledge and on the building of the hogan. The following song burdens complete, in a general sense, the basic idea of the song and the ceremony:

(2)   I had full knowledge from the very beginning.
(3)   Long ago he was thinking of it . . . of origins he was thinking.
(4)   Long ago he spoke of it . . . he speaks of origins.

(Wyman 1970: 113–114)

And after thinking of it and speaking of it, he brought it into being and he placed it. The songs continue describing the building of the house and of the world. There is one other verse in the same sequence that is important, although not so much for this chapter as for a later one. As the hogan is finished, and as the completion of the various parts is described, each section of the description is followed by:

Now long life, now happiness, it has come to be. . . .

The point here is that to be sạ'a naghái bik'e hózhǫ́ is, in a sense that is still undefined, to be complete.

The events described have been planned for and known about by First Man from the very beginning. The song verbally, and the hogan physically, summarize and encode everything that is Navajo. What remains of hózhǫ́ǫ́jí is merely an elaboration of this summary description, just as the universe is, in turn, summarily described by hózhǫ́ǫ́jí.

In response to Reichard's point then, First Man is neither fumbling nor ignorant. His actions were purposeful and carried out with the knowledge of their ultimate result. In answer to the dualists, let me reiterate that hózhǫ́ǫ́jí, their essential "good way," was

[49]

created in the underworld, their "hell," by their "personification of evil." I suppose one can accept such a view, but it seems rather inexact.

First Man, then, represents almost a distillation of what it is to be diyin. The essence of diyin is knowledge and, in a way, wisdom. In particular this is knowledge of the future which enables you to predict and at the same time create, or at a minimum appear to create, future events. As already noted such knowledge or such an ability is not an inherent feature of diyinii; it is something that is achieved ritually. Thus, if one wants knowledge of the future, he employs a divination ritual; if one of diyin dine'é wants to create something he uses hózhǫ́ǫ́jí (or another ritual). First Man does this, as do the other diyinii. And it is the same thing that earth-surface people do today in the same circumstances. First Man is exceptional only in the completeness of his knowledge; everything that came after him, everything that is known about today was known and, if not created, at least allowed by Átsé' Hastiin.

A final point to begin to consider is how we, earth-surface beings and ourselves the creation of First Man, can best or most accurately view the quality or nature of creation in general. The dualists have made one attempt at this. And, they have basically adopted a view utilized at one time by Christian theologians, the key question or dilemma centering around the existence of evil. Or, to phrase it more specifically, "Why do witchcraft, disease and poverty (to give a few examples) exist? Why are not things totally good and totally pleasant?"

No one has ever come up with a convincing answer to this question. In general, it is the wrong question. From the Navajo perspective, it is simply the most inaccurate way to look at it. First Man is not much of a god, as we are used to using the term, nor is he benevolent. He created what he did primarily for his own, selfish reasons. In this he is much like man. The fact that it benefited (or harmed) people today is a consequence of, not the reason for, his actions.

A second answer derives from this explanation. He created what was necessary for things to exist as they do today. Wealth is very important to the Navajo; but, for reasons to be given later, there could be no riches without poverty. For health to exist, there must be disease. A thing that is joyous for us, or good or positive or whatever, exists as part of a larger whole which also includes something that is not so joyous or good or whatever. There is no justification or reason for the "evil" existing. Evil was not created but came about as a part of and as a necessary consequence to the creation of something else. Further, "evil" is not an entity or a "whole" but always a part of something else. One can ask why the whole exists, and the reason is again teleological. It is the way life is today, and the whole, whatever it is, exists and was created so that life could be that way.

NAYÉÉ'

The story of nayéé' further demonstrates First Man's character and purpose. In addition, it introduces us, and the Navajos, to Changing Woman and relates the reason for which she came into being. Finally, the way in which the term "nayéé'" itself has been analyzed by various researchers gives us some insight into the source of Western "theories" about the religions of others, particularly the Navajos.

Nayéé' has always been translated "monster," and in the story and ceremony nayéé'ee ("Monsterway") many of the beings satisfy this description. But, other less tangible beings are also mentioned—old age, poverty, and disease to name three. It is this intangible, relatively abstract usage that is most common today.

Navajos use nayéé' to refer to and describe anything that gets in the way of a person living his life.* It refers more to the subjective than to the objective, more to the internal than to the external. Examples include obsessive thoughts—worry, fear, and jealousy; the states that we label depression and paranoia, as well as all physical illness. Note that the words that we employ to describe these pro-

---

*Allen Manning, personal communication.

cesses do, in fact, objectify without necessarily externalizing. The verbal creations alter that which one is passing through, or that which is passing through someone, to states that are, implicitly, relatively permanent features of the individual. For example, consider the statements "He is paranoid," or "He is psychotic."

The Navajo term's initial and immediate referent is to process; but the term takes on additional, or even alternate, meanings in curing. Hóchxǫǫjí-type ceremonies are basically intended to exorcise nayéé' or, if not to do away with them, to make them manageable or put them under control. Thus, nayéé'ee describes the death of some of the "monsters," while the others (e.g., old age, poverty) are left living. But even the ones that were killed are dangerous today as their bodies, their blood, their ghosts, and their memories remain on the earth's surface and potentially affect those of us who live here.

The initial step in any cure* is to objectify that which is nebulous and intangible so as to be able more easily to externalize it or place it outside the patient. This is (at least on one level) what the ritual is all about. The stories describe nayéé' in incredibly vivid terms, the battle between them and the hero twins is re-created, and the bodies of these beings (and their other remains) can be seen all over the Reservation. The curing, then, first describes and objectifies. Then there is a battle and the externalization which results in either the death of a particular nayéé' or in its management by the patient and the singer. Finally, there is a celebration of what is basically a new way of looking at the world.

The singer is quite aware of this process. Some singers, in addition, believe in the "literal" truth of what the stories describe. Others take nayéé'ee as "metaphorical," the real "monsters" being intrapsychic processes. Most Navajo theoreticians, however, do not make this distinction. There are things that are in people, or that enter into them, or there are processes that are experienced that hinder their lives for a moment, even though, in the larger moment, they may transform. As to the source of these things, their true

---

*In *Persuasion and Healing* (1961), Jerome Frank describes this beautifully.

identity and their names, no one really knows; but a persuasive statement on source and identity is, at a minimum, necessary so that a cure can be effected.

At this level, we have a view akin to our own entity notions of disease. There is an important difference, however. As already noted, most Navajo practitioners regard the "monsters" as metaphorical or heuristic devices that simplify a very difficult and complex process. I have never met a physician who regarded the notion of disease as metaphorical (although I have certainly met medicine men who see the Western notions of illness in this way, and who can further see the usefulness of this device).

In the summary description of nayéé'ee that follows, I will discuss mainly the objectified entities, as they would be described in a ritual or curing. Later, in Chapter 5, the more abstract meaning will be considered.

Nayéé' (or at least some of them) were a fairly direct result of the separation of the sexes in the underworld. At this time, the women* had intercourse, or "sexually abused" themselves, with rocks, various kinds of cacti, some kinds of animals, and who knows what else. Nayéé' were the "children" of these acts; this is the origin that one primarily thinks of for nayéé', despite the fact that other, perhaps separate, origins are mentioned in some stories.†

These beings almost totally destroyed diyinii. The few that survived went to live at dził ná'oodiłii‡ (one of the "sacred" mountains of the Navajo). There, Changing Woman was born and was raised by the primal couple. Upon maturing, she either married or became the consort of the Sun (and perhaps the Moon and, in a way, Water). Of this (or of these) union(s), twins were born—nayéé' neezghání, "Monster Slayer," and tóbájishchiní, "the one born for water" or

---

*The men also masturbated, but nothing was born of it. Additionally note that these people were not yet of human form; they were still diyinii.

†The Sun is the Father of at least yé'iitso. But in some versions, he is given a primary role in the paternity of other nayéé' (see, for instance, Wyman 1970: 139). Such "responsibility" is not incompatible with the above statement. There can be, and usually is, multiple causation.

‡This location is referred to later in the texts as Gobernador Knob (not a translation of the Navajo).

simply "Born for Water." These two[6] rid the earth of most nayéé', so that diyinii and other beings could again live on it. Today it is these twins that are invoked in serious illnesses to again undertake the dangerous journey to the underworld in order to rid the seriously ill patient of nayéé'.

First Man was responsible for the separation of the sexes in that he was the creator of sexual desire and, therefore, of the jealousy and adultery* that went with them. These in turn were the immediate cause of the separation. In this way, First Man is indirectly linked to those nayéé' born as a result of the women's sexual acts that occurred at this time. But, an even more direct role is assigned to him by Frank Mitchell in the creation of certain other "monsters":

> Now it seems that even before White Shell Woman† had been picked up First Man, usually after dark, would go to the top of Chief Mountain at the point which extended northward. Apparently, he had made ugly kinds of monsters (in addition to those already existing) which, it seems, grew up on the slope of Mount Taylor. And when these began to devour people on that side this was known to him. Most likely it was for (to destroy) those people mentioned before who had not kept things holy, that these monsters appeared, and in this way his (First Man's) wish that these (monsters) should do this to them was being fulfilled. These (the disrespectful ones) be abandoned to them (the monsters), that happened to be his purpose. (Wyman 1970: 418)

It is not clear from the text as to whether these are the nayéé' from the underworld or whether they have been newly and separately created by First Man (I lean toward the former view). Whichever view is correct, his reason for allowing or for creating nayéé' was to eliminate "the disrespectful ones," who did not keep things and did not do things in a diyin manner. Having achieved this, or, more precisely, having brought about the conditions that resulted in

---

*In certain contexts, particularly when adultery is frequent and jealousy chronic, these are viewed as nayéé'.

†For the moment, the reader should take White Shell Woman and Changing Woman to be identical.

this, he and First Woman set about planning for Changing Woman's birth:

> First Man, First Woman again discussed matters. Now this Earth's inner form which, as said, he had made from his medicine corn bundle, he would repeatedly hold up in the direction of Gobernador Knob. At dawn, he would do this and hold it up in that direction four times. (Wyman 1970: 140)

Changing Woman was (somehow) born of these actions and was found lying within Gobernador Knob. She was then presented to diyinii by First Man, an event described by Slim Curley:

> You can see now that this is the child of the young woman and young man of exceeding beauty who, as mentioned earlier, had arisen from that medicine bundle which he never laid aside to become the inner forms of earth. It is clear, too, that she originated here at Gobernador Knob when he held that same medicine bundle up in that direction, as they say. (Wyman 1970: 143)

In this version of the story, the young man and woman of exceeding beauty are są́'a naghái ashkii* and bik'e hózhǫ́ at'ééd* who arose from First Man's bundle earlier in the story. In Frank Mitchell's description of this event, basically the same theme is developed, but the parentage of Changing Woman is presented slightly differently. The primal pair are again angry at and worried by those who do not respect anything. They want to eliminate them while preserving those who do keep things diyin. They then instruct Earth Woman and Sky Man to think about these things. At this time, First Man's foreknowledge of the birth of the twins is confirmed:

> Now it seems that when First Man had spoken of his intention of thinking about the loafers some way, he really had reference to dangerous enemies (monsters) that were to come into being but he had directed his words at those disrespectful ones (who kept nothing holy). And when he told the Earth and the Sky that they should think it over somehow, he was referring to the manner in which Changing Woman would come into being. For that reason

---

*Ashkii may be glossed "boy"; at'ééd as "girl."

he had said that this should be done according to Blessingway. As for the other things planned for the time beyond (this event) about which he had said that he who is the Sun will somehow think of it, it seems he had reference to Monster Slayer and Born for Water. For the one who will make monsters, others will be born (i.e., if anyone produces monsters, a monster slayer also will be born), that was his purpose in saying this. (Wyman 1970: 403–4)

The Sky can be called są'a naghái, and the Earth can be labeled bik'e hózhǫ́.* In the first version it is sky phenomena that seem to impregnate the mountain within which Changing Woman is born. These views, although different, are therefore not totally incompatible. At any rate, Changing Woman can be described as the child of są'a naghái bik'e hózhǫ́; she can be spoken of as Earth's child; she can call the Sky her father; and she is also the child of the mountain. She is the daughter of First Man insofar as he, at a minimum, planned her birth and, in Slim Curley's version, brought her birth about by holding up the bundle toward the mountain. He also raised her and, as we shall see below, taught her many things. But there is a more immediate sense in which First Man and First Woman are her parents as they are, very literally, the parents or creators of są'a naghái and bik'e hózhǫ́. Therefore, Changing Woman is, depending on one's perspective, their daughter or their granddaughter.

I am considering in some detail Changing Woman's parentage, because (to a degree) one understands a child by knowing her parents. This is neither deterministic nor is it unimportant. From this perspective, there is a final version that is instructive. Black Hat, one of my teachers, was adamant in insisting that the Sun was the father of Changing Woman and that their subsequent marriage was therefore incestuous. This was not a view that anyone else would discuss or admit knowledge of, preferring instead to define her father as one of the unnamed yáádiłhił dine'é (dark sky diyinii) and professing ignorance as to his precise identity. I present this as a possibility, not as definitive. Such an incestuous union, however, is a possible explanation for Changing Woman's power and the great power of her children.

---

*These labels are far from unique; any "animate" being or pair of beings can be referred to this way.

When Changing Woman matured, she, in relative ignorance, had intercourse with the Sun. That is, she, at least at first, did not know the identity of her lover, nor did she seem to understand completely what was going on. But although she might have been ignorant, First Man was not, for it was he who planned and arranged this union. After visiting her, the Sun spoke to Changing Woman about what was happening: "It is not according to my mind that I am doing this. Your father, First Man ordered me to do this" (Wyman 1970: 196). Similarly, the Sun did not know the purpose for which the twins were going to be born, "This was known to First Man alone" (Wyman 1970: 196). The purpose of the twins existing then, as now, was, of course, to slay nayéé'.

First Man is, as previously noted, the prime mover or, at a minimum, the prime knower in these and almost all other acts of creation, but to view the sequence just recounted, or any other, in Manichean terms or to impose other human ethical perspectives just does not work very well. He, being evil, creates the evil monsters to destroy the ones who are disrespectful (evil?). The all-good Changing Woman is born of a union that transcends human norms of propriety, she is raised by the evil primal pair and learns from them, but somehow she maintains her aloof sanctity. She has sexual relations with the Sun, a union which may be incestuous, and gives birth to the good twins who slay the evil monsters. This view lacks a certain consistency.

First Man does what he does because his actions are necessary (in ways that are not totally known) to bring about future conditions. He alone has (relatively) total knowledge of how conditions will turn out. Often the reasons behind what he does are unknown, and, when they are known, intellectuals are reluctant to discuss them both because of the fear of being accused of witchcraft and because of the value of such knowledge. To share in his knowledge is to have the very power of creation, the awareness of how to bring about future conditions that will be to one's direct and immediate benefit.

As noted above, a primary theme of the dualists is First Man's place in hózhǫ́ǫ́jí. Since they view it as a rite that is oriented toward maintaining or restoring "good" or "benevolent" conditions, First Man's involvement presents a serious problem. They therefore interpret the story as a struggle over the control of the rite between the good forces, as led and represented by Changing Woman, and the evil forces, as represented and led by First Man, with Changing Woman ultimately being victorious. Thus, Haile had a strong preference for Version I (given to him by Slim Curley) precisely because it allowed for less interference and control on the part of the First Man group.

It is quite correct to say that the process of hózhǫ́ǫ́jí is one of a gradual relinquishment of control on the part of First Man and the concomitant take-over by Changing Woman and her associates. But to look at this as a struggle between good and evil distorts the theme of the story. From the very beginning of time, First Man is concerned with creating the conditions that are necessary for life to exist, as we and the Navajos know it, on this earth. At various times in the story he says that conditions are not yet established or that the establishment of future conditions is not yet complete. In general, First Man lets the other diyinii proceed with hózhǫ́ǫ́jí and with creation in general. He exerts a very light touch and he, or members of his group, do not intervene unless the others deviate from the course he has in mind.

For example, in Frank Mitchell's version, Talking God tried to "sanctify" and give life to the Sun and the Moon carriers when they were assigned this task. This effort was without result, presumably because it was thwarted (somehow) by First Man. Finally, Coyote and Be'ghochidí (both members of First Man's group in this account) enter the hogan where the ceremony is taking place and are spoken to by the diyin dine'é who are present:

> "Go ahead, old man, you must be of use here," he (Coyote) was told. . . "from now on any plan which you propose to add to those of others will not be overlooked again," he was told. "Then, too, over such various things of which the powerful (Holy) People are in charge you will partly share in their authority," he was told. . . . "And as time goes on in the future, you will partly be in authority over things which are going to be made on the surface of this earth. . . ." (Wyman 1970: 367)

On the heels of their failure then, Coyote "sanctified" the Sun, the Moon, and the Grand (twelve-eared original) Cornstalk, along

with the plants which had been placed in position to clothe or to
decorate the Earth. Where nothing had happened before, the Sun
and the Moon jumped up and the plants grew and in general
showed signs of movement; at which time, Frank Mitchell, speaking for his predecessors, said, "This it seems had occurred just as
First Man himself had it in mind, Coyote, I suppose alone being
aware of it" (Wyman 1970: 368).

As things proceed, First Man takes less and less of a role in the
creation of things, and the power or control is passed to Changing
Woman. But she is, or at least occupies the role of, his daughter, as
they live together and he teaches her. In short, he willingly passes
the potential for control over to her. The exact content of these
teachings is never made quite explicit, but Frank Mitchell does say:

> And so it seems everything was now told to her, it was told to
> White Shell Woman, it seems that First Man told her, "Back
> yonder, who knows how far back, I began thinking for the benefit
> of all of you. That was from then to the time of coming up to the
> (earth's) surface, and from then on I have prepared all conditions
> on its surface for your benefit. So from now on you must make
> yourselves useful, your thoughts must be used for that purpose. It
> is for this purpose that we have given birth to you," he told her.
> "You must now think of conditions as they should be in the future
> my child, my grandchild!" he said. (Wyman 1970: 421)

At a certain point in all versions of the story the control is explicitly transferred to her, and with it all knowledge. One has to
assume that with this "total knowledge," First Man transmitted to
her the knowledge of "witchcraft." In Slim Curley's story this
transfer of authority takes place on the occasion of the second
puberty ceremony of Changing Woman, which Haile saw as being
introduced to ". . .wean Blessingway away from every influence of
the First Man group and place it under the direction of Talking God
from White-Earth-Streak so that he, jointly with Changing Woman, could control the entire rite in the future" (Wyman 1970: 9).*

At this time, the Moon speaks to her concerning the control
that First Man has ordained for her:

---

*Oswald Werner (personal communication) notes that this may all be a meta-
phor to describe a paradigm shift.

[59]

"Now in this manner, First Man has ordered that all giving birth (reproduction) will be yours (i.e., you will be in charge of it), vegetation and everything that exists on the surface of the earth shall give birth, and you shall be in charge of fabrics of all kinds, jewels of all kinds. . . ." (Wyman 1970: 197)

There is, of course, a corresponding change in attitude and behavior on the part of First Man and First Woman, and the separation from their daughter is not always described as an amicable parting:

But from here on First Man and First Woman began to plan differently. "It is up to yourselves, use your own judgment now, my children" she (First Woman) said. "Back in time I have planned for you, as you know," she said. "To direct conditions as they should be from now on ahead, for that you (Changing Woman) have come into being. Therefore, you yourselves will discuss conditions from now on," she told them. "You know that everything has come into your possession. Is anything still lacking? In places where you live various kinds of means of living are all yours. You can discuss these (things) at my daughter's place here. . . ." (Wyman 1970: 432)

In this separation between First Man and Changing Woman, Haile sees the battle between good and evil and the subsequent victory on the part of the good as the primary theme. I have tried to emphasize the transfer of control from one being to another. This transfer does not take place without ill feeling and threats, particularly on the part of First Woman. (See, for example, Goddard 1933: 156–57; Wyman 1970: 440–41.) The question is, how is this hostility to be explained if not in terms of an ethical duality?

Frank Mitchell, in his version of hózhǫ́ǫ́jí, emphasizes the social-familial aspects of the separation. From the point of view of First Woman, Changing Woman has stolen herself; that is, taken a husband without the approval or even knowledge of her parents, particularly her mother. This deprives her family of bridewealth. Note also that the Sun is not the ideal choice to marry one's daughter. He is a notorious adulterer, and he is often disrespectful in other ways. Finally, he takes Changing Woman away to the West to live with him, thus depriving First Man and First Woman of the services of their son-in-law. Remember that this is a society that

[60]

emphasized matrilocal residence. It is when Changing Woman says she is going to the West, with the possession and knowledge that the primal couple have given to her, that First Woman really gets angry, but she also communicates hurt at the disrespect she has been shown. In short, it is very difficult to see her as the culprit in this situation: the Sun and Changing Woman are not doing the correct thing. At this time, Coyote comments on what has occurred and on its implications for the future. He says that the break between the people has occurred according to the mind of Sun, that before this time they had not had ugly intentions toward each other, but that with marriage and people growing old such things were perhaps inevitable. Thus, in a sense which he does not totally explain, Coyote indicates that the pattern of the marriage between Changing Woman and the Sun will be at least one pattern for marriage in the future, and a common cause of strife (Wyman 1970: 437–45).

Here he is describing things that to a degree are inevitable parts of being human. At some point, the child separates from his parents; there is always a debt that cannot be paid back, so inherent in the separation is a sense of guilt on the part of the child and anger and sadness on the part of the parents.

Changing Woman attempts to reduce these feelings by obtaining support from her "uncle" Talking God, and by using parts of hózhǫ́ǫ́jí to free her mind—something she has learned from First Man. It is also expected that First Woman will feel hurt and sadness; therefore, her expression of anger is not surprising. On the other hand, perhaps the anger and hurt of the primal couple are feigned. First Man arranged the marriage and certainly knew that the separation would occur. If this is so, their behavior is intended as instructive of what can, or of what is likely to, happen in marriages in the future.

It is useful to remember also that Navajos are all the children of First Man, and his statement, "It is up to yourselves, use your own judgment," is directed at everybody. When he relinquished control, he seemingly withdrew completely from human events. As far as I know, there are no prayers or songs that enlist First Man as an ally. This theme of the separation of the all-powerful creator from the conditions that he has created, combined with the doctrine of free

will, is a fairly common one in many religions. But, generally omniscience and free will are rather uncomfortably resolved, as in
Christianity. In the Navajo situation, the solution is more sophisti-
cated. As already noted, power is not an inseparable attribute of a
being. One has the potential for power through the possession of
knowledge, but power is actualized or achieved through the ritual
exercise of this knowledge. Thus, when First Man separates himself
and relinquishes control, he ceases to exercise his ritual knowledge.
In a sense he is still omniscient (or he has at least the potential), but
in an equally important sense he is not. The solution is, of course
not absolute, nor is it perfectly logical; but it does make the omniscient creator/free will conflict somewhat less severe. Similarly, it
allows for other beings (including ourselves) to have the same
power (since the same knowledge is available to us) as First Man
had. By his teaching others, he therefore irrevocably gives up
control.

Finally, the story is instructive of what it is to be a teacher, primarily as expressed in the parent-child relationship. At a point in
teaching it is necessary to relinquish control over the student—to
put him on his own. When one does this, the consequences are
unpredictable. When one raises a child, one takes him to a point,
but beyond that he is on his own. When this happens one must
accept what ensues. This separation, as epitomized (for the Navajo)
in marriage, is both joyous and sad, filled with love and anger, and
is both beautiful and ugly. There is beauty and ugliness in this and in
all things, and a side that is beautiful and one that is ugly in all
beings. Entities are never one-sided, and entitivity is defined essentially by that two-sidedness that is completeness. Coyote alone is
wise enough to see and express this.

THE "GOOD" DIYINII

The last point to be considered in this chapter is the character and
place of Changing Woman, who (as already noted) the dualists regard as "the embodiment of goodness." Most people equate asdzą́ą́

nádlehíí (Changing Woman) with yołgai asdzą́ą́ (White Shell Woman). In addition, there is a strong association (and, in many contexts, an identity) between her (or them) and Earth Woman—nahasdzą́ą́. The primary difference between Changing Woman and First Man today is the immediacy and constancy of contact that she has with the earth-surface dwellers. For the Navajo, she is shimá. In fact, she is the essential shimá. She is the nurturer, the giver, the provider. One feels primarily warmth, trust, and safety in her presence, and the earth-surface dweller is always in her presence.

She has "responsibility for all those giving birth," and for the Navajo this includes almost everything. The increase of the sheep, of the corn, and of the plants that clothe the earth are all hers. The births of human beings started with her as she created them, and one still refers to her as "my mother" or "my grandmother." The seasons that both mark and bring about this growth are her responsibility, her creation. She "changes" from a young girl in the spring to an old woman in the winter. This cycle is continuous. Her annual cycle is the cycle of humanity—the movement of the Navajo population from birth to old age, generations repeating continuously.

This all came about according to First Man's plan, but it is Changing Woman who has the immediate control over things, who is actually the doer in this master plan. When one thinks of her and of the earth, the primary emotion, as stated, is one of warmth, trust, and safety. However, it is not total safety. She is, in some limited contexts, báhádzid (dangerous).

In a camp where I lived, two children were killed in the cave-in of a tunnel they had dug. Several individuals and certain other beings were deemed responsible; included were Earth Woman and Changing Woman. Her reason for taking the children was, in part, because they were not being taken care of properly by their family. So, "Their mother took them back." Her motives are usually too complex to be described simply in terms of goodness. Here she protected her children by killing them and by bringing intense sorrow to others who are also her children. Similarly, when yee naaldłooshii (skinwalkers or werewolves) travel, they pray to Earth Woman and to Changing Woman for protection, just as one, in

[63]

normal travel, prays to her. She again is protecting her children, but here her one child is often doing harm to her other children.

Changing Woman is also subject to emotions like anger and jealousy. When she goes to the West, she takes the things she is in charge of with her. Slim Curley summarizes some of these possessions:

> That way, it seems the decision was made as to what, exactly she would settle down with; she was to be in complete control of vegetation and male rain. She would have a turquoise basket. which would give out a sound and cause epidemics whenever she got into it, it was said. . . . (Wyman 1970: 190)

Later he further describes the same incident:

> "As for these baskets here that were secured, Monster Slayer will continue to stand for them. If there be no disorder then they will not sound with (for) him, but if through your own fault over there you abuse your songs, if you disrespect them, then they will give a sound (of disapproval) whenever he steps on them; kaal it will sound. A change in condition will then occur." By that, they say, she meant fevers, even colds, and various other diseases which would remove (by death) many young men and women. . . . (Wyman 1970: 234)

Haile interprets this control over sickness in general and epidemics in particular as a punishment which she would inflict upon the race for non-observance of customs. But, of course, if one chooses to reduce diyinii to these parameters, then the creation of nayéé' by First Man to rid the earth of "the disrespectful ones" must be viewed in the same way.

CONCLUDING REMARKS

The view that I have referred to as "dualism" is not simply a Western, Christian view superimposed on a native religion. The duality that Haile and Witherspoon describe is most certainly a Navajo view as well as their own. What I, in contrast, am arguing is that it is, in the terms of Western science, a theory that does not fit the facts, the facts here being the body of knowledge found in the stories. This, incidentally, is the way that Navajo thinkers would argue about their ideas in general and about these concepts in particular.

In the preceding argument I have implied or stated that there is "good" in First Man, and "evil" in Changing Woman and that there is "good" and "evil" in almost everything else. This constitutes more of a reply to Haile and Witherspoon than a statement that is correct in itself. To reduce to concepts like "good" and "evil" is simply the wrong way to look at it. And, to say that there is "good" and "evil" in all things is very little better than personifying these qualities and embodying them in beings called gods as Haile and Witherspoon do.

There are two concepts that are strongly associated with diyin. The first of these is adziil, about which Reichard (1970: 34) says:

> Normal adjustment of the body gives a person atsee, "strength, firmness, physical dependability." Add to these attributes power derived from supernatural experience and he is "strong, enduring, powerful, capable of controlling good and warding off evil" (adziil).

Bidziil is concrete strength and it is abstract power.* In this latter sense, it is power based on knowledge which is acquired through learning the stories and the ritual. It is virtually identical to diyin. Both terms, adziil and diyin, apply most strongly to First Man. He is, in a sense, the personification of these ideas.

The second concept that is a part of the intention of diyin is báhádzid, a term usually, and not incorrectly, glossed as "dangerous." Bidziil and báhádzid are obviously complementary, a part of the same whole. Where there is power, there is danger, but the danger can be mediated through knowledge.

The stories of the Navajos reflect the relationship between the concepts diyin, báhádzid, and bidziil. The world, for the People,

---

*Personal communication from Oswald Werner.

begins as a very dangerous and frightening place. When they learned the names of the powerful ones and other information about them, the fear was reduced and the danger mediated. An initial stage in this mediation was the learning of taboos. Through this process the world was made manageable, but only barely so. There are simply too many taboos, and it is too easy to breach one of them. In fact, the most common example that people today give of illness etiology is the inadvertent violation of such a rule. Fortunately, for the Navajos there are still "fixers"—ritual experts who can remedy such errors. But they are forgetting and their prices are becoming quite high. In some ways, the world now is more fearful than it was in the time of ignorance.

The interrelationship between these concepts also is reflected in the change in attitude toward diyinii that takes place through an individual's life and through learning. A youth, particularly an adolescent boy, will violate taboos with impunity to show that he is not afraid and that he has courage. Then a misfortune occurs and he begins to believe. It is at this point, when one begins to believe but has no knowledge, that the world is most fearful. One then begins to learn the stories and the ceremonies in an effort to transcend this fear. During the initial phases of this learning, the teacher protects his pupil, until he has acquired the control himself. Subsequently, a point is reached where fear is no longer the predominant emotional coloring of one's relationship with diyinii. That fear is replaced with respect. This respect describes a relationship between equals or near equals, whereas fear characterizes a relationship of subordination.

According to the chantway stories, the acquisition of knowledge is, in itself, an incredibly dangerous undertaking. The knowledge of detail that a singer needs it quite vast, and a mistake can bring harm to the singer and the patient, or to their families. The báhózhǫ́ǫ́jí part of a chant is designed to correct most mistakes or to patch them up after they occur. Individual singers in addition have their own private devices to protect themselves. In general, the learning of some things and the concomitant association of certain knowledge with certain diyinii is relatively safe. But, the acquisition of some knowledge necessitates an alliance with very powerful forces and is, therefore, very dangerous.

There is the social aspect to this danger as well. If a man chooses to practice as a singer, he inevitably becomes involved in "battles" with certain other human beings (as well as with "ghosts" and diyinii). In general, these antagonisms are long-term and escalating. In the camps in which I lived, some conflicts had gone on for generations.

Diyin contains both bidziil and báhádzid, "power" and "danger." It is helpful to view this as a continuum. All beings in the universe, whether they are in the realm of diyinii, human beings, natural phenomena, or whatever, can be placed on this continuum and differentiated according to the particular knowledge and concomitant power they possess.[7]

But, the power/danger continuum view is that of the "user" of diyinii. That is, it is the outlook of the ritual specialist, the one who purposefully attempts to alter the process. There is, however, a rather more profound way of looking at things. Those individuals who are the most knowledgeable, as I have already noted, often are not ritual practitioners. They seem to be rather satisfied with things, not totally satisfied by any means, but accepting of the way things are. They do employ ritual, not to alter but in the form of minor celebrations for what exists. At the same time, the relationship of these men with diyinii is rather more intimate than is the relationship of the ritual practitioner. They have a direct experience of the "powerful ones" as a part of them, and themselves as a part of the "powerful beings."

A way of talking about this is in terms of níłch'i.[8] This is the term for, among other things, "wind" and "air." Additionally, níłch'i is diyin. Therefore, the act of breathing is in itself a very "sacred" or "holy" thing. There is a constant exchange and alteration of boundary. On inhaling, the powerful ones enter one's lungs and are both a part of the breather as well as his being a part of and linked to all other beings.[9]

With these more knowledgeable men, this boundary between self and diyinii, never very strong for the Navajos, has become nearly non-existent. The men I knew who attained this state were very old, and I suppose that death brought the final dissolution of this boundary. But, their state of mind on approaching death was one of peace, not of anxiety.

Diyinii then can be regarded as both "good" and "evil." They can better be described as both hózhǫ́ and hóchxǫ́. For the user, they can be looked at in terms of relative power. But, the view that is the most correct is the one that leaves us with the least control—diyinii simply are.

CHAPTER 3

CREATION

THE OVERRIDING THEME of Navajo religion is creation. The stories describe the establishment of the conditions and processes that ensure that growth on a generational basis will occur. This is ultimately achieved by bringing hózhǫǫ́jí into being. Creation of earth-surface conditions was brought about through this ritual, and today earth-surface beings perpetuate growth through it.

The ultimate source for all that is brought into being below, on, or above the earth's surface is First Man's "magic bundle." It is this "medicine" that provides temporal and spatial continuity for the Navajo. In the stories and their exegesis there often appear to be spatiotemporal disjunctures. But, First Man's "medicine," which began in the underworld, which guided the movement upward and out onto the earth's surface, and which is the source of all created beings, provides the thread that ties everything together.

NIILYÁII

Niilyáii is usually glossed as "the things" or "the entities that were created," presumably by diyin dine'é. A more literal rendering is "those entities that were placed," the creation stories being not so much concerned with creation from nothing as they are with the transformation of "primal" life stuff and the placement of the result.

Most often this placement involves another alteration in that the created being is animated for a specific purpose by having another created being placed inside him.

The time of the beginning and the primal beings are variously described, but a point on which the stories agree is on the primacy of gender as a universal quality:

> The First World, Nihodilgil, was black as black wool. It had four corners, and over these appeared four clouds. These four clouds contained within themselves the elements of the First World. They were in color, black, white, blue and yellow. The Black Cloud represented the Female Being or Substance. . . . The White Cloud represented the Male Being or Substance. He was the Dawn, the Light-Which-Awakens, of the First World. (O'Bryan 1956: 1)

These beings are more usually described as "Mist," "Haze" or "Wind" dine'é, or, in translation, "people." They have substance, but they lack form. They are gender essences and, as stated, the primal life stuff from which all other living beings will derive.

> The conception was of a male and a female being who were to become man and woman. The creatures of the First World were thought of as Mist People; they had no definite form but were to change to men, beasts, birds, and reptiles of this world. (O'Bryan 1956: 2)

Form was achieved through reproductive transformation. Gender existed in the beginning and therefore "creation" was assured. This mechanism provides the purposefulness essential in a creation story without a purposeful creator, at least at the outset, being necessary.

The gender difference described here is not identical with the sexuality that we know in the present world. Sexuality in its present form was created much later. The pure gender substance of the First World, however, does have the ability to "mate" or combine, and to reproduce.

> In the East, at the place where the Black Cloud and the White Cloud met, First Man was formed; and with him was formed the

white corn, perfect in shape, with kernels covering the whole ear.[1]
(O'Bryan 1956: 2)

At the same time:

> On the western side of the First World, in a place that later was to
> become the land of Sunset, there appeared the Blue Cloud, and
> opposite it there appeared the Yellow Cloud. Where they came
> together First Woman was formed and with her the yellow corn.
> (O'Bryan 1956: 2)

The beings described here as "clouds" are in other English
translations referred to as "pillars" or "columns" of light. They are
the prototypes of what become the light phenomena of the cardinal
directions of this world. Today these entities retain the reproductive
power described here. Similarly, the corn, originally formed from
their union, may be reproductively transformed through ritual.*
There are, in addition, other sources of life substance which will be
described below.

This transformation is a central theme in the Navajo and, I suppose, any creation story. The amorphous, primal gendered beings
repeatedly give birth to beings that more and more come to approx
imate the living things on the earth's surface today. Reichard (1970:
16–17), in fact, sees this "perfection of form" as the primary theme
of the underworld creation. She says that it reflects a movement
from relative ignorance (in the underworld) to a more complete
knowledge on the earth's surface. But, as noted in the previous
chapter, this "creation" occurs ritually. Thus, the knowledge of
form and the concomitant ability ritually to produce it must precede the form itself. There is, of course, a paradox here, but all
theories of creation of necessity include such a paradox—a "knowledge" of some sort concerning form must exist prior to form itself.
Evolutionary theory is a good example. It works only if one assumes a primal "natural selection" or form-perfecting mechanism.
Stated differently, the knowledge of perfect form, or a more perfect
form (really the same thing), must exist somewhere and precede
even primal substance for an evolutionist.

---

*See the section on First Man's bundle later in this chapter.

A second (and the primary) aspect of Navajo creation is animation, especially after diyinii reach the earth's surface. Often the entities that are "created" in hózhǫ́ǫ́jí have existed from the beginning; the story then describes the placement within them of a life force. Thus, for example, the mountains and the cardinal light phenomena are generally described as existing (in some form) from the First World on. But, on the earth's surface they are animated; that is, living beings are placed inside them. The beings that go into the mountains are yé'ii, and each has a relationship that may be described as bii'gistíín to their respective mountain. Similarly, many of the things that we regard as natural phenomena have bii'gistíín.[2] Haile (1943: 68) analyzes the term in this way:

> The term is composed by bii' in its interior, gi there, and sitι̨, it lies, which becomes –stíín "an animate object lies." We render the term with "inner form of it. . . ."

The placement of these inner forms within natural phenomena (e.g. the Earth, the Sun, the Moon) is described in the story, and brought about through the ritual, of hózhǫ́ǫ́jí. In addition to being yé'ii, these inner forms may also be referred to generically as Talking and Calling Gods. They are diyinii; they transform what is an inanimate object into a living being. Most importantly, the natural phenomenon becomes something that can be communicated with by and be useful to the earth-surface people. This purposefulness is emphasized by First Woman when she argues for the placement (and animation) of dził ná'ooditii and ch'óol'į́'į́* on the earth's surface. By following through with this example, we can see not only what "placement" entails, but also how creation usually occurs both in the stories and today among human beings. First Woman first stresses the potential use of these mountains:

> "You see, these (mountains) will string along among all songs and among all prayers. At some time in the future the earth people will make use of these very ones," she said. After that they began

---

*These are two "sacred" mountains in addition to the four of the cardinal directions. For a discussion of their location and meaning, see Haile (1938), especially pp. 38 and 51.

to give it thought, then held a discussion about it. They (the two mountains) were then placed in position. "I wonder by what means they will be (made to be) alive!" was said. Then it seems it was announced, "Let (some beings) take standing positions within them! In matter of fact, *if there be none standing within them they are nothing but things that lie around without a purpose,*" was remarked. (Wyman 1970: 357; emphasis added)

They then discussed the form of these beings who were to stand within the mountains. Since this is hózhǫ́ǫ́jí[3] it was agreed that they would be made in the form of Talking and Calling Gods. This decided, "Talking God" sets about making them:

Thereupon it seems that he (Talking God) immediately began to think of the manner in which it should be done. He then laid down a white shell, also a turquoise which he had. Over the turquoise which he laid down he made a motion with the dew collected from Blanca Peak, while over the white shell which he laid down he again motioned with dew collected from Mount Taylor. (Wyman 1970: 359)

The dew and the jewels are common sources of life stuff in acts of creation. Jewels can be described as "living" and, in the underworld they "grew" (Stephen 1930: 88–91). Dew comes from the Sky and the cardinal phenomena as well as from other sources. The dew, along with other water phenomena, is bigą́ą́sh, the generic term for sexual fluid (usually semen). Thus, yádiłhił bee dahtoo' can ceremonially be called yádiłhił bigą́ą́sh—the semen of the Sky. Other water phenomena can be described in a similar way. Dew is also associated with other kinds of reproductive fluid. In the following, Frank Mitchell describes the general purpose of the dew of the cardinal phenomena in the placement of the Earth and the Sky:

Now these dews (of the cardinal points) just mentioned were mixed together (by them) they say. You see, (the dew) of the horizontal sky blue was a male, while that of the darkness was female. These two were mixed together and the one called Calling God performed over them. After placing a spread over them he tremble ran towards it from the four sides, which caused it to move nicely. It became known that this (the dews) was to be the menstrual flow of the Earth by means of which vegetation will become possible.

Again the dew of the dawn and of evening twilight already mentioned were also mixed, a spread was laid over them, and for this
Talking God repeated the performance, he tremble ran towards it
from the four directions. This was to be the gastric juice (amniotic
fluid?) by means of which everything was to receive moisture.
Then that was placed into the root of growing things, after which
they now began to move (have life) on the surface (of the Earth)
and to grow up from there. (Wyman 1970: 345–46)

In resuming the story of the creation of the inner forms of
ch'óol'į́į́ and dził ná'oodiłii, note the similarity between the following and the preceding account of the creation of birth-associated
fluids:

These (the jewels) were covered with a spread for Talking God
who sanctified them from the four sides. When he had tremble
run toward them from the east side they began to move. This was
repeated again from the south, they almost raised up. Again it was
repeated from the west side, it poked its head out towards the east
direction. He repeated the same from the north side, at the east a
(being) in Talking God form crawled out. He arose . . . and he
(Talking God, his maker) blew his own voice upon him. (Wyman
1970: 360)

After Talking God made these replicas, Calling God did the
same. The material out of which they crawled (which was derived
from dew) is then described:

It . . . was much like soapsuds, it was white, but somewhat
speckled here and there with yellow streaks. (Wyman 1970: 360)

This fluid was saved. Today similar material is used in the ceremonies and is made from yucca root suds that are strewn with corn
pollen. Often such material is used in "baths."* In some sense, or in
some contexts, these baths are primarily acts of creation. Perhaps
this dual aspect is always present; washing clean is an act that commonly denotes the passing to a new status or a reanimation.

The inner forms of the two mountains were then dressed and
given names. The reason for the naming and their future relationship with earth-surface people were then told to them. Note

---

*This description is sometimes folk and sometimes analytical.

here the emphasis on the "partnership" between diyinii and earth-surface dine'é that was commented on in Chapter 2:

> You see when later on in the future people have come into being and they use these names in calling upon you and call you by them in the proper way, they will make you strong partners with one another, their songs will be holy, their prayers will be holy. (Wyman 1970: 360)

The material "like soapsuds" that had been saved was then combined with mountain soil (that had previously been brought up) and with mirage and haze stone. Then the four beings just brought into existence as inner forms of the two mountains "sanctified" these materials and, in doing so, "created" the mountains.

This example is quite typical. The creation described is based on reproduction. It is overtly sexual, although it is seldom described in explicitly sexual terms.* An exception is found in McNeley (1973) in a story given to him by Curley Mustache. This story segment describes the meeting at which Earth, Sky, Sun, Moon, and various animals were animated. Other diyin dine'é who attended were the primal pair, dine'é of the cardinal light phenomena, and various nílch'i:

> These "winds" back then were Holy People, they were Mirage People. These different kinds of "winds" gathered together. All of them back then would give life. In this way horses were made then, sheep were made, sun was made, moon was made. In this way these were made together.
>
> So these Holy People: Sunrays there were, rainbows there were, Mirage People, Mirage Haze People, Haze People in dark haze, blue haze, yellow haze, white haze, the sacred haze—these back then did it.
>
> Here Dawn Woman and Dawn Man placed a basket and beneath it and on top of it spread the dawn. Female Skyblue was spread beneath it (the basket) with Dawn underneath. Dawn Woman, Dawn Man, Skyblue Woman, Skyblue Man, Evening Twilight Woman, Evening Twilight Man—these were spread beneath it (in

---

*The primary exception to this is in stories of "witchcraft" creation where the sexual aspect is emphasized.

that order). They were spread beneath sheep, horses, hard goods, these being set inside the basket.

Then they sang Blessingway towards it. Not many songs were sung—they sang only four (which were) really the ones by which they moved. So these were spread beneath it and some were placed on top: Well, Skyblue Woman (and) Man joined together and here it seems, they "bothered one another" (had intercourse—being covered they bothered one another beneath it). Here movement began under where they were spread—some underneath and some male ones on top. Here, beneath it, something formed. (McNeley 1973: 103–5)

Curley Mustache went on to explain that what was formed was "the same thing as the nłłch'i that forms inside of us (when we are conceived)" (McNeley 1973: 106). But, of course, this "same thing" is also bigą́ą́sh, in this case, the seminal fluid of the cardinal phenomena. The sexual nature of these acts is usually disguised or at least not mentioned explicitly, but it is always present. Perhaps it is simply obvious to those involved. The stories are constantly describing the "covering" of substances and/or beings with "blankets" or "sheets" of jewels or light, and "new" beings always result.

A second point worth reiterating is that even with diyinii these acts of creation are achieved ritually. They first think about it and then perform the appropriate ceremony. The emphasis is again on their performance rather than on any innate quality that they might possess.

The creation ritual as well as the story of creation is hózhǫ́ǫ́jí. The ones referring to it as the "good way" tend to underestimate or overlook this aspect which is, in fact, primary. Hózhǫ́ǫ́jí is both the creation of the things and beings necessary and valuable to humans and the plan or outline for their use. The ritual is used in the same way today by earth-surface dwellers as it was by diyinii. By means of it, one creates. It is not just a remembrance or a reenactment of mythical time, nor is the singer simply "identifying" with the gods. It is a repetition of the act itself. The story is the teaching, the transmission of knowledge; the ritual is its performance.* Today, if one

---

*This atemporality of myth and ritual has, of course, been frequently noted.

wants to increase the number of sheep he owns, for example, he does hózhǫ́ǫ́jí.* He thus creates the sheep ritually just as they were created in an earlier time. The same can be said for all valuables— fabrics, jewels, horses, water, plants. All increase through reproduction, and all "giving birth" started with and continues by means of hózhǫ́ǫ́jí.

Contrasted to this symbolic sexuality is the very emphatic sexuality of the "witchcraft" stories or, more accurately, anecdotes about current "witchcraft" practices. The following is a segment taken from a fairly typical story. Note the similarity between the acts described here and those of the hózhǫ́ǫ́jí creation described above by Curley Mustache.

> One reason the other witches will be glad to kill the man is after they kill him they'll make more medicine, fresh medicine. When they kill him they go out and get him and bring him inside to this bad hogan. For a man they can be made into that medicine. If they kill a woman, a good woman, they'll bring her down here inside the hogan and one man can have intercourse with her. Maybe two, maybe three, maybe all of them can have intercourse with her. Put a little pot of something underneath her and catch the stuff. (Kluckhohn 1968: 133–34)

More often people describe this "little pot" as a basket or, occasionally, a jeweled basket. The material collected is, as it is in the hózhǫ́ǫ́jí creation described above, bigą́ą́sh and/or nítch'i. The substance is also ánít'į̌ (which, as noted, Haile and others gloss as "witchcraft medicine"). Thus, at a superficial level of analysis, there is an identity between "evil way" acts of creation and "good way" acts.

There is another source of ánít'į̌ (as noted by Kluckhohn's informant), and that is the corpse. Thus, ánít'į̌, apart from its qualitative connotations, is very literally life (and/or death) stuff. From such substance, other life can be created or destroyed. It brings about increase and it can cause decrease. Most commonly it is mentioned

---

*Hózhǫ́ǫ́jí may be done in many different ways, depending on the goal. Thus, in this example, one would emphasize the livestock parts.

as being used to promote increase in the sheep, but since all valuables increase through reproduction, it can be used on anything. In fact, there would not have been, nor could there have been, any creation and wealth without ánít'į.

The point of all this is, first, that the Navajo place a strong emphasis on increase. This point is so obvious that I mention it only because it seems to have been overlooked in the literature and because it is essential for an understanding of what follows. Further, all creation is sexual or reproductive. Finally, the difference between "witchcraft" and "good way" acts of creation is not to be discovered at the level of the typing (good versus evil) of knowledge. The knowledge (and its concomitant ritual) is unitary.

Hózhǫ́ǫ́jí describes and subsumes all of this. Further, it created creation in that through it the potential for birth was placed in all beings. The purpose of the second performance of the ceremony was "to enable all beings regardless of size, to give birth (reproduce) in days to come, it was made a very sacred thing." As such, "The Blessingway" has had incredible success.

FIRST MAN'S MEDICINE

The source from which all beings derive and by means of which all animation was (and ultimately is) accomplished is First Man's medicine bundle.

A means of conceptualizing quality in the Navajo universe is in terms of this bundle, its source. Thus, it is not surprising that the dualists maintain that there were (and are) two of these bundles—one of "magic" corn which is the dził łeezh* or hózhǫ́ǫ́jí bundle prototype, and the other which was used (and kept) by First Man for "witchcraft" purposes. Thus, they argue for a dual source and, by implication, a dual creation—the quality of "evil" in the universe

---

*Dził łeezh is literally "mountain soil" or "dust."

deriving from the "witchcraft" bundle and the quality "good" coming from the magic corn bundle.

Nor should it come as a surprise that I maintain that there is but one bundle from which all else derives, thus making the universe at this, its most abstract, level either without quality or possessing all qualities, depending on one's perspective. As is probably already apparent, this both simplifies and complicates the problem of Navajo epistemology.

In most published accounts, the bundle is first mentioned "at the rim of emergence place," that is, immediately after diyin dine'é emerged from the underworlds. The major features of the incident are fairly widely known:

> First Man and First Woman came up through the Earth. Water came up right behind them.* First Man says, "We forgot something underneath." First Woman says, "What is it my husband?" "It is medicine" (He didn't say ánt'į because there were some more people with those two people. So he just called it "medicine"). "We left it down there." "Well, we shouldn't do that," says the woman. "They cannot stay without it". . . . "Go in the water and look for that thing and bring it up." They sent that bird in there and pretty soon he brought this thing up. The man and his wife was feeling bad about it. After it was brought up, they feel good again. First Man says, "When you have this thing, man will get rich easy. This thing is sheep, horses. All the same as having lots of hard goods, including different kinds of shell. . . ." (Kluckhohn 1968: 133)

Note here the objectives of the ánít'į—horses, sheep, hard goods.[4] In short, the primary objectives of hózhǫ́ǫ́jí.

Curley Txoaheedliini gave Father Berard an essentially similar but more complete version of the same event. Again, the incident occurs immediately following the emergence; the water had stopped rising, but there was still water all around:

> "This is really too bad my children! What now! How shall it be?" said First Man. "We have started out without the thing that regulated our lives, by means of which the earth, the sky were setting

---

*From this it is fairly obvious that the emergence is the Earth giving birth.

firm. We went away without the thing, which had made things firm, by which they had life in them, which regulated the ripening, which regulated the raining, which regulated giving birth, which regulated our progress, with this thing missing, we have come up." (Haile 1932: 48)

Again, these are the functions of hózhǫ́ǫ́jí—this ceremony is used at birth and, in fact, created birth. It was used to animate all the things we refer to as "natural phenomena." Today it regulates the seasons and other temporal phenomena which, in turn, "regulate our lives," and which regulate ripening, the rain, and so on. But First Man does not here explicitly mention hózhǫ́ǫ́jí (he really does not have to mention it, as he could not be talking about anything else). At a literal level he is still talking about his medicine or the bundle. The account continues:

"Let's see who will go back there? If it remains where it is, how will conditions be without it? Whereby will there be life in things? What can make them firm? What will regulate our progress?" he said. "For this is everlasting one, it is happiness (one)," he said. So it seems here then of those who were flying beings, one after another volunteered. He then spoke again: "Somewhere in the conicle hogan, it is clear, it lies (you'll see)." Having placed it in position somewhere between the poles of the hogan, he had remarked this. (Haile 1932: 43)

Here he again stresses the importance of what he left behind and says that he left it in the hogan in the lower world. As an aside let me note that the hogan is one of the things created, in the sense of animated, by hózhǫ́ǫ́jí. This occurs after the incident described here; but, as with all "created" things, the hogan exists in the underworlds (in some form) as well. Finally, and most importantly, note that the term that Haile glosses as "everlasting one, happiness one" is są'a naghái bik'e hózhǫ́ in the text. Thus, what is being sought is, in some sense, są'a naghái bik'e hózhǫ́. The story continues:

And so one of them tried to go in but did not (go) far before he came back out (of the water). A certain number tried without success. The diving heron then finally dashed off and appeared as a white speck far down in the water. From his position here, he was looking at him. "Plainly as a black spot he moved along. Yonder he has entered," he said. From there again the black spot appeared

and came out close by. He had brought it up (again). His magic*
he had had reference to. "Thanks" he said. "We can regulate our
lives by it, it will regulate ripening and giving birth in the future,"
he said. In this way it happened, they do say. (Haile 1932: 48–49)

The term that Haile glosses as "his magic" appears as 'bee'ńt'į
ááhiłníílá in the text. Roughly, this glosses "by which witchery is
done" (Haile 1932: 94 n. 23) or literally by which áníťi (if we assume that we do not yet have an adequate gloss) is done. It is rather
interesting that Haile translates the text as he does, for he accepts
áníťi as always referring to witchery. Later in this version of the
story, the bundle is spread over the earth or "placed" everywhere:

> ". . . that magic,* which had been brought up for him, be placed
> in the center for (the seeds). Having forgotten this at the crossing
> of the stream and dispatched someone for it from this end, this it
> was which he put there for them, and over this, the no-sleep was
> held,* during the fourth night. Immediately at daylight, First
> Man said: "You must now plant that on the entire surface of the
> earth." Immediately, they left in all directions, some starting away
> right from the emergence rim. All planting was finished, thereby
> learnt. . . . (Haile 1932: 54)

There is one other point about this incident that needs to be
stressed and that relates to our discussion in the previous chapter.
My teachers constantly emphasized the fact that First Man did not
forget the bundle, as some versions of this story say; he left it behind for a purpose. The exact nature of this purpose they were quite
reluctant to discuss, but it has something to do with inflicting harm
on others through witchcraft. This is characteristically carried out
by placing or enticing a part of the victim to the underworld. There
are different ways of doing this; one can use the red ant, for instance, to carry it there. A cure is effected by bringing that part of
the person back to him on the earth's surface and making the patient
whole again.

"The Prayer of a Navajo Shaman" recorded by Matthews (1888:
149–71) illustrates the nature of this journey and of the restoration.

---

*Note that the magic, the áníťi or the bundle, is the "patient" in the no-sleep,
that is hózhǫ́ǫ́jí.

The "shaman" had just finished telling Matthews several weeks' worth of stories about this region. Thus, his mind, his thought, and his speech had been directed there or in a sense traveled there in the telling of the stories. The prayer then was aimed at getting him back "together" on the earth's surface. The prayer, or ones like it, can also be used to cure victims of "witchcraft" or of untoward acts against the beings of this region.

The text describes in great detail the journey of the hero twins to the underworld to retrieve the part of the person that is there. It is a dangerous journey; hence, these two must be the ones to carry it out. It also must be a journey that is similar to the one the diving heron undertook. The final destination is again the hogan, but it is now the home of Woman Chieftain, who is also known as First Death Woman[5]:

> Again on this side thereof, in the back of the lodge, Nagaynezgani [*sic*] with his black wand opens the way for me. He arrives for my sake. Behind him, Thobajishcheni [*sic*], with his blue wand, opens the way for me to where my feet are lying, to where my limbs are lying, to where my body is lying, to where my mind is lying, to where the dust of my feet is lying, to where my saliva is lying, to where my hair is lying. (Matthews, 1888: 155–56)

Perhaps, then, leaving the bundle behind was intended as a kind of instruction by First Man. On the one hand, he was demonstrating how others could be harmed or how "witchcraft" could be effected; but by retrieving it, he was also demonstrating how a cure could be accomplished. More basic, perhaps, is the fact that the journey to the underworld could then, and can today, be undertaken to gain wealth. The underworld is still open; thus, one can travel there. The journey and the result are very powerful and very dangerous. Once First Man demonstrated that the journey was possible and, in a sense, necessary, then the results, whether they be "good" or "evil," "automatically" follow. It is all part of a single package; the potential for harm as well as good are both parts of a whole, whether that was intended or not.

The bundle is the source of the valuable things on the earth's surface. As a part of this it is "in charge" of birth and increase. As previously noted, from the Navajo perspective all valuables (with the sheep being the prototype) "give birth." Therefore, the fact of increase in wealth and of reproduction are one and the same thing.

Thus far, then, the bundle has been called azee' (medicine) and są'a naghái bik'e hózhǫ. This final association is of some interest. Są'a naghái bik'e hózhǫ is, for the dualists, the master symbol of the good way. Opposed to it is ánít'į which is the master symbol for the evil way.* But here, they are equated. Haile (1943: 76), in an effort to resolve this, argues that there are two są'a naghái bik'e hózhǫ, the one being called simply są'a naghái bik'e hózhǫ and being associated with hózhǫ́ǫ́jí and the second one being called ánít'įįjí są'a naghái bik'e hózhǫ, which Haile glosses "witchery way long life and happiness."[6] This pair, he further says, are the children of the primal couple.

I could find no support for this view. And my teachers were quite adamant in stating: "There were not two bundles, there is just the one, the ánít'į, it is są'a naghái bik'e hózhǫ."

The story of the bundle after it is brought to the earth's surface is the story of hózhǫ́ǫ́jí. After the emergence and after the land had somewhat dried, First Man and First Woman discussed how things were going to be in the future. At this time, the first moments on the earth's surface, First Man showed the other diyinii the bundles:

> He (First Man), it seems, carried something on his person which he would never lay aside.[7] When he opened it to show them there was a perfectly kernelled white shell corn ear, a perfectly kernelled turquoise ear of corn, a perfectly kernelled abalone ear of corn, and a perfectly kernelled jet ear of corn, they say. (Wyman 1970: 110)

The wrappings of the bundle are then displayed:

> He now allowed them to look at it. They found it wrapped in white shell. In the presence of all he named this white shell in unwounded form. And there was a wrapper of turquoise which in the presence of all he named turquoise in unwounded form. There was a wrapper of abalone, in the presence of all he named abalone in unwounded form. There was a wrapper of jet which, in the

---

*I will devote all of Chapter 5 to są'a naghái bik'e hózhǫ; thus, I do not want to go into great detail here.

presence of all, he named jet in unwounded form. (Wyman 1970: 110)

Earlier in this chapter, I discussed corn and the cardinal phenomena as sources for ritual creation. The jewels mentioned here are related to both of these but are themselves sources for growth. When "wrappers" are mentioned, however, the primary association is with the cardinal light phenomena* as these are likewise viewed in terms of flexible wraps of "blankets."

First Man then "opens" the bundle again, but before he displays the contents he carries out a short ritual. An interesting question is whether or not the "jeweled corn" described above is all that is in the bundle. If so, then the other contents are derived from these almost basic forms. If not, then all the things described are contained in basic form in it:

> He now opened it, moved his hands over it, then rubbed his hands over himself (with their breath as it were) and across his lips. After that, while merely moving his hands over it each time, he said, "This one is called White Shell Boy, this one Turquoise Boy, this one Abalone Boy, this one Jet Boy. This one is called All-kinds-of-fabrics-Boy, this one All-kinds-of-jewels-Boy," he announced as he seated each one in real human form. Then he again moved his hands over them four times. With this he again rubbed himself all over and across his lips. Again, he motioned over them with his hands (and said), "This one is called Rock Crystal Boy." Again he passed his hands over it (saying), "This one is called Mirage Boy." Again, he passed his hands over the entire lot (saying), "This is called Pollen Boy." Again, he passed his hands over them (saying), "This is called Corn Beetle Boy." Again, he moved his hands over it (saying), "This one is called Dewy Boy," he said. Again, he moved his hands over it, "This one is called Dewy Leaves," he said. . . . (Wyman 1970: 111)

All of these beings are mentioned quite commonly in hózhǫ́ǫ́jí and, like the others already discussed, are what we would label "creation symbols." There is a slight anomaly in the above, however. It is more common to speak of half of these beings as being

---

*See Chapter 4 for more on these phenomena. In English we refer to these light phenomena as dawn, daylight, twilight, and darkness.

male and half as being female. Thus, more frequently one hears of "Pollen Boy" and "Cornbeetle Girl." But there is a "Cornbeetle Boy" just as there is a "Pollen Girl," although, as stated, they are rarely mentioned. Perhaps by stating the male member of each dyad, one implies the female member. Or perhaps half of these beings are altered into females. This, in fact, is a fairly common theme in ałkéé naa'aashii stories, and it will be discussed in the following chapter.

Note now, however, that these twelve (or twenty-four) are presented in the context of a ritual acted out by First Man. The goal of this ritual is the alteration of the form of the beings in the bundle. In doing this, First Man is not just displaying the contents of the bundle. He is also demonstrating its use, its potential, as well as the rituals that will come to be associated with it, as is made clear in the ensuing text:

Then he unrolled (unfolded) that unwounded white shell, then placed it, the unwounded turquoise, the unwounded abalone, the unwounded jet, all four, one above the other. At once, he placed these humans* upon them. Over there, he spread (sheets of) dawn, evening twilight, sunlight (instead of horizontal blue to the south)†, a spread of darkness. He then prayed in a whisper, they did not hear him.‡ They too prayed for it. After some length of time, he withdrew the covers and also replaced them. And again, he silently prayed, they too again prayed for it, "may conditions be blessed," they were saying as time passed.

When he had covered them four times as described, a young man and woman first arose from there. Absolutely without their equals in beauty, both had long hair reaching to their thighs. *The two happened to be those various things which he carried about tied up in the bundle.* To fix your gaze on them was impossible, the glare from them was surprisingly bright. "This is the only time that any of you have seen them, from now on none of you will ever see them again. Although they are right around you, even though

---

*Probably "in human form" would be a better gloss.

†This "substitution" in the sequence of cardinal light phenomena will be discussed in Chapter 4.

‡This is unusual; prayer is almost always aloud and public. Haile and Wyman have both mentioned this and noted the association between silent prayer and witchcraft in other contexts.

they are taking care of your means of living (subsistence) to the end of your days right around you, none of you will ever see them again," he told them. . . . (Wyman 1970: 111–112; emphasis added)

As already noted, the beings and processes described are fairly typical and frequent in acts of creation. Life substances are covered with spreads of jewels or of the cardinal phenomena and then ritually altered.

The male and the female of exceptional beauty are the ultimate alteration or, in fact, reduction of the contents of the bundle. Thus, the bundle contents are made up of twelve (or twenty-four) beings, or of four (the jeweled corn) or of two. But, in addition, the bundle is all things. The two beautiful ones are są'a naghái ashkii and bik'e hózhǫ́ at'ééd. They are the essence of the bundle. They are also the bundle itself. Everything that has life on the earth's surface, including the earth itself, is animated by the bundle and is są'a naghái bik'e hózhǫ́, which is quite literally the Source, as the inner forms of all things derive from it.

Są'a naghái bik'e hózhǫ́ (and the bundle) were created in the underworld. By the time the earth's surface was reached, the bundle's contents had already been altered in form. In extracting these two, First Man was reducing living form to its essence, to są'a naghái ashkii and bik'e hózhǫ́ at'ééd. In doing this, he was also reversing and re-creating time, but, of course, this is the function of ritual. In displaying the contents of the bundle and in altering it as he did, First Man was (or is) setting the stage for the subsequent creation. He begins by showing the items and their potential; what follows in the story is a description of the exercise of this potential and, necessarily, the instructions for future generations of how to do the same. In doing this, he does not create the conditions as we know them on this earth; instead, he creates the preconditions (or perhaps presuppositions) that make the creation of current conditions possible.

In Slim Curley's version of hózhǫ́ǫ́jí, the creation of earth-surface phenomena begins after the contents of the medicine pouch have been displayed. The hogan is the first thing created, but with the hogan one quite literally creates the universe.

As always, it seems, it is Father Berard that has written the best description of the meaning of the hogan in his unpublished introduction to Hózhǫ́ǫ́jí, but even this version is quite incomplete, as I am sure that he would agree.

As briefly noted in the previous chapter, the hogan is one of those master encodings; by this I mean that it is an economical starting point for understanding the whole of Navajo world view. A complete understanding of the hogan is complete understanding. Older Navajos will, in fact, occasionally refer to this encoding saying, "Everything I know is here in this hogan," implying both our notion of "my home" and the more general encoding of the Navajo "place home." There had, of course, already been the creation of a hogan in the underworld. So the creation of this hogan is intended more as a demonstration for future generations and as an animation of what existed previously in an "inanimate" form or a form that was of no use to the earth-surface dwellers.

As a part of the creation of the hogan goes the creation of the inner forms of the cardinal light phenomena, the mountains, and the Earth. In addition, many other related beings are animated at this time as well.* The source of these inner forms is always First Man's medicine bundle.

As described in the previous chapter, Changing Woman is also born of the bundle. So she is the child of sǫ́'a naghái bik'e hózhǫ́ or of sǫ́'a naghái ashkii and bik'e hózhǫ́ at'ééd, and she is the child of the bundle, and she is the child of the primal pair, and she is the child of the Earth. She later takes the bundle with her to the West where, with it, she creates the Navajo and many of the things on which the Navajo depend for livelihood. Whereas Slim Curley barely mentions what First Man brings into being, he goes into extensive detail about the beings that Changing Woman produces and often describes her means of doing so. One of the reasons for this is quite simply that Changing Woman's acts are repeated by Navajo today. They continue to reproduce, grow corn, and raise sheep. All are acts centered in hózhǫ́ǫ́jí. Upon obtaining the bundle from First Man, she first "mates corn":

---

*Frank Mitchell includes important attention to the Sun and the Moon.

> She spread down one of those white shell unwounded skins, one
> of turquoise, one of abalone, and one of jet, four unwounded
> skins she laid down. Then by running her hand over the white
> shell corn,* she made a drawing of its roots, she drew its legs and
> its leaves, its leaves she let extend opposite each other. She drew its
> tassel and its face, she made markings for its mouth and eyes, its
> ears and nose, and by moving mirage over it four times, she
> formed its genitalia. And by moving her hand over the blue corn,
> she reproduced its parts in the very same manner, but for this one
> she made the genitalia of rising haze. . . . (Wyman 1970: 201)

The ritual that Changing Woman is beginning is essentially similar to all acts of creation whether carried out by her, by First Man,
or by the present-day Navajo. The knowledge of how to perform it
was given to her[8] by First Man, and she is now teaching it to us
through the story told by Slim Curley. There are things that separate us from Changing Woman, but this ability to create is not one
of them. One final point: the "sexual" nature of corn (and of other
plants) is made explicit here in the reference to the genitalia.

As this story continues, Changing Woman now sings, at which
point the "inner forms" of the mountains arrive. These beings were
summoned by the song just as they are called by ceremonial singing
today when they are needed to animate or to reanimate a being:

> "Arise!" the two [that is, the corn dine'é] were told. The two arose
> there, a young man and young woman unequalled in beauty arose
> side by side. At once she (Changing Woman) applied pollen to the
> young man's feet along the skin coils, then upward as she went
> along she applied it to his legs, his genitalia, his chest, palms,
> ending at the tip of his tongue. Then she put some into the mouth
> of that young woman wiping her tongue at the same time. Then
> she repeated the same on the woman's side and also put some into
> the young man's mouth. . . . (Wyman 1970: 201–2)

Slim Curley goes on to say that this is the prototype wedding
ceremony. Again, there seems to be a certain repetitiousness in the
way these two are described. They are those "beautiful ones," but

---

*As Wyman and Haile point out, this is the "corn" from First Man's bundle.
Above I quoted Slim Curley's description of his exhibition of it. The same is, of
course, true for the unwounded jewel spreads that are used here.

they are not identical to the ones initially identified as sa'a naghái ashkii and bik'e hózhǫ́ at'ééd (although they do have a closer relationship to them than any other earth-surface beings). Yet, at the same time, they are sa'a naghái and bik'e hózhǫ́ or sa'a naghái bik'e hózhǫ́; this has yet to be explained. Changing Woman now directs these two "corn people' to mate, at the same time taking a quite active part in that herself:

> That done she then put the two under one cover. She moved her hand down from head to foot of the male and said, "This represents dark cloud and male rain." On the female she moved her hand upward from head to foot, and said, "This represents vegetation, dark mist, and female rain." She then moved her hands behind her back, hiding them from the two, and placed (a figure) on the ground. In this very same manner she put twelve (figures) on the ground. . . . (Wyman 1970: 203)

These twelve are the "children" of the corn pair. They are also the children of Changing Woman and the children of the Earth. These are the corn and vegetation dine'é, those things that will become of primary importance to the Navajo way of life. Changing Woman instructs us now on the proper attitude toward these twelve:

> "Now this represents something that will take care of you, regularly it will clothe you, and you will eat it," she told them. "If through your own fault, you are instructed uselessly, if you do not take care of it, it will cause you suffering," she told them. (Wyman 1970: 203)

She then goes on to name each of the twelve, to explain how each is to be used, and to describe the proper attitude that one should display toward them. With the bundle she later creates the other things that will be of use to earth-surface people. Finally, she creates the earth-surface people, the Navajos themselves. They are created in part from her own epidermis, in part by means of, and with, the contents of the medicine bundle, in part from other life substance, and in part in a way that is kept secret, at least in the text we are now considering. Thus, the story of Changing Woman here is the story of her creation of the earth-surface people and of the things that they need in order to exist.

The following rather lengthy passage is important in that it summarizes and exemplifies the multiplicity of levels in the creative endeavor. There is, first of all, the literal act of creation itself—that is, the creation of a tangible entity. At a second level, it involves the creation of conditions that are in themselves necessary preconditions for future creation. This includes the creation of gender difference in earth-surface beings, reproductive fluids, and birth. Finally, the passage enumerates at all levels those things that can be used creatively, that is, those things that we would label "creation symbols."

There are two other, related reasons for the importance of this passage. It first points up the relationship of Changing Woman to the Navajo, and secondly, it describes the most important tangible creation for the People in the last two hundred years—the bringing into being of sheep. The following incident occurs after Changing Woman has made the Navajos. They ask for a means of living that they can depend on and that will be theirs, for although there is game, it is really the property and the pets of diyin dine'é.

> She busied herself with what is called earth mirage and earth rising haze. This she rubbed (on her hands and then) on the white shell, the turquoise, abalone and jet (jewels) while they followed her with their eyes whenever she moved her hands with it away from them. She again reached behind her back with it, then produced one in each hand saying, "This one is male, this one female," and laid them here side by side again. "This one will give birth," she said when she again sprinkled that other one with water's child. Here there was some confusion, the one she had called the female became the male.* That water which she had sprinkled upon them "will be called amniotic fluid," she said. Inside of those (two pools of water) they began to wiggle, one crawled out of the side the other also crawled out to the side, but *the amniotic fluid of both soaked into the soil right there. From this soil soaked spot herbs grew up which eventually were to be* (future) *sheep.* What was to be future goats she made in exactly the same manner, both crawled out again in the same manner from their amniotic fluid in the soaked soil herbs again grew up. (Wyman 1970: 245; emphasis added)

---

*Gender change and gender ambiguity is a common and important theme in the stories.

In the preceding section, I quoted Frank Mitchell's account of the transformation of the dew of the cardinal phenomena into the reproductive fluids of the earth. By means of that "amniotic fluid," everything was to receive moisture. I also quoted the description of dził łéézh[9] being made from the combination of mountain soil (dził łéézh literally) and the dew. All these fluids are są'a naghái bik'e hózhǫ.

These herbs then become sheep; but they are not just mutton and wool sweaters; they are much more. They are capital, what the gold is to the gold standard, the silver to the silver standard:

> She then took a pinch from the plants* that had grown up there and inside she took a pinch from every fabric and all jewels found there.† All of this she rolled into small balls which poked into their hoof clefts and into the corners or her eyelids. "By means of these you will be able to live on. Time and again it will transform into fabrics of all kinds, into jewels of all kinds. It represents your pets from the tip of which fabrics and jewels of every description will begin to sprout, thus making life possible for you. . . . (Wyman 1970: 246)

For a pastoralist these statements are, of course, quite literally true. If one takes care of the sheep then good things will come to him. But there is rather more to it than that. There is a feeling or sense of security that is obtained from the sheep; this is not just a feeling of economic security, although it certainly includes that, but also a sense of physical safety and well-being. Witherspoon (1973: 41–42) quotes a statement from *Son of Old Man Hat* that nicely illustrates this aspect:

> About this time I began to herd around the hogan in the morning and evening when the sheep came home. But I was so small. I went out with the sheep like a dog. I just walked along with them and stayed right in the middle of the herd. I was afraid to go around them, but while I was in the middle of the sheep I wasn't afraid of anything. (Dyk 1938: 8).

---

*Nanise' is used here.

†Either these jewels are also derived from the above-mentioned plants, or she is referring perhaps to the sheep as their source.

The sheep also reflect, or very literally are, kinship and social relationships. In summary, then, the sheep are all forms of security and safety. They are a "sure thing," if they are handled in the right way. Or, at least they were until recently, but that is another story.

But one must also look at the Navajo "hunter tradition" as the contrast to the coming of the sheep. By means of this contrast one may understand a little bit more about the relation of Changing Woman to the present Navajo. At one level we have almost a pure raw/cooked antithesis. The game are whimsical, in part because they do not belong to the Navajo but rather to diyinii. Game at one level are, in fact, diyinii. But, in addition to the insecurity and undependability of relying on game, there are other forms of danger as well. The person who lives as a hunter is very like the beings he hunts. As part of this, a hunter is not simply seeking animals (from our point of view), he is seeking to kill beings that are quite literally his kinsmen and his gods.

In a sense, the hunter has no choice but to create (if we assume it is, in fact, created) this relationship with the game and, having created it, he places himself in a very dangerous, very anxiety-ridden situation. Put very simply, the more human or godlike he assumes game to be, the more potential he has for controlling and therefore capturing them. If they are speakers (and they are), then they can be spoken to and persuaded, and he can also listen to them. If they are reasonable, then they can be reasoned with. The hunter is in fairly desperate need of such control if he is to survive. He therefore seeks it, creates it, or perceives it, depending on your point of view. But the controlling and killing of gods and kinsmen are incredibly dangerous. Investigation of the taboos, restrictions and rules associated with hunting ritual can only lead to the conclusion that the hunter is a paranoiac, and, from the Western point of view, he is, in that he is assuming order where there is only arbitrariness.

The sheep, the corn, hózhǫ́ǫ́jí, and Changing Woman at least partly changed all that. They provided things of relative safety which could do away with much of the anxiety and the fear that went with a reliance on hunting. It really is not difficult to make a living from sheep, and there is almost no danger associated with it.

But that obviously was not and is not enough; what is lacking is the power, and the only place to obtain power is from the hunting tradition. Almost all that is álílee is associated with the hunting; all "witchcraft" uses this; the forms of sensory intensification that are used in divination originate as parts of the Game Way.

To return to hózhǫ́ǫ́jí and Changing Woman and the sheep: After the previous incident, Changing Woman goes on to assure that increase will occur:

> Then having shaped a gourd like a skull, she buried this in the ground down below the side corners of the entrance. From there a big reed grew up. Plants had also grown from the soil soaked with the amniotic fluid of both sheep that had previously risen (to life). "Of these one is male, the other a female plant," she explained. She then blew the male plant beyond the animals and behind them, and also sprayed them with it. She repeated the same with the female plant. She then took pinches from the four sides of the big reed and pinches too from those plants which, combined, she chewed. This she then blew in all four directions and four times around in a circle. "This will be found everywhere on earth, by means of it they will desire (mate) each other. . . ." (Wyman 1970: 246–47)

So, the mating and, therefore, the increase of the sheep is assured and a means of controlling it is given to the Navajos. Following this ritual, the sheep and the goats reveal their names and are then placed. The process is complete; yet, it is just beginning.

CONCLUDING REMARKS

The primary goal of this and the previous chapter was to introduce the reader to the realm of Navajo "gods" and "religious symbols." This introduction has obviously not been exhaustive. Reichard (in her concordances) lists hundreds of deities and symbols, and there are thousands of pages, both published and unpublished, on the subject.

My primary goal, however, is synthesis, not inventory. From this perspective, only two points made so far are essential. First, the realm of Navajo "religion" is not to be divided along the dimension separating good from evil. There are dimensions of contrast, certainly; in fact, the notion of contrast is central, but good/evil is neither very correct, elegant, or important. Second, the Navajos and their gods are obsessed, to slightly overstate, with creation, since their creation is always "sexual," with fertility. The subsequent discussion is concerned only with how creation on a repeating or continuing basis (that is, as long as Navajo culture exists) was and is assured.

We now turn to the consideration of two very abstract, very synthetic notions. The one is ałkéé naa'aashii, the other sạ'a naghái bik'e hózhǫ́. Sạ'a naghái bik'e hózhǫ́ is the central concept in Navajo philosophy. Ałkéé naa'aashii appears less often in the prayers and songs and is rather more difficult to get people to talk about. But, one cannot understand sạ'a naghái bik'e hózhǫ́ without first beginning to understand ałkéé naa'aashii. In the final analysis, they are different perspectives on the same idea.

CHAPTER 4

AŁKÉÉ NAA'AASHII: UNIVERSAL PROCESS THROUGH OPPOSITION

THE SUBJECT of the previous chapter was creation or placement. It was incomplete because of the limited temporal perspective that I adopted to describe it. The Navajo emphasis is on repeated creation which is often, if not always, cyclical. It is to be contrasted with the lineal, progressive view of time that characterizes our own evolution and/or genesis.

In overview, the movement of and within the universe is described in terms quite analogous to (if not identical with) our concepts of information and entropy. Before the time that is the "in the beginning" of the stories, there was no movement and therefore no sound or light. From the perspective of a knower there was nothing to be perceived. Of course, neither was there, nor could there have been, a perceiver. At some point, this stillness was broken, and so began the growth of the universe and, as part of this, the growth in different ways of thinking (different cultures). The entire process is one of increasing complexity as reflected in the amount of difference in the material world, as well as in the different ways of thinking that are a part of the human (and, for the Navajo, animal) world.

At a point in time already reached this process reversed. Physically today the movement is toward entropy—a return toward the primal stillness. Culturally, the movement is toward sameness or a reduction in different ways of thinking.

Within this overall process are lesser repetitive processes that are of rather more immediate interest for earth-surface dwellers, especially human beings. In following through the stories, for example, it appears as if many of the beings are created more than once. Or, it seems as if beings cease to exist or move into a state of partial existence and are then reanimated. This reanimation, in fact, continues today and is the main purpose of the ceremonies.

Many Navajo concepts express it. Hááhat'eehii is a word that appears frequently in the stories. I am not totally sure of its analysis, but it may be as follows: Háá comes from ha (start) + náá (again); ha is probably a third person marker; t'ee(h) is the stem which literally glosses something like linear movement but which is more often used idiomatically to refer to the movement of thoughts or of stories; (h)ii is a nominalizer. So, roughly it is something like "by means of it his thoughts began to move again." This describes a common purpose of hózhǫ́ǫ́ji—to start one's thoughts up again or to redirect them along happier and more productive lines. Also recall that a medicine bundle (as well as "objects" we regard as inanimate) can be a "patient" in hózhǫ́ǫ́jí and that this term can refer to that. Another word is nahinii'na, which glosses "made up" or "came back to animation." Again, it describes what happens to patients in a ceremony. Finally, one can say nahoo'nii', that is, "he or some animate being came back to life.

But, the most important context and the most powerful use of the notion of reanimation is with the concept ałkéé naa'aashii. The literature that purports to explain this idea is not very good. It uniformly reduces it only to the concrete—e.g., masked gods, prayersticks. And only a very literal gloss of the term is offered— "follower pair," or "the two that follow each other." Additionally, Haile (1947) associates the concept with the underworld and with witchcraft. None of this is exactly wrong, except insofar as it is incomplete. Ałkéé naa'aashii is as abstract a notion as one can find. In content, or in lack of content, it closely resembles Jung's (1916) notion of pleroma.

There are two published versions of ałkéé naa'aashii stories. They are sketchy, but they offer us a starting point to understanding the concept. The first was elicited by Father Berard as a segment in "Upward Reaching Way."

Two "non-sunlit struck" girls left their seclusion and were killed by Utes. Many years later, the twins Nayéé' Neezghání and Tóbájíshchíní went out in search of them. On the fourth morning of the search they found the skeletal remains of the girls. The twins then spoke to what remained of these two:

> "Are you the two that disappeared here twelve years ago?" The skulls replied by rubbing themselves against each other. Monster Slayer picked up one skull, his brother picked up the other skull, and they brought them back to the hoghan.
>
> At the hoghan the skulls were placed on buckskins and questioned as to their identity with the two missing girls of twelve years ago. Each supernatural promised to restore a specific part of their bodies. . . . (a footnote by Haile in Wheelwright 1949: 107)

A list of what was restored and who did the restoration can be found in Haile (1947: 100–1). Thirty to thirty-five parts of the body are mentioned, but the accounting is far from exhaustive. Other parts of a person commonly mentioned in restorative rituals include, but are not limited to, bíni' (his mind), bizáád (his speech), bígááł (his moving power or his characteristic way of moving).

Prior to these incidents, anaa'jí and hóchxǫ́ǫjí medicines were administered. The "redressing" began at daylight and was completed around noon. At that time it was discovered that one of the girls had become a boy. Additionally, they wore dawn and evening twilight masks which initially were too small and which then were blown on to be enlarged.

The other published ałkéé naa'aashii story is also important. It combines the theme of reanimation with that of personal mortality. The following account was given to Wheelwright by "Klah" (Tł'aáh). The events occur in the second world, and the key actors (which is rather unusual) are Haashch'ééshjinii and Be'ghochidí:

> In the second world Begochiddy made twin women and twin men.

[97]

Hashjeshjin* did not like this world or the creatures there and told Begochiddy* that he wanted to kill the male twins and Begochiddy answered: "Why not kill both the male and female twins? Hashjeshjin answered him twice in the same way and then he killed the twins. So Begochiddy had made two laws.†

Then Begochiddy slit the bodies of the male twins from the neck down to the legs, and cut the flesh into small pieces, and cut off the ends of the fingers and toes and put all the pieces back into the heads. He then did the same to the female twins, starting at the feet and cutting upwards, and the pieces he put into the heads as in the male twins. Both the male and female twins were called Ethkay-nah-ashi.* He put the Lukatso* (bamboo) into the male and female bodies from the head to the legs and he put a small bamboo across the mouths of the male twins, a large sunflower on the right-hand side of the face, a big bamboo across the forehead and on the left side another sunflower. On the heads of the female twins he put a reed across the chin and forehead and a small sunflower on each cheek.

Begochiddy then took a piece of bamboo a foot long and put it into the mouth of the male twins and held the other end in his mouth and then he breathed his spirit into the dead male twins and a great sound began in their bodies. And while this sound went on, in the east near the mountains the white cotton began to move, and in the south the blue cotton moved, and in the west the yellow cotton, and in the north the black cotton, and then all the cotton rose and changed into clouds.

. . . Begochiddy breathed into the bodies of the female twins and then the great sound began in their bodies. (Klah 1942: 41–42)

As noted earlier, "cotton" refers to the protypical light phenomena. At this point, various plants grow up under these "clouds" and the rain begins in the east and moves around the earth. With the rain, the plants flower and everyone is pleased. Later on, Be'ghochidí is involved in the creation of various other beings and it is always ałkéé naa'aashii who are the source of, or the mechanism for providing, life in these acts of creation. Be'ghochidí would first provide the form and then ". . . he took bamboo and breathed through

---

*As elsewhere, in quoting a text I leave the transcription intact.

†The word used here for "law" is very likely saad (bizáád) which is usually glossed "word" or "language." Witherspoon (n.d.) discusses this translation label.

the Ethkay-nah-ashi and gave life to all that he had created" (Klah 1942: 42).

"Witchcraft" stories also have reanimation as a primary theme. Many Navajos, in fact, see a strong relationship, or even an identity, between ałkéé naa'aashii and "witchcraft." There is, however, a key thematic difference. As seen in the above example, ałkéé naa'aashii stories combine the notion of renimation with personal mortality, whereas "witchcraft" stories combine reanimation with personal immortality. That is, the life force of others is used to perpetuate oneself rather than to animate new beings.

These examples, although conspicuous, obscure what is perhaps the central feature of Navajo world view. Reanimation or renewal is not an isolated feature of the universe; it is its essential attribute. Its primary expression is found in the persons of Earth Woman and Changing Woman; in the concepts ałkéé naa'aashii, sạ'a naghái bik'e hózhǫ́ and "increase with no decrease"; and in the ritual hózhǫ́ǫ́jí.

Haile, via Wyman, comments on this notion of "increase with no decrease" and, along with it, sạ'a naghái bik'e hózhǫ́, in the context of a description of the leading members of the so-called "twelve-person group":

> The Corn Man, the leader of the pair, possesses an enduring increase of the goods of life which is equivalent to continuance in time, or in other words, long life [sạ'a naghái]. His inseparable companion, the Vegetation Man, possesses perfect contentment which has no fault, it never decreases, or in other words it is happiness [bik'e hózhǫ́]. (Wyman 1970: 398 n. 292)

This is close to the mark but does not quite capture it.* It correctly emphasizes "an enduring increase of the goods of life" but should go on to stress the generational increase and continuance of the beings that reside on the surface of the earth. It is the continuance through time and the generational increase that are the key to the Navajo term. Their source is sạ'a naghái bik'e hózhǫ́. And as we have already noted it is sạ'a naghái ashkii and bik'e hózhǫ́ at'ééd

---

*Witherspoon also discusses these notions but in a different fashion.

who themselves animate the Earth, and who, according to Slim Curley, are the parents of Changing Woman. But they are also the parents/grandparents of everything on the earth's surface. Similarly, Changing Woman is the mother/grandmother of all living things. She is, in some sense, the Earth. The kinaaldá associated with her becoming fertile was the celebration or signal for the reproductive power of all beings.

But, Changing Woman (the Earth, Earth Woman) does not just reproduce. She reproduces time and again. Her life cycle and the life cycle of the Earth are characterized by a death or hibernation in winter and birth everywhere in summer. This happens repeatedly; it is continuous. It is one aspect of są'a naghái bik'e hózhǫ́ and "increase with no decrease." These ideas concern not the perpetuation or immortality of the individual but the continuance and immortality of life itself. What is emphasized in these concepts is the non-egotistic perpetuation of process, which is partially achieved through individual death. This idea is expressed by Coyote and reported by Frank Mitchell:

> "As for that which lies at its (Earth's) interior (its inner form) you have made long-life [są'a naghái] to be that," he said. "Therefore, if things exist on its surface without any special order and grow up time and again anywhere on its surface, it (Earth) will thereby become young again," he said. (Wyman 1970: 347)

Hózhǫ́ǫ́jí creates, reinforces, and celebrates the process of renewal. By means of it, other beings were created that take part in this cycle of reanimation. In the following, according to Wyman and Haile (Frank Mitchell as told to and recorded by Father Berard and as published by Wyman 1970: 378 n. 274), First Man is describing the main objectives of hózhǫ́ǫ́jí. Actually he is describing quite a bit more.*

> "Obviously in our present doings here we have not as yet made those things which will join things together, as it were," he said. "So who knows how much time will be required to put things in

---

*This point has semantic difficulties and other self-reference problems. Hózhǫ́ǫ́jí includes and subsumes everything; but in this context, Wyman is referring only to the ritual.

order. You see, as you go along there working on them, your thoughts will come to an end. Should this happen there should be a means to restart it, a means to sanctify it again, a means to restore its energy," he said. (Wyman 1970: 377–78)

This statement alludes to a multiplicity of things. In the first place, it refers to the Sun and the Moon who are about to be named and/or created. The Sun and the Moon, by punctuating time diurnally and seasonally, very literally restart things. These two along with the Earth and Changing Woman are the most notable re-animators, and they work together to assure continuance in time. The hózhǫ́ǫ́jí story chronicles their creation, and the ritual itself was used to create them. Thus, hózhǫ́ǫ́jí was and is used to assure that "things will continue" by creating the creators, but hózhǫ́ǫ́jí is itself a continuance. When the world ends for the Navajos, hózhǫ́ǫ́jí will disappear from the minds of the people.[1] It will be forgotten as if it never existed. The fact of the final ending, or the non-continuance, in itself makes hózhǫ́ǫ́jí self-referentially invalid.

But hózhǫ́ǫ́jí does not deal just with continuation and rebirth abstractly; it also assures a sort of renewal for individuals. Personal transitions—birth, female puberty, the objectification of an important life goal—are marked by it. Similarly, the recovery from an illness or the prevention of an untoward occurrence, in general, the re-establishment of completeness, is achieved through hózhǫ́ǫ́jí. This is described in the story:

> By means of that pollen your speech will become (blessed) again, thereby it will be blessed before you, thereby it will be blessed behind you, thereby it will be blessed below you, thereby it will be blessed above you, thereby it will be blessed in all your surroundings, thereby your speech will go forth in blessing, thereby you will be made to be long life, happiness [sąʼa naghái bikʼe hózhǫ́]. (Wyman 1970: 425)

To be complete is to be sąʼa naghái bikʼe hózhǫ́. The person who is ill is not described this way. In anaaʼjí,* for example, he is sąʼa naghái until the completion of the ceremony, at which time he

---

*Usually translated as "Enemyway."

"becomes sǫ'a naghái bik'e hózhǫ́ again." But, to be "sǫ'a naghái bike'e hózhǫ́ again" is not necessarily to be the same individual again. Transitions are in a sense rebirths, but the other side of the coin is that they are partial deaths. To become a woman is to give up being a girl; to be a warrior and to have killed an enemy is to have become different—to have become at once more powerful and more dangerous to self and others. To survive a serious illness is to approach death and to be reborn. The most conspicuous token of the newness is a new, or additional, name. To become sǫ'a naghái bik'e hózhǫ́ is to become complete, and perhaps to become more than you were before. It is not a return to the same person.

The overriding theme of this discussion and of all of the stories is the creation of a way of life that will last. But, paradoxically, continuation can be assured only if change is built into the system. This in turn assures that things or the way of life will not last "forever" but will continue for a while and then come to an end. An understanding of the specifics of this general theme is achieved through an understanding of ałkéé naa'aashii.

A Navajo initially comes into contact with this concept through the so-called "cardinal phenomena." Minimally, these include the lights and the mountains of the four directions. At first glance, these phenomena seem to be associated primarily with the punctuation and use of time. As we look more closely, however, it becomes apparent that rather more is being alluded to in the discussion of time. When diyinii are planning for the specifics of temporal difference (e.g., night and day), they are more generally talking about the abstract phenomenon of difference. In addition, the discussion is structured hierarchically.

At one level, diyinii are talking about social and personal difference. That is, the difference within and between people and within and between social units. An important theme in the stories is the creation of a society that will allow for such difference, and the creation of a process that will promote it.

At another level, this discussion is concerned with creating certain oppositions that will assure that the abstract phenomenon of difference will continue and the complexity of the universe will increase. These oppositions, as with everything else, are encoded in

the entities of the cardinal directions. The primary sets of oppositions are, on the one hand, birth and death, and, on the other, maleness and femaleness. These sets generate differences and assure that
other differences will be created in the future. Finally, this "guarantee" of difference is, in itself, an assurance of "things not coming to
an end."

TEMPORAL PUNCTUATION

There are three related sets of markers for the division of time—the
cardinal light phenomena, the Sun and the Moon, and the seasons.

The Cardinal Phenomena

The cardinal lights today, on the earth's surface, are hayoołkááł, the
dawn, followed by náhodetł'izh, which glosses something like
"horizontal blue" and refers to that layer or band of relatively darker
blue that lies on the horizon during the day. Next is náhotsoi, which
is usually glossed "evening twilight" but which is more literally
"horizontal yellow"; it refers to the horizontal yellow band that lies
on the horizon in the west just after the Sun has set, and before it
becomes dark. The final one is chahałhééł, the darkness.

The prototypes of these light phenomena were either primal or
very nearly so. In the underworlds, there being no Sun or Moon,
light was provided, and day and night were marked, by these four.
In translations they are variously described as "clouds of light,"
"pillars of light," "columns of light" or as "mists." In tł'aáh's story
cited above, they are referred to as "cotton" and then as clouds."

As noted above, these "lights" contain the elements of the First
World within them, as well as containing the elements for creation.
They are also described as "mating" and as "giving birth" to various diyinii. Thus, the light phenomena are the source of matter
(or life stuff) and mechanism (gender difference[2]) for the Navajo
creation.

The other published descriptions of these entities are in essential agreement with those cited previously. One other (unpublished) text is worth quoting in some detail. It was elicited by Haile (1932) and recorded in Navajo. Its importance is in its completeness and in its description of the relationship between the cardinal light phenomena and the other important features of the cardinal directions—the "sacred mountains":

They were living when there was no sun and no moon. From what was (supposed to be) the sunrise (direction) a white column usually arose and the sunset a yellow one. When these columns met they spread light and people went about in it. You see in that way it was day (time), in the same manner as we now go about in daytime. From the north a dark column arose, from the south a blue one. When these met it became night and people would go to sleep in the manner we now sleep at night.

This white column, mentioned as rising in the east happened to be the dawn, they say. Inside of it one just like a real breathing human lay, and as usual, his position was sunwise it was found. Inside of the column too, mentioned as rising yellow out of the west, a human like person lay sunwise. This yellow rising column mentioned happened to be evening twilight. The column mentioned as rising dark from the north showed a person in human form inside of it. That turned out to be the darkness. The column which, as mentioned, rose blue in color from the south showed a real breathing person in human form lying within it. This happened to be the skyblue. You see, then, those four were really lying sunwise as usual, one behind the other. In a holy way unequalled anywhere they lay there. According to these, people were living (at their homes). You see, when that white column met in rising, as said, it brought daytime, and the time had come for their various occupations by which their lives could be preserved.

Sisnajini mountain already stood there, here on the east side. On the south side stood Mt. Taylor, on the west side San Francisco Peak, on the north side La Plata range, it was found. This (thing) that rose as a white column in east time and again, is the inner form of sisnajini by which it breathes and this we know is the dawn. In the west (the rising column) is the inner form of San Francisco Peak by means of which this breathes. This, we see is evening twilight. When they joined the one from the east, you know, the people had made it daytime. (The column) from the south, the inner form of Mt. Taylor by which it breathes is, we know, the sky blue. The one from the north, the inner form of Perrin's Peak by which it breathes, is really the darkness, they say. This, when it would meet the one from the south, they had made (it) the night. Here towards the south stood a mountain yellow in color, and right opposite, towards the east there was a dark mountain. So you see that was the condition of their country.[3] (Haile 1932: 1–3)

The light phenomena were brought up to each subsequent underworld and, finally, to this world. They are associated, usually quite directly, but occasionally indirectly, with all acts of creation. For instance, when First Man displays są'a naghái ashkii and bik'e hózhǫ́ at'ééd to the other diyinii (described in the previous chapter), the bundle was covered with "sheets" of the various cardinal phenomena. They were an essential part in this first act of creation (or, as I argued previously, extraction) on the earth's surface.

At each stage in the emergence this placement of the lights into the mountains is repeated until they are finally put into the mountains on the surface of this world and made useful (as well as making the mountains useful) for the Navajos. The mountains can be viewed as the hogan for each of the light phenomena; conversely, the light can be referred to as the bii'gistíín (inner form) of its respective mountain. It is in this sense that the mountains are living things. Finally, the light is often conceptualized as the smoke from the mountain or hogan.

But, the cardinal light phenomena also have diyinii within them which animate them, as the lights animate the mountains. Slim Curley describes the ceremony where these "real breathing humans" that animate the light are identified or "placed" for the benefit of the earth-surface dwellers:

> Then from the midst of dawn pairs of Dawn's children began to arrive. Now the leading pair, Boy-who-returns-with-a-single-turquoise and Girl-who-returns-with-a-single-(ear of)-corn, were to leave for the interior of Blanca Peak to stay (live) at its interior, a purpose for which, "We two are called, 'two (begin to) sit for a name, two are seated for a name.'" By explaining this the two mentioned themselves by name. . . . (Wyman 1970: 211)

The same is repeated for the other mountains. The following is a list of the mountains and their associated pair:

Boy-who-returns-with-a-single-white-corn   and   Girl-who-re-
turns-with-a-single-yellow-corn: Mt. Taylor
Fabrics Boy and Jewels Girl: San Francisco Peak
White Corn Boy and Yellow Corn Girl: Herperus Peak
Pollen Boy and Cornbeetle Girl: Huerfano Mountain
Dewy Body and Dewy Leaves: Gobernador Knob
(Wyman 1970: 211–12)

The translation then finished with, "In this manner they got to
be called Two-who-followed-one-another (Follower Pair)" or, ałkéé
naa'aashii (Wyman 1970: 215).

These beings are all members of the twelve-person group,"
common participants in hózhǫ́ǫ́jí. As is obvious in the text, the
identifiers used in the story are not the important use names[4] for
these beings, who, depending on their function in a given context,
have several ways of appearing. In hózhǫ́ǫ́jí they are "Talking and
Calling Gods," the male member (Boy) of each pair being
haashch'ééłtihí, the female (Girl) being haashch'éé'oghan. In
tł'ééjí,* they are referred to as yé'ii, and in the public dance portion
of that ceremony, they appear dancing one behind the other.

Published accounts identify the beings within the cardinal phenomena in other ways as well. Hayoołkááł bii'gistíín has been variously referred to as hayoołkááł asdzą́ą́' ("Dawn Woman") (Haile
1943: 72), simply as "Talking God" (Wyman 1970: 369), and as the
pair "Dawn Man" and "Dawn Woman" (Franciscan Fathers 1910:
354). In addition, níłch'i łigai (white wind) has been identified as the
níłch'i bii'sizíinii ("in-standing" wind) of "Dawn Woman" (Haile
1943: 72; McNeley 1973: 73). Haile (1943: 72) says that náhodetł'izh
bii'gistíín is náhodetł'izh at'ééd ("Horizontal Blue Girl"); the Fran-
ciscans (1910: 354) have it as the pair "Azure Man" and "Azure
Woman." Blue wind is the animating force for "Horizontal Blue
Girl." For náhotsoi bii'gistíín, there is náhotsoi ashkii ("Horizontal
Yellow Boy") (Haile 1943: 72), "Calling God" (Wyman 1970: 369),
and the pair "Twilight man" and "Twilight Woman" (Franciscan
Fathers 1910: 354). Yellow wind is said to stand within "Twilight
Boy." Finally, chahałhééł bii'gistíín is identified as "Darkness Man"

*The most usual translation is "Night Chant."

and as the pair "Darkness Man" and "Darkness Woman" with dark wind standing within "Darkness Man."

This list is by no means comprehensive, however. As previously noted, there are dine'é of all generations and both sexes for all of the cardinal phenomena (as, for example, hayoołkááł dine'é). Further, some would say that all of the beings are the children of the dawn, and, for others, the Darkness as well. Finally, there are those that stand within those that stand within the light phenomena. For example, nítch'i łigai is nítch'i bii'sizíinii for hayoołkááł Asdzą́ą́. Thus far then, we have the mountains, the cardinal phenomena that are bii'gistíín to each of the mountains, the diyinii that stand within the cardinal phenomena, and the various nítch'i that stand within these. The hierarchy is certainly not infinite, but it is very difficult to concretely bound.

Of these, we already know that the pair of beings within each of the lights are ałkéé naa'aashii. On one level this is descriptive of and encoded in their spatial relationship as exemplified by the public dance portion of the major ceremonies. The same can be said for their, or for any, nítch'i bii'sizíinii; these exist as pairs, one behind or one on top of the other. Thus, for example, the nítch'i within each human being can be (and is) called ałkéé naa'aashii. In prayers and songs, it is indicated verbally by the sequence "before—behind" (and, "behind—before") or by approximately synonomous spatial descriptions. Such descriptions are incredibly common, and, in each case, it marks an explicit ałkéé naa'aashii relationship.

A second aspect of an ałkéé naa'aashii relationship, is that these pairs derive from the prototypical ałkéé naa'aashii of the underworlds. (In fact, we shall soon see that all living things derive therefrom.) These beings are the ultimate (or at least one step away from the ultimate) source of life in the universe. This process continues today as the cardinal phenomena, themselves ałkéé naa'aashii, are a primary animating force for created beings.

But, although each of the lights has these pairs within it, it is also a whole, and these wholes are related to each other as ałkéé naa'aashii. The spatiotemporal encoding of this is perceivable by anyone: Dawn is followed by Horizontal Blue, which is followed by

Evening Twilight, which is followed by Darkness, which is followed by Dawn, and so on, ad infinitum. The order is important (clockwise or sunwise), but the starting point is not.[5] Each of the "wholes" is sexed and the gender sequence alternates male and female, although there are differences of opinion as to which light is which sex. As noted earlier, the ałkéé naa'aashii within each of these can, and do, reproduce, but the light phenomena are themselves mated with each other. Most commonly, Dawn Woman is paired with Darkness Man, and Horizontal Blue Girl is coupled with Twilight Boy. For example, in Sandoval's (O'Bryan 1956) version of the creation story quoted earlier these couplings result in the birth of First Man and First Woman, and of Corn.

But, this sequence has much more than just an abstract spatiotemporal meaning. It summarizes and brings about the entire pattern of Navajo life. First, the four are associated with certain patterns of behavior and thought; second, they are a reduction of or a model for larger temporal units (months and seasons) which are themselves associated with certain activities and thoughts; and, finally, they summarize qualitative difference (good and evil for Haile) in the universe.

Changing Woman speaks very generally to the first of these points:

> "These things all of you will make use of. These exclusively will be your future guides in life! Darkness will instruct you. It will say to you, 'My grandchildren, go to sleep now.' You will act accordingly!" was said. "Dawn will instruct you. It will say to you, 'Arise, all of you, prepare your food to gain strength for your work,' you will act accordingly and make progress in life," was said. "Evening Twilight will say to you, 'Eat this, it is food which will strengthen you for your work to be done,'" they said to each other. (Wyman 1970: 165)

Certain times of the day, then, are appropriate for certain types of activities. This has two aspects. On the one hand, it is "natural" to behave or to feel certain ways at certain times. On the other hand, the cardinal phenomena and their inner forms instruct earth-surface creatures by transmitting thoughts and feelings to them (McNeley 1973: 110–40).

Frank Mitchell goes into quite a bit more detail about the meaning and use of the different times of the day. He again emphasizes the fact that the cardinal phenomena will serve as a guide to people's movements and activities. Dawn is the one that will cause people to stir, to awaken. Coyote* speaks on its characteristics:

> "You see, I myself will remain in charge of this first one here," he said. "Whatever is good, exclusively for that alone it will exist," he said. "Offerings made in that time (at dawn) will all be holy, and in the future young men and young women who are to come into being will all be put in shape (so that) he (or she) who has walked in it (the dawn) will enjoy every possession," he said. (Wyman 1970: 370)

People who walk in the Dawn, who arise early, will be assured of attaining possessions. Ritually, one assures this by a prayer and an offering to the Dawn. One stands facing the east and strews corn meal perpendicular to the first light, or along an east-to-west line. But the pragmatic aspect is also to be emphasized here. Rising early and planning the day make it very likely that one will attain wealth. The planning and the prayer are a means of objectifying and making concrete one's goals. The objectification makes the goal more immediate and more obtainable, as well as creating a feeling of success in the attainment. The feeling of success is sought again on the following day, and so on. The native teacher is aware of and emphasizes both of these aspects; in fact, they are really not separable. The sacred and the pragmatic do not intermix; they are part of the same package.

Skyblue or Horizontal Blue serves as a guide to the earth-surface beings in their daily activities. When the Sun is up, it is the time to carry out the activities and pursue the goals that one has set in the Dawn. But, it is also a time of danger and death. Coyote again is the spokesman on this:

> "Concerning the next one again, although good to some extent it will remain two sided. Whereas it will be a protection particularly

---

*It is interesting to note in passing that Coyote of the supposedly "evil" First Man group is "in charge" of the "all good" Dawn.

for one's journeys, bad things (deaths) will repeatedly occur in that time, (so that) half of it will be good, the other half will not be good," he said. (Wyman 1970: 370)

The deaths that occur in this time are the payment demanded by the Sun carrier for his journeys (this will be discussed more extensively below). One ritually and physically (planting, herding, etc.) cultivates the Earth at this time. It is a time when the products of the Earth grow, not just the plants and the livestock, but the jewels and the fabrics and money as well. All are nanise' in the most general sense. All are her wealth and benefit the ones that live on her surface. The Sun is, of course, also necessary to this growth, and in the sense that he is required, the death that is his payment is necessary as well.

The third light or temporal phenomenon is Twilight or Horizontal Yellow. It is the time when activity ceases, when people come together again, and when one reflects on the day's activities and accomplishments.

"The next one will also be good, and offerings too will be made in that time (at dusk), it will be a time of bringing people together again. Should any of you not act properly, should anyone disbelieve and continue (travel) through it, that also will not be quite proper," he said. (Wyman 1970: 370)

The last one is the Darkness. The Moon also demanded deaths as payments for his travel and it is these that Coyote makes reference to below. The Darkness is exceptional in the fact that it is not a limited phenomenon. It covers the whole sky and is not just a horizontal band. The dippers (the constellations), of which there are a male and a female, are in some sense representative of Darkness (or are the ones that animate it) as well as being associated with the deaths that occur at this time. Coyote continues his instruction:

"As for the very last one, only a small portion of it will be good. Merely the resting part in this time period, in this small point only will conditions be good. Otherwise, there will be more of whatever is bad (death) in this time than in others. And should you desire this same (time) above the others (i.e., sleep too much) you will suffer want of everything. That is the purpose of these things," he said. (Wyman 1970: 370)

The cardinal phenomena, then, function in part as a guide, a model, and as instructors for activity on the earth's surface. But they also protect the Earth and the living things. Dawn and Evening Twilight, which in Frank Mitchell's account are male, are singled out for this. Here also is a general statement on the difference between male and female thought:

> "The two of you who are the males will keep watch over the people with whatever is good, while you who are females will simply be in the rear, since planning far ahead which is to be done everywhere has not been given to you in full measure. Those who are the males do thinking on a broader and larger (scale), therefore that (part) has been assigned to them," they were told. (Wyman 1970: 371)

The individual chooses which of these primary aspects, wealth or protection, he wants to draw upon at any given time. There are two distinct types of offerings to the Dawn; the one for wealth has been described above. In order to call upon the protective potential, one faces the east but strews the corn meal horizontally, that is along a north-to-south axis, between himself and the Dawn. One can make similar offerings to the Twilight; the color of the corn meal used is different, as well as, of course, the prayers, but the prayers are always fairly distinct, as one's wants and fears differ.

Jóhoonaa'éí and Tł'éhonaa'éí: The Second Set of Temporal Phenomena

Jóhoonaa'éí, the Sun or Sun carrier, and Tł'éhonaa'éí, the Moon or Moon carrier, are also ałkéé naa'aashii.[6] This pair, and the set of the cardinal light phenomena, are the two most common and perhaps powerful examples of ałkéé naa'aashii. But, of course, they do not exist as mutually exclusive groupings. The light phenomena existed before the Sun and Moon, but today the two sets are quite obviously related.

The pair originated in the underworld. The stories differ on many points but agree in describing them as mysterious and powerful. Stephen (1930: 104) cites one version where the two are created by Talking God and Calling God. In the other version he relates, First Man is responsible for or associated with their creation. Two other published stories (Matthews 1883: 80; Wheelwright 1949: 39) associate the pair with the big reed, or bamboo, by which diyinii moved up to this world. In all versions, this pair is distinguished by alone having strength to carry the weight of the sun and moon discs.

Sun carrier is usually identified as "He-who-returns-with-a-single-turquoise" (Wyman 1970: 366), "Boy-who-returns-with-a-single-turquoise" (Wyman 1970: 167), or simply as "Turquoise Boy" (Goddard 1933: 135). Moon carrier is usually identified as "He who returns carrying one corn kernel" (Wyman 1970: 366) but is sometimes portrayed as female—"Girl who returns with a single corn kernel" (Wyman 1970: 167). In Goddard's (1933: 135) version, the Moon carrier is mentioned both as a male (White Shell Boy) and as a female (White Shell Girl). Other identifiers are summarized by Wyman (1973: 91).

The varying gender assigned to the Moon carrier points up an extremely important feature of the ałkéé naa'aashii concept, namely, the relative strength or maleness on the part of one member of the pair, and, a corresponding relative weakness or femaleness in the other member. These are not, however, fixed attributes of either entity, but relative to and descriptive of the particular relationship. The one who is the leader in one pair may just as easily be the follower in another pairing. The most common, but not the only, means of expressing such a relationship is by means of sexual differentiation. Occasionally, however, two males or two females will be paired in this way. Then, as often as not, the sex of the "following" member will be a point of disagreement.

An example of this is the way the Sun and the Moon are related to the light phenomena. In the recitation of the cardinal sequence, the Sun, or Sunlight, is often substituted for Horizontal Blue; similarly, although less frequently, the Moon is substituted for Darkness. The most common description of the cardinal sequence that I heard was—Talking God (who, as already stated, is associated with, or the inner form of, the Dawn)—the name of the Sun carrier—Calling God (the inner form of Twilight)—the name of the

Moon carrier. The Sun is the leader or the "chief" relative to the Moon, but Talking God is the leader of all the cardinal phenomena and therefore necessarily the leader or chief in relationship to the Sun. Similarly, Calling God leads the Moon and the Darkness. So far, this is a fairly straightforward relativistic concept. Later we shall see that it becomes more complex, for there are differences of opinion as to how time should be used.

The Sun and the Moon carriers instruct diyin dine'é and the earth-surface dine'é in the same manner as do the light phenomena; thus, Changing Woman says the following:

> "Sun will teach you workers, 'Be quick about it,' he will say to you. You will make use of Talking God, you will pray to him. You will make use of Calling God, you will pray to him. You will make use of Boy-who-returns-with-a-single-turquoise, you will pray to him. You will make use of Him-who-returns-with-a-single-corn-(kernel), you will pray to him." (Wyman 1970: 165)

The whole sequence of temporal phenomena, and the various alternative ways of describing them, are, then, ałkéé naa'aashii. But, there is much more involved in the meaning of this concept than the simple punctuation of time. The stories of the appointment of the Sun and the Moon carriers aid us in beginning to understand this larger meaning. Many different versions have been published and the details vary, but the essence of the story remains constant.

Before these two are placed, and immediately after the cardinal phenomena are vitalized, First Man speaks on that which is still lacking, about that which is yet to be created:

> "So it really is, my children," said First Man. "Obviously, in our present doings here we have not as yet made those things which will join things together, as it were," he said. "So who knows how much time will be required to put things in order. You see, as you go along there working on them, your thoughts will come to an end. Should this happen there should be a means to restart it, a means to sanctify it again, a means to restore its energy," he said. "Now although this be so your thoughts on this point have become somewhat confused. So you see for the present we will devise the means to make things holy again. Therefore, you must appoint two persons for this, one of them (to stand) for work

which is being done, for journeys which are being made, and for assistance you are to get in the future, such a one you will appoint to do the thinking for you. There are not a few things in this connection, the future ahead is far from being completed. Is this the only thing that will represent your holy (things)? Many things which will cause you pain or make you immune to it are increasing. Therefore, think it over well (before) you appoint some person for this purpose," he told them.[7] (Wyman 1970: 377–78)

The Sun and the Moon assure or, in fact, are continuity through time. They first join the other temporal phenomena together. Their travel connects and defines days and nights as well as the larger temporal units—months and seasons.[8] The Sun and, to a lesser extent, the Moon give life to the earth-surface beings; by doing so, they assure the continuity of life on the Earth.

But, says First Man, ". . . your thoughts will come to an end. Should this happen there should be a means to restart it, a means to sanctify it again, a means to restore its energy." In the underworld the twins are slaughtered, and their life substance or ánít'į started life up again and animated that which followed. Life comes to an end on the earth's surface in the night and in the winter; there is sleep and there is hibernation, both of which are a kind of death. The Sun, rising in the morning and moving northward in the spring, restarts or re-energizes living things on a daily and seasonal basis; the Moon does the same on a monthly basis. The primary symbol for this renewal and for the Earth is, of course, Changing Woman, and through her person, we have (in Chapter 2) seen an additional dimension to First Man's statement.

After the events described here have occurred, the earth dwellers, at that time diyinii, are almost totally destroyed by nayéé' (First Man refers to them at the end of the above quote "Many things which will cause you pain or make you immune to it are increasing"). It is the Sun* who will father the twins who will rid the earth of most of these creatures so that human beings and other living things may be safe there again. The Sun also provides the weapons

---

*In some versions of the story both the Sun and the Moon have intercourse with Changing Woman prior to her giving birth to the twins.

that allow the twins to slay nayéé', as well as the armor that protects them. Finally, the Sun strikes the first and most lethal blow against Yé'iitso, the most frightening of nayéé', who is also his own son.

The Sun then starts and ends the day; the Moon is responsible for the night and the monthly cycle. The Sun's north and south movement is associated with, and a part of, the literal death or hibernation of the Earth in the winter, as well as bringing about and signaling seasonal activity cycles for the ones that live on the earth's surface. A human being's daily, seasonal, and life cycles are a part of this, just as it is with Changing Woman. The Sun is the male giver of life and will continue to perform as such in the future. The Sun and Changing Woman, who is the Earth, gave life a new start by providing the ones that slew nayéé'. So the Sun and the Moon renew and re-energize, but they are also responsible for bringing things to an end, both from an immediate and from an historical perspective.

Their work is not for free. They demand a payment, and it is in the lives (or the deaths) of living things. In the meeting where the Sun and Moon* are appointed, the Sun makes this very clear:

> "Well you are just now saying that dying will come into being! And since you are telling me, 'You shall be going for (travelling with) the Sun,' I will not go down (set) without a man's death. Every time I make this journey, let a death occur accordingly. . . ." (Wyman 1970: 379)

The Moon is then asked for his opinion.

> "What about you?" he who was to stand for the Moon asked. "I am too of that opinion," he said, "I will be in charge of the happenings in daytime, but more so of whatever occurs at night," he said. "Moreover, I will be in charge of whatever may happen to vegetation," he said. "And I will have more control over those of the night side," he said. "And you may be thinking, 'How is this? Is it only for things which are deadly that we are making him (to be) a certain thing?'" he said. "At any rate, I am now in control of

---

*In this story the two are identified as the inner forms of the Sun and Moon; but in the narrative, there seems to be some confusion about this. I refer to them simply as Sun and Moon.

this night (part)! And, concerning what you say about future giv-ing birth, births in the future including any and every kind of birth will mostly occur at night, births will be more frequent at night. That will be a cause for rejoicing. Oppositely too, deaths will occur only at night. . . ." (Wyman 1970: 379–80)

It is in this statement that we begin to understand and get a feeling for the opposition inherent in the concept ałkéé naa'aashii. There will be births and there will be deaths. Correspondingly, there will be joy and there will be sorrow. Along these same lines, the Sun, who is responsible for fathering the twins that killed the monsters, is also at least partially responsible for the monsters' exis-tence. When the twins come to him and ask for weapons to kill Yé'iitso, the Sun says to them, "That is your brother, that is my son, you cannot kill him." The Sun is greatly saddened by what they want to do, but he also in some sense fears for the twins, and recognizes the need for their action. He finally agrees, and himself is instrumental in the killing.

First Man also has a hand in the creation of nayéé' and in their destruction. They were created, at least in part, to rid the Earth of those "that didn't keep things holy." The death of these "unholy" people clears the Earth for the future Navajo. But, nayéé' must also be brought to an end. Changing Woman and the twins are needed to do this. The twins are heroes, but they kill their brother; the Sun (along with First Man) fathers the monsters, but he also causes their destruction. He cleanses the Earth, but, in doing so, he kills his own son. He feels joy for the future and great sadness in this death.

The temporal entities and temporal punctuation then are a part of emotional differences in general and emotional cycles in particu-lar. Along with this they describe the death-rebirth cycle of the Earth.

So far, however, Coyote has described only what one might la-bel the "orthodox" daily activity cycle. It is the kind of statement one would be likely to get as a first approximation if one asked a Navajo about proper behavior. But, if there is value in and respect for difference, we would expect it to go deeper than what Coyote has just described. That is, it would be self-referentially invalid for everyone to be in agreement on difference. If there is difference, there should be differences of opinion on difference, differences of opinion on differences of opinion, and so on. To this the narrative of Coyote and the other diyinii now turns. The discussion takes the form of what Bateson (1972) has called a metalogue on difference in thought in general, and difference of opinion in particular.

DIFFERENCE ON DIFFERENCE

After he had described the use of time, as summarized in the preceding section, Coyote asked the other diyinii what they thought. There was no answer which, in this context, implied dissatisfaction. He then commented on the reasons:

> "As I see it the cause for this [the dissatisfaction implied by the silence] is right here. This one time for travelling to be is not good, clearly here is the cause for (this difference of opinion)," he said. "I can see that this one time for travelling which is (proposed) is not a sensible thing. *Where will thinking of various kinds of plans come from?* Clearly this present single way of talking, the single manner in which plans have been made, the work expended on them and the journeys made for them will cause things to last just so long in my opinion," he said. "But, if travelling be done at different times, from that thoughts and planning could then be renewed. . . ." (Wyman 1970: 372; emphasis added)

So, instead of everyone traveling during the day, some should travel at night and rest during the day. This fact of difference will assure that things will continue, whereas sameness will allow existence only for a relatively short period.

On one level this is an allusion to the differences in emotional and behavioral states associated with the temporal cycles described above. But, as Coyote begins to indicate above, there are not just differences in thought with different times, there are also differences about such difference, especially differences of opinion about how such difference should be used. After diyinii vote on how they want the seasons in particular and time in general divided,[9] Coyote comments on the result:

[117]

"Now in this matter, I see half of you are of a different opinion, but this will not be the only thing on which you will disagree since various ways of thinking are now here to stay," he said. "See for yourselves, the Sun and the Moon which you have just made here constitute a similar point (at issue). That these two should travel in one way again is not approved by some of you. . . . Then too you say that there will be births, and say that there will be deaths of old age, and you are saying that deaths will occur, about which you probably have different opinions," he said.

"Besides there will be months about which, too, you probably differ in your opinions," he said to them. "But should you decide one way about these things it really is not a good thing to do in my opinion. . . ." (Wyman 1970: 373)

So, first there is the fact of temporal difference which both causes and is a part of different ways of thinking. Second, Coyote argues that differences of opinion about temporal difference and its associated activities are both a fact of existence and something that should be maintained. But he takes this one step further. After trying to persuade diyinii of the need for and desirability of difference, he notes their reaction:

"I see that some of you are not satisfied with what I am saying in this regard, and some of you are satisfied. Now thus far, what is day has come into being with night, birth too and death have originated together, winter and summer also have come into being. But on this point (the existence of opposites) you have become divided and thus you cannot come to a friendly understanding among yourselves. . . ." (Wyman 1970: 382)

This anticipates our next section on opposition, that is, on the sources and ongoing types of difference in the universe, but it is, of course, the definitive argument on different ways of thought. Diyinii cannot agree on whether or not to allow disagreement. So there is difference, and there are differences of opinion about difference, and there are different opinions about different opinions about difference.

There are several levels of reasoning on why difference exists or on why it should exist. One is simply that there are very few issues that are clearly one way or the other. Most often one can see some merit in both positions. The social rationale, very much a part of

Navajo thought and behavior today, is an extension of this: "Even if one person be arguing, the matter is not an easy one if he favors one side, since the other would feel hurt" (Wyman 1970: 372). This is a very important notion: the premise that a society can exist only if it allows for individual difference.

But, there are really very few arguments made for this in the stories. The process of differentiation, on the one hand, and the existence of certain oppositions, on the other, are taken as givens. They *are* existence—the most general theme of hózhǫ́ǫ́jí and the emergence stories.

The primal state, the time (which, of course, could not be a time) "before" the "in the beginning" of the stories, was one of stillness. And since there was no movement, there was, of course, nothing to be sensed and, therefore, nothing to think about, and no language or behavior. Then, a differentiation was made: "It was as if a stone was thrown into a still pond; the ripples that are time started from this point and moved (and continue moving) outward." The thrower of the stone is not identified. He is not, of course, really a "he" or a being at all, but some abstract initial force. This force, of course, comes from outside; it has to come from outside. There has to be an outsider if information is to be produced in a previously entropic state.

At this differentiation point, one can begin to talk about the "in the beginning" time. It is described as "one language," and, by implication, there was one way of thought and one set of behaviors. Then the number grew. The rate of increase varies in different versions of the story. Some say to two, then four, then twelve; some say to four and then twelve. Twelve is given as the final figure but is not necessarily to be taken literally; it usually simply implies many. This differentiation in language is a differentiation in culture, society, and ways of thought as well. Most of it occurred in the time prior to the emergence, and significant stopping points on this journey are named, as the initial point is named in reference to the number of languages spoken.

This increase is not only essential, it is a very positive thing. It is growth, noot'iił, the increase and perpetuation of living things and systems of thought through time. But it did not stop with the emergence; the process of diversification continued on the earth's surface and continues today with hózhǫ́ǫ́jí. In Chapter 3 we described how this notion of increase applied to the beings we know as living, but from Coyote's discourse on difference it is apparent that it applies to much more. Hózhǫ́ǫ́jí is about noot'iił, about increase and diversification in all things, including that which we label culture. And, it is equivalent to that pattern of existence that we label Navajo culture.

Today this process is reversing. The ripples are returning to their source: "Time is turning back around." The English language is viewed as that one language, and one way of thought, that is replacing others, including Navajo. It is, of course, not the same language as that of the beginning time, but it is the identical process in reverse. As a part of this, the ceremonial knowledge is being forgotten; the culmination of this process, and the end of the Navajos, will be the loss of hózhǫ́ǫ́jí. But with hózhǫ́ǫ́jí go the processes of increase and of differentiation. The state of the one language, probably English, will be followed by a return to the primal or, in this case, final state of stillness.

At a rather mundane level, this macrotheory has rather interesting implications for anthropological theory. Culture is commonly defined in terms of a shared belief system or of shared knowledge. Here we have a people who share the "belief" that belief is not and should not necessarily be shared, that differences of opinion, differences in ideas, and differences in behavior are a part of human society in general and Navajo culture in particular. Individual difference presents a rather serious problem for notions of culture and for the ideas of anthropologists. But, of course, it presents no problem for Navajo theories. At one level, this is a function simply of where one begins, or what one takes as given. The anthropologist begins with the notion of sameness at the level of culture, whereas the Navajo begins with the idea that differentiation is the essential prerequisite to the existence and growth of all systems.

Western theory at the very abstract level shares this basic assumption. However, Western disciplinary theory is founded on the assumption of a delay or a disjuncture of some sort in the basic differentiation process. This disjuncture is then equated with, or defined in terms of, sameness of some sort. Thus, for example, the disciplines that have evolutionary theory as their basis assume that the differentiation that is the core of the theory stops or slows down when the level of sameness labeled "species" is reached. Similarly, anthropologists accept the process of differentiation up to the level of culture and linguists to the level of language. All, of course, also accept intermediate levels of sameness—"families" being the first one to come to mind.

Navajo culture then identifies differentiation as the process that pervades all entities. It is identical to being. In contrast, we create disciplines by assuming that differentiation is stopped or delayed at some level, and at that point there is created a "field," a "profession," or something else. It is less a question of which is more correct than it is a problem of what is more interesting. The one emphasizes boundaries, but it never (to my knowledge) makes a very good specific or general case for entitivity. The other emphasizes relative (but not exclusive) boundlessness—a "unity" in all things by de-emphasizing "thingness" and emphasizing process. The Navajo allows potentially for an understanding of all things. The Westerner emphasizes expertise which may be seen as relative ignorance on almost everything.

OPPOSITION

Different ways of thinking both create and are caused by certain sets of oppositions in the universe. Thus, night and day produce different ways of thinking, but they are themselves a product of more primary polarities. But, ałkéé naa'aashii is a concept that can describe *any* two phenomena that are in an ongoing, permanent relationship of opposition to each other. All of these are manifestations of a single phenomenon, which is the ałkéé naa'aashii pair of the underworlds. Their representations in this world include not only fairly concrete entities but also ideas and emotions.

After his discussion of day and night, Coyote goes on to identify other "opposites" in the world:

"And concerning births (it is likewise), some children are males and other females. Vegetation too is similar, some plants will not grow rapidly, others will show a rapid growth. And so, on the part of those children, when they are seen, and on the part of vegetation which shows a rapid growth, it is a fact that these will cause gladness and be much kept in mind." (Wyman 1970: 374)

This statement is much more general than this translation indicates. The word glossed "children" is áłchíní, which primarily does refer to human children but which can also refer to at least the children of diyinii and, I believe, in certain contexts to the young of most animate beings. The words glossed "male" and "female" are bik'ą and ba'áád, which only very unusually apply to human beings but which are probably the most abstract gender designators. Absolutely everything in the world can be divided into ba'áád and bik'ą. Finally, nańse' or nanise' is the word that Haile (in the above quote) glosses "plant." That is, in fact, its most common referent. It is more literally the neuter form of the verb noo sééł which refers to growth (it is growing). Utilizing this as a starting point, Werner, Manning, and Begishi (1979: 22) found that there was a more general usage, which they glossed as "live things" and which includes both nanise' with the "plant" referent at a lower taxonomic level, and hiináanii which they gloss both "moving thing" and "animal." But, nanise' can be taken even more abstractly. It can refer to any of the "growing things" in hózhǫǫ́jí: not just livestock, human beings, game, and plants, but jewels, fabrics, language, and ideas, as well.[10]

A better translation of the above (but, still quite inadequate in its concreteness relative to the Navajo) would go something like this:

> (And here are some other important differences). Concerning the ones that give birth (the plants, the animals, diyinii, jewels, fabrics to name a few). The ones that grow all around are similar in the fact that they too show a difference; namely, some will show a rapid growth, and others will not grow rapidly. And so, when one sees those young ones, and when one sees the rapid growth, it will cause gladness (a form of hózhǫ́ is used in the text) and be kept much in mind.

The growth referred to is not just that of individuals; it is also that of populations and generations. So growth, increase, births, maleness and femaleness, and happiness exist together or are a part of the same phenomenon. But, there is another side to it as well:

> "Then too on the side of those that die and continually are dying, grateful feelings will continue on the one hand and sorrow for it will be immense (on the other) which, as you see, again shows a difference." (Wyman 1970: 374)

Joy and gratitude then, on the one hand, and sorrow, on the other, are ałkéé naa'aashii, as are many other sets of emotions including strength, or the feeling of strength, and weakness; love and hate; passion and jealousy; and so on. The immediate point of the stories is that the affect labeled negative and the affect labeled positive are parts of the same package. One can do away with the negative (in the case of emotions) only by doing away with affect.

But these oppositions are not confined to the realm of affect; they exist with other rather abstract phenomena, as well. Coyote includes this in his description of future conditions:

> "Besides, there is still another point," he said. "That, you see, concerns the fact that you are clothed," he said. "But of this being clothed in just one kind of thing as it is now (continues), it would represent acquisition of property once only. Now that just does not seem sensible to me," he said. "And as I think of the matter, I have in mind that poverty should exist," he said
>
> "And I have in mind that acquiring property also should exist," he said. "The reason is that these clothes will be subject to wear and tear, and this will be called poverty," he said. "As for the other (circumstance) called acquiring property, this will apply when different kinds of new clothes are acquired, and because of it satisfaction will be felt. Besides thinking about it will continue, so that there will be differences concerning it, as it were. You can see that on this point there is again a difference. . . ." (Wyman 1970: 374)

Similarly, in anaa'jí (Enemyway) poverty is one of nayéé' usually mentioned as being spared by the twins. The reasoning is essentially similar to that outlined above:

> Poverty also spoke up here, "Let me live on, my grandchildren! Should you kill me nothing will be threadbare, there will be just one kind of clothing in use all the time! Why is it that he should wear just one garment indefinitely!" he said. "While if I live on it

will become threadbare on persons, after which they will clothe themselves in good kinds of goods. This will be similar to giving birth as days go on in the future," he said. "Therefore you must let me live on, my grandchild," he said. (Wyman 1970: 573)[11]

The clothing, of course, represents property in general. This theme is repeated in the discussion of hunger and food:

"There is another thing, foods which sustain lives, of this too I now want to say a word to you," he told them. "You see, you have made plants and what is called grand (original) corn, and these are to continue as food," he said to them. "And of these, too, there will be (enemies that) bother them," he said. "Of these, there will be two in existence as though they were inside of one another," he said.[12] "You see these plants will be in a good shape only when it is warm," he said. "And too, with the cold there will be hunger which will serve as a lesson as time goes on. Because if it were always warm and continued warm there would be no planning ahead. But if cold bothers a person at a certain time it would cause thoughts to be directed towards it. And if hunger likewise bothers a person, there would be repeated thoughts concerning it." (Wyman 1970: 374)

These oppositions, and many others, are ałkéé naa'aashii. The "negative" state exists in part as a lesson, to ensure that the "positive" side will occur. For instance, the worry and unhappiness associated with and brought about by poverty assure the happiness and comfort brought about by work and acquisition. Further, these "negative" states assure that there will be planning for the future. At this level, and at the level of the associated emotions, different ways of thinking are produced. But, the "wear and tear on clothing" produces other differences as well. If one's property lasted forever, there would be very few goods and very little variation in them. The fact that things do not last assures both a variety and varied thoughts about possessions (in the sense that there is more to think about). It further assures that earth-surface dwellers will be active (as well as occasionally, but not chronically, inactive), which in itself is a difference and (the activity) a source of other differences.

These oppositions do not, however, exist solely as isolated distinct phenomena but are instead a part of larger "packages" of oppositions. The sets can be summarized thusly:

"Besides, those of you that have chosen the night (know) that death will occur in that period, therefore you will travel in winter.* . . . Concerning those of you that have chosen daytime, in this period everything will take care of itself, therefore you will do your work on plants which will always come into being in the summertime*. . . . This will represent acquiring property, it will be called providing for one's self. Those of you that have chosen winter and night time, this will be called laziness (which) keeps things out of one's reach. . . ." (Wyman 1970: 374)

We therefore have the set night, death, winter travel, poverty and laziness, on the one hand; opposed is the set daytime, growth, summer, acquisition of property, and work. There is nothing particularly esoteric about these associations. They merely describe the way things are for the day dine'é, particularly human beings. If a person sleeps too much (values the night), he will be poor. He will then have to travel in the winter in search of food because he has stored no provisions. The opposite is also true. If one values (by rising with the dawn) the day and uses it and the summer (the times of growth), one will acquire the necessary things along with, very likely, a surplus.

Time and temporal punctuation then describe the process ałkéé naa'aashii, and these (and many other) oppositions describe the content. But there are two *primary* oppositions, two pairs that are themselves ałkéé naa'aashii, which are the source of all of this and the source, both literally and symbolically, of all the other entities that are today regarded as ałkéé naa'aashii. They are gender opposition and the pair birth/death, two sets that are closely related.

BIRTH AND DEATH

That temporal punctuation both reflects and is a part of the birth/death cycle is the essence of the previous discussion, which

---

*Wyman thinks that these are non sequiturs; I obviously do not agree.

was nicely summarized by Coyote near the conclusion of the preceding section. The beginnings of this association and, of course, of everything else are in the underworld and are described in the ałkéé naa'aashii stories of this time. One good example was given near the beginning of this chapter. As the reader will recall, it dealt with the ritual slaughter of twins (who were diyinii) and the subsequent use of their life stuff to animate other beings. This theme of death being a necessary prerequisite or a part of life continues today with the Sun and the Moon, the seasons, and the daily temporal cycle. All are ałkéé naa'aashii, all have encoded within them the birth/death polarity, and all derive from or, more literally, are the "children" of these twins sacrificed in the underworlds.

The stories of the creation of (or, more precisely, the choice of) death by diyinii continue with this theme. After they emerged, diyinii were troubled by and questioned the fact that there was no increase in their numbers. As described in Chapter 2, there is a divination to see whether or not people will live forever. First Man initiates it by throwing a hidescraper or some other piece of wood into the water proclaiming, "If this floats up, people will not die, they will live forever." Coyote, either simultaneously or immediately afterward, throws a stone ax or some other stone into the water while he makes the same statement. The stone, of course, sinks; the wood floats. Initially, diyin dine'é are quite angry at this, but Coyote explains it to them thusly:

> "If there be no deaths, there shall be no births. In that case, you will number as many as you are now." (Wyman 1973: 119)

Similarly, in anaa'jí, "old age" (sá) is one of nayéé' that is spared by the twins. "Old age" speaks for himself in the following quotation, but the reasoning is identical to that of Coyote:

> "In spite of it all, I am going to live on, my grandchild," he said. "How surprisingly little sense you have, my grandchild!" he told him. "You have not the right thing in mind, I see," he told him. "Should you kill me dying would cease," he said. "Then too giving birth would cease," he said, "and this present number of people would continue in the same amount for all time to come. While if I live on, old age will do killing and giving birth will go

on in the future. As giving birth goes on ahead, so deaths will go on in the other way," he said. "The various birth beings, all without exception, should continue to give birth in the future, every kind of moving being, none excepted." . . . (Wyman 1970: 573)

The aspect of death which lives on has both a corporeal and a "spiritual" part[13]:

The ax sank but the stick floated. Because it floated, a person's soul* comes to life again. Because the ax sank, people die. . . . (Goddard 1933: 138)

It is on the fate of this life force or "soul" that there is fairly serious (although not usually intense, as the subject is viewed as too speculative) disagreement among Navajo philosophers today. And, it is in these disagreements that we can begin to understand another polarity, that between behavior which is bąąhágii, or socially unacceptable, on the one hand, and that which is encouraged or allowed on the other. The disagreement centers on the degree to which ego or identity is maintained within the nítch'i bii'sizíinii after death.

The view that I prefer has a being's nítch'i going at death to hayoołkááł dine'é and being "washed clean," becoming, as it were, a part of a kind of undifferentiated pool of nítch'i. It is in this sense that McNeley's (1973) informants could say "all nítch'i is one," and it is also in this sense that McNeley likens nítch'i to the "Great Spirit" concepts of the Plains Indians.

Some say, however, that certain attributes of the life force are maintained or are inseparable from it. Thus, Haile (1943: 74–79) can say that there are nine to twelve "types" of nítch'i; and McNeley's informants can say there are four. Among those features commonly mentioned as continuing as a part of the life force are longevity (or, in contrast, short-livedness), and certain character (e.g., insanity) and physical (e.g., deformities) traits. In addition, there are some that say life forces are transmitted only within clans, or even within more restricted units of kinship. Those that accept the

---

*Nítch'i is the word glossed "soul" here; one should be aware of it, as it is the most common, but very incomplete, translation, for this very important concept.

"washed clean" hypothesis, however, brand such a view as "witch-craft," and this example leads us to the presuppositions underlying such an accusation. But these can be understood more easily if we diverge for a moment and look at what happens to the body after death. It provides an exact but simpler parallel to what happens to the "soul." The "normal," as well as appropriate, state of the corpse is decomposition. In this rotting, the Earth and the beings of the Earth benefit. The corpse both directly animates the Earth Mother and fertilizes the plants, thus improving the entire food chain.

The essential feature, and the ideal at death, is the freeing of the life force and the life substance to aid in the formation of and growth of new life. This is what noot'iił, "increase" or "increase with no decrease" or "generational increase" is all about. The Sun and the Moon are a part of it. They use the life force, and perhaps the substance, freed in certain types of death as both payment for and as the energizing force which enables them to continue their journeys. Their journeys in turn bring the benefit of growth and, of course, the sadness of death. The Earth, the seasons, and Changing Woman are also part of, and primary symbols for, this process. The death—rebirth cycle of the universe, this is ałkéé naa'aashii.

"Witchcraft" short-circuits this process, and that is its essence. The typical story describes how a corpse is stolen from the grave-yard fairly soon after burial. It is then taken to ánít'į́ báhoghan, which is always hidden and usually located under the Earth. The people who do the stealing, or others at the hogan, are closely re-lated to the deceased. The participants do one of two things. They either render the body, or they have intercourse with the deceased (in all the stories told to me, the corpse was female) and collect the combined sexual fluids in a basket. Before they do this, however, the one who has died is in some sense brought back to life but not necessarily to that state of awareness of consciousness that he or she enjoyed previously. Further, there are usually others sitting around the hogan who had died. Again, they are described as "zombies" of some sort, or in a state of limited awareness or, perhaps, possession.

The following story, which describes an incident which oc-curred in a family I lived with, is typical. An "aunt" was suspected and made to confess, and she (not surprisingly) blamed it all on her ex-husband:

That night he made me go with him. I didn't know what it was all about. We walked to a tree and stood by it and down under the roots we could hear something and see kind of a faint light. All of a sudden, I don't know how it happened, we were down in there, in the ánít'į́ báhoghan. [Lists names] all of these that had previously died, they were all there sitting around, but they kind of looked different or strange, kind of like they were hypnotized.* Then there were others [gives names] who still live around here. We got down in there and there were wild animal skins around. They put them on us, but I don't remember how, all of a sudden it just seemed like we were in them. I don't remember much of the rest either. We were outside again and it seems like we just thought of this place that this girl who just recently died was buried and we were there†, even though it was several miles away. Then my husband, with only a small stick, dug her out. And then somehow he made her body real small, so that I could carry her back under my armpit and under the skin that I was wearing. In an instant, we were back at the hoghan. We got inside and somehow the skins were removed. The girl was kind of brought back to life again, by her real brother, he was there. She just kind of sat there, smiling and looking around; she was kind of half-conscious.

She was lying there on the buffalo robe, then the men, one by one, had intercourse with her, even her brother and her other close relatives. They collected the fluid in something like a Paiute basket placed under them, only it was made of white shell instead of sumac.

The corpse and the reproductive fluid are ánít'į́. In fact, they are the only sources of ánít'į́ that I know of. As noted in the previous chapter, the term is usually glossed something like "witchcraft medicine," or "evil medicine" or "corpse medicine." This labeling is correct as far as it goes, but it is quite incomplete. In the underworlds, ánít'į́ came from the bodies of the twins who were slaughtered. All subsequent life derived from this source. Further, the association between twins and this medicine is maintained today. Kluckhohn describes it thusly:

> (It) . . . is made from the flesh of corpses. The flesh of children and especially twin children is preferred, and the bones at the back

---

*This is the word people use, in English, to describe the state.

†As noted in Chapter 1, rapid movement is a feature mentioned with regard to diyinii, but attainable by man. Here we have álílee bagáál; just thinking about a destination and instantly being there, moving in a "supernatural way."

of the head and skin whorls are the prized ingredients. When this "corpse medicine" is ground into powder, it "looks like pollen." . . . (Kluckhohn 1968: 25)

The whorls on the palms, the feet, and the top of the head are the imprint of one's nítch'i bii'sizíinii or animating force and are the interface between the nítch'i that is within one and the nítch'i that is everywhere. Further, the nítch'i exist within us in pairs; and it is partly in this sense that one's animating force is ałkéé naa'aashii.[14] But, it is also ałkéé naa'aashii in that the life force derives ultimately from the ałkéé naa'aashii of the underworlds and, more immediately, from another being's animating force being freed at death.

Additionally, note that ánít'į has more than the visual association with pollen that Kluchkhohn mentions. Both substances are a part of, and themselves bring about, the increase in the numbers of animate beings on the earth's surface. After the ánít'į was brought up, First Man described this aspect of its use to his companions:

> "When you have this thing, man will get rich easy. This thing is sheep, horses. All the same as having a lot of hard goods, including different kinds of shells." When it was brought up, there is the place where it starts. People keep on with it and we are still hearing about it yet. (Kluckhohn 1968: 133; Kluckhohn is here quoting an informant)

The identical statement can, of course, be made for pollen. Ánít'į and the corn were brought up in the bundle. This was the flesh of the twins, and it was used in the underworld to "renew" First Man's medicine bundle. So, the twins died so that the bundle could "live again" or continue to live. This, of course, is the distillation of one-half of the essential meaning of ałkéé naa'aashii. This bundle lies in the Earth today; it is nahasdzą́ą́ bii'gistíín. And the flesh of those who die repeatedly continue to renew the bundle in the same way. Finally, all living things, all things that are created, derived from and are continuing to derive from this bundle; this ánít'į, the flesh of the twins, the source of it all.

This birth/death cycle, the process of reanimation and rebirth, is what hózhǫ́ǫ́jí chronicles, directs, and produces. This ceremony and this process belong to no one, but they, and the goods that result, can be used by everyone.

The witch is one who subverts or disturbs noot'iił or, stated slightly differently, interferes with and interrupts the cycle described by the concept ałkéé naa'aashii. There are several facets, and they are all found in and essential to the story of the ánít'į báhoghan. Fundamentally, the grave robber is stealing from everyone. The corpse, in decomposing, is to the benefit of the Earth[15] and therefore to the benefit of everyone. The witch takes these benefits for himself and uses them exclusively for his own egotistic gain and thus "steals" from all. The same is true for the life force. To not allow it to be freed again denies or inhibits generational increase. Personal immortality in some form replaces this generational increase and continuation of life. This is what the choice of death or the choice "to live only so long" by diyın dine'é was all about; this is what the life force being "washed clean" by hayoołkáál dine'é is a part of. And, conversely, this is why those who believe in the maintenance of some life force attributes may be labeled a "witch." Finally, people who live too long (beyond a certain age, usually given as 100 or 102) are not looked on very fondly. The only egocentric immortality in Navajo is in the context of witchcraft (and, one would have to mention, Christianity)—those people sitting around the ánít'į báhoghan, in a zombie-like state who had previously died. To summarize, witchcraft is egocentric and immediate in a context that should be generational and populational.

Finally, the "witch" is one who "steals" a woman of his own clan (in the example above it was also the real brother, but the clan relationship is the one that is emphasized in these stories). The women of one's own clan, in fact, very literally are said to "belong to" others.

There is an additional differentiation that can be made, according to the motive one has in using ánít'į. It can be used to gain wealth or to harm others. If the latter, the person is labeled a "witch" or as "evil." If the former, it is, within bounds, acceptable, or even appropriate. Very knowledgeable (and, usually, very old) people will say, "You can't have much increase without ánít'į." And, they will point to a particular individual as possessing it with an attitude of admiration and respect, mixed with fear. However, it is not something that one talks about publicly.

But, this differentiation, in practice, no longer exists. The land is too crowded and the grazing too poor. The situation has become too clearly zero sum.[16] The gain (the livestock are to be emphasized) of anyone is too clearly the loss of others. Acts of "witchcraft" are everywhere.

To reiterate, the "witch" is one who uses ánít'į for his private gain. He takes what should be public, impersonal, generational increase, the gain of all, and subverts it to his own selfish ends. Thus, at a minimum, ałkéé naa'aashii describes this cycle of rebirth, or of birth and death. But, there is an additional element, for, as already noted, an essential aspect of the concept is generational increase, noot'iił, or "increase with no decrease." So far, we have only a rebirth sequence with no mechanism for the growth of a finite amount of life stuff. The mechanism for this growth is, of course, gender. First Man describes the package in a kind of contrary talk at the time he divined for death:

> First Man said, "They will not die for all time. Women will not have periods.[17] They will not give birth to babies." . . . (Goddard 1933: 138)

Thus, if the divination had "succeeded" (that is, if people had lived for all time) these conditions would have prevailed. But, of course, it failed so that today we have births and deaths, males and females, and increase. The next section then is about gender and sexuality, the increase they bring about, and the problems they create.

GENDER

The gender we have discussed as existing primally was more abstract and less defined than that quality that we are familiar with today. To put it slightly differently, since gender was the only quality in the universe at that time, it had to be highly abstract. The only state that is more abstract is the one that preceded it, without division, or without quality, and therefore containing all qualities. Today, however, this is only part of the story. Gender still has this abstract side, but, in addition, it has a concrete and more superficial aspect, very like our notions of sexuality. Later it will be apparent that this distinction is more heuristic than real.

Everything,* as any Navajo will tell you, can be divided into male and female. This includes not only those things that we regard as living, but all other entities as well—stories, ceremonies, "jewels," and "fabrics" being a few examples. Matthews (1902: 6) commented on this distinction early:

> Of two things that are nearly alike, or otherwise comparable; it is common among Navajos to speak of or symbolize the one which is the coarser, rougher or more violent as the male, and that is which the finer, weaker or more gentle as the female.

This does not quite capture the spirit of it, but the emphasis on the relationship is correct. The qualities of "maleness" and "femaleness"[18] are positively correlated with, but by no means determined by, the superficial division of living things into males and females on the basis of external sexual organs.

As described earlier, ałkéé naa'aashii, when used concretely, refers to pairs (usually expressed as "twins") who show a difference in their gender relationship if not necessarily a sexual difference. The light phenomena and the beings that animate them along with the Sun and the Moon are important examples. Nayéé' neezghání and tóbájíshchíní are an example in which the gender relationship and the sexuality are not congruent. The former occupies the male role and the latter the female role in the ałkéé naa'aashii relationship, and yet both are males.

There are certain features associated with each of these gender essences. Male thought is characterized as strong and capable of "traveling great distances." Female thought is pretty much limited to the hogan and the things associated with the home. This is usually described in terms of the smoke from the mountain tobacco.

---

*Peyote may be an exception, being only female; but, on this, there is disagreement.

Male thought, as if it were the smoke being exhaled, travels as far as the most distant of the sacred mountains; female thought, when "exhaled," lingers around the smoke hole of the hogan. Planning far ahead and thinking or perceiving great distances are, of course, synonomous. There is another aspect to this as well. The strength and power of male thought is opposed to the stability and relative safety of female thinking. Thus, it is male thought that is the source of irresponsible behavior (e.g. chasing around, drinking), on the one hand, and the ability to learn and be able to "control" ritual knowledge on the other. The female thought is "the cooked"; it is associated with the house and domesticity, and the things associated with the hogan—the sheep, the corn, and the family.

Completeness or entitivity obviously results from a combination of the two. Thus, married couples are referred to ceremonially as ałkéé naa'aashii. Similarly, nádlee (the hermaphrodite) is strongly (I think as strong an entity as can exist) complete, as he possesses both and therefore has all potentials. But, as already noted, almost all beings that we regard as monads are ałkéé naa'aashii as well. Although their entitivity may not be as strong or as conspicuous as nádlee, they (and we) all have at least the potential for this completeness.

The gender that manifests itself today, particularly as reproductive potential, and its twin, sexual desire, were created in the first world and brought up to and placed in each of the subsequent worlds. The "final" placement on the earth's surface and into the beings that lived there is described in hózhǫ́ǫ́jí. The source of this reproductive potential was and is the medicine bundle. In describing creation in Chapter 3, it was made clear that an essential part of animating a being is to place within it the ability to give birth (and to conceive) and, as a guarantee that birth will occur, to also place sexual desire within it.

Sexuality was created by the primal couple according to First Man's plan. The published accounts of the emergence story include partial descriptions of this. Goddard's (1933) version emphasizes the function of sexual desire in keeping men and women together; it also reiterates the differing aspects of male and female thought. The following episode is preceded by First Woman being caught at, and causing a lot of trouble for herself and others through, committing adultery, an incident that is chronicled more completely later in this section:

First Woman thought about it and resolved to be the leader in these matters. She concluded that she would not be the only one to commit adultery, but that women in general would do that. She planned that it would be hard for men and women, once attached, to separate again. She decided that both men and women would have medicine to attract each other. Then she made a penis of turquoise.* She rubbed loose cuticle from the man's breast. This she mixed with yucca fruit. She made a clitoris of red shell and put it inside the vagina. She rubbed loose cuticle from a woman's breast and mixed it with yucca fruit. She put that inside the turquoise penis. She combined herbs with waters of various kinds which should be for producing pregnancy.† She placed the vagina on the ground and beside it the penis. Then she blew medicine from her mouth on them. That is why when people marry nowadays the woman sits on the left side.

"Now you think," she said to the penis. It did so and its mind extended across Mesa Verde. When the woman's organ thought its mind went nearly half way across and returned to her hips. That is why her longing does not extend to a great distance.

"Let them shout," she said. The penis shouted very loud, but the vagina had a weak voice. "Let them have intercourse and try shouting again," she said. When they tried again penis could not shout loud, but vagina had a good voice. The penis had lost its voice. As the organs were being put in place between the legs Coyote came. He pulled some of his beard out, blew on it, and placed it between the legs of both the man and woman. "It looks nice that way," he said. (Goddard 1933: 138–39)

From this story one can begin to see that the set adultery and sexual desire are ałkéé naa'aashii. Although this is correct, it is not the best way to look at it, as we shall soon see. A second version of

---

*Everything has a male and female. In the world of ńtł'iz (jewels), dootł'izhii (turquoise) is bik'ą (male).

†This is important. In Chapter 2 Haile translates this as "amniotic fluid"; here Goddard more literally describes it as fluids that produce pregnancy. These are, of course, the semen for the male and, for the Navajo, the coital fluid of the woman. Note here that they are part of the means of attraction that First Woman is creating.

this story was elicited by Haile.[19] It is more philosophical in nature and more immediately relevant to the concept we are trying to define:

> First Man and his eight companions took counsel together and decided that there should be more creation. . . . All the principal people came in (to the hogan created for that purpose). . . . None of the people, except Coyote, knew what was to happen, and he whispered to his neighbors about it while he ran from one side of the door to the other. He whispered to the people that the bunch of mixed stones would be the genitalia of a man and the pile of mixed jewels the genitalia of woman. Then Coyote went to First Man and told him what the various things were to be created, but First Man did not answer, and Coyote said to the people, "No one of you seems to be able to guess what these things are. I roam about and have little sense, but I have guessed all of them. You must all pay great attention to this ceremony since it concerns you all for this is the *Creation of Birth*.". . .
>
> Now they began to give power to the male and female genitalia and all the people were to contribute. Wolf, Wildcat, Kit Fox and Badger gave their vomit, and male and female organs made of Red-White Stone, and while they did this seventeen songs were sung. Coyote came to First Man and said, "What have you made here?" First Man answered, "You run around in the dark everywhere; you ought to know what it is." Coyote said, "These things are not alike." And then he gave the male organ four hairs from his left beard, and to the female organ four hairs from his right beard. First Man then put away his precious stones which had been used to create the genitalia of Man and Woman, and distributed the created organs *so that Man and Woman might give birth to children. First Man is the source of the evil that did not exist before. After this rite was finished, Coyote said. "We have done well to let new ones come into the world."*
>
> First Man then collected all his treasure and also the Magic Hogan, and made them into a little ball. Then he folded up the Turquoise columns of Light and raised up the columns of Twilight, and all slept. When the day came again the women were pregnant and chiefs made speeches to the people about the future crops and also about the children to be born. After four days, twins were born, then a male child, and then twins, then a girl child, and after that many more babies were born; the people flourished and had meat and crops in storage, and this was the seventh season in this place. (Wheelwright 1949: 13–15; emphasis added).

This then is the creation, or a creation, for there seem to be several, of birth. Two things are done. The first is to rigidify the form of what was previously a much more diffuse kind of gender difference. The second is to create and place the mechanism that will ensure that births on a repeated basis (noot'iił) will continue. And the mechanism is, of course, sexual desire, which not only ensures the increase of population but also is responsible for bringing about "different ways of thinking." There are first the sex-linked differences in thought already described. Second, new beings are continually coming into existence and, therefore, individual and generational differences are created. But the thing to be emphasized more is the oppositions or polarities that we have already partly discussed. In fact, all difference can be reduced to this particular act of the creation of creation. This is summarized in the portion of the story that I emphasized; let me repeat it:

> (He) . . . distributed the created organs so that Man and Woman might give birth to children. First Man is the source of the evil [read ugliness or unpleasantness here] that did not exist before. After the rite was finished, Coyote said, "We have done well to let new ones come into the world."

At first glance, this seems to be a rather unusual juxtaposition of ideas. But, it very nicely ties together and summarizes many of the things we have been discussing. First of all, it very clearly states that the pair hózhǫ́ and hóchxǫ́ are ałkéé naa'aashii. The ugliness referred to is, at an abstract level, death and dying (and their companions—poverty, old age, and disease). By creating birth, the other side is necessarily created. But a more immediate reference is being made to the jealousy, adultery, worry, and negative affect in general that accompany sexual desire. We began to approach this in Goddard's version of the story, which pointed up adultery and sexual desire as ałkéé naa'aashii. But, the set jealousy and desire form a much stronger opposition or entity, albeit worry and adultery must be included as part of the package. The final aspect of the ugliness are nayéé' (the "monsters") that come into being as a direct result of this reproductive potential and of passion. All of this is brought together in the story of the separation of the sexes. The separation occurs immediately after, and as a direct result of, the creation of sexuality.

The event that precipitates the separation is the adultery of the wife of an "important chief." In the version that I will cite, it is First Man's wife. Every day, she feigns sickness so that she will be carried to the riverbank where she meets her lover. First Man follows her one day and sees what is going on, at which point he returns home to wait for her. In most versions, he then pines over it and worries about it for several days. In this version, he immediately informs the other chiefs about what has taken place. When his wife returns home, he strikes her. She enlists the aid of her mother who, in this version, is Woman Chief, the one who later becomes First Death Woman. An argument ensues; Woman Chief is here the speaker:

> "Shall anyone abuse what is mine? Shall anyone strike what is mine, my babe?" she said. "Who is it that lives by him? I do not live by him" she said. "I (can) make everything. I make anything that is necessary for life" she said. "Everything exists through me, everything that ripens exists through me," she said. "While through him they do not exist" she said. . . . (Haile 1932: 8)

Woman Chief then goes over to talk to her son-in-law:

> "You certainly have no pity. Without any cause at all you have abused my daughter" she told him there. "You usually begin your talks by saying all things exist through me! All things that are planted exist through me you say in your talks. My feet stick through the earth and my head through the sky, you say in your talks. Furthermore of the holy beings I am the very highest you claim in your talks." Yet, although this line of words was strung out and so much was said to him, he had still not spoken a word. "Everything without exception I have made, you say in your speeches, and everything continues firm through me you claim in your speeches" she told him. And on top of that also: "All things necessary in life I know of, I am master of all things, I am responsible for them all" she said. "With my feet sticking through the earth and my head sticking through the sky I think of myself" she said. "Therefore I do not live by you. Who lives by you anyway? I myself, by myself, make myself live!" she told him. "What, now, do you think of yourself?" she asked him. Not even a word did he say to her. Then it seems she left him. (Haile 1932: 9)

I often think that anthropologists who try to explain mother-in-law avoidance are commenting on the obvious. All published versions of the story, and all versions told to me, make the women the culprits,* and the men the victim/heroes. Here, for example, First Man is behaving in an extremely socially appropriate way, while both his wife and, particularly, Woman Chief are not. I do not believe that this is essential to the story. My teachers accepted a qualitative male—female difference, it is true, but an aspect of this was not one being better or worse than the other. Additionally, note that all published versions and all accounts that I elicited were from men. I have it on good authority that women tell the story quite differently, although my associates and I were never able to get a woman to tell it to us.

A subsidiary theme being explored here is the strength of First Man's power and control, something very appropriate to this work if very unusual in this particular story. Finally, note that, since First Man is responsible for the creation of sexuality, he is also directly responsible for the trouble and the worry he is now experiencing. Not only did he bring this on himself, but, according to my teachers, this entire episode—the adultery, the separation, the reunion—all happened according to, and as a part of, First Man's plan. Had there been no separation, there would have been no increase on the earth's surface.

Following this discussion with his mother-in-law, First Man spent a sleepless night worrying about his wife and about the challenge to his authority:

> With this on his mind he spent the night. So the fact that I make everything, that I always thought I am master of all things that grow and ripen, and the thought through me that the earth's position is firm and the sky's position is firm through me, so all of that does not exist through me, I am not then master of it! With such thoughts he spent the night.
>
> Now he usually spoke at dawn, but when the time for it arrived, nothing was heard. Without having eaten food the sun set.

---

*Tł'aáh's version is the harshest to women. This is interesting as tł'aáh was, at least socially, nádlee.

No speeches were made. He walked about just worrying about it all day long. Another dawn appeared but again nothing was heard. . . . Up to that time four nights had passed without his having made even (a single) speech, not even did he eat anything for four nights. Another day passed. . . . (Haile 1932: 9–10)

He is then sought out by another chief to whom he tells his story; they then assemble the men (or, more properly, the males) and First Man repeats his story to them. He finishes his address with these words:

"So now think this over. You have heard all the particulars of what I told you. Now think it over, because of us, who are men, it was spoken in a manner, as though we are unnecessary in life," he said. "And so my mind is on this, mine is" he said. (Haile 1932: 10)

They then call upon First Man to decide what to do. He says simply that since we men are unnecessary to life, we may as well separate from the women and have each sex live by itself. The males can live on one side of this river and the females on the other side. But, First Man knows what is going to happen, and so he arranges it so that nádlee will accompany the men. First Man calls nádlee to the meeting and asks what tasks he can perform. Note here also the way in which First Man addresses him[20]:

"But what are you able to do my grandfather, my grand-mother?" he asked him. "I myself (can) plant, I myself make mill-stones, that's settled" he said. "I myself make baking stones. I make pots myself and earthen bowls, gourds I plant myself. I (can) make water jugs" he said, "and stirring sticks and brooms" he said.

He was counting up it seems the things women usually do. "Liquid corn mush" he mentioned, "still corn mush" . . . You see up to there he had counted up all in the line of woman's work without omitting one. "What she said I alone keep up life I can also say" he said. (Haile 1932: 15)

Nádlee is both male and female. Although the term is usually glossed "hermaphrodite," today people will often, perhaps jo-kingly, translate it as "queer" or "homosexual." Nádlee used to be, and should be, a person who is respected, not one who is made fun of. This is still a very important and very common teaching. I think the term refers less to external genitalia then to the potentials one exhibits in behavior. On this point, some very knowledgeable younger Navajos disagree with me, saying that traditionally it referred only to the true hermaphrodite. At any rate, a person who is nádlee "can do anything." He can do both male and female tasks and can (except for childbearing) fill both, or either, sex's roles. Nádlee is also associated with great riches; the person who knows the stories concerning him "gets rich easy."

But let us now return to the story of the separation. The people now prepared to move apart, the women being allowed to stay on the land that they had shared with the men and the men moving across the river. Each side retained their belongings, including, quite importantly, the tools that were a part of the sexual division of labor. But, of course, the men had nádlee and the female skills and tools that he possessed. So, while there was only the female element on the one side, the men had at least a partial female element with them. There was great sadness on both sides at the parting.

On the men's side, they did their work, while nádlee cooked and raised the male children (the women kept the female children):

> At nádlee's (place) the pots were boiling. The skin part of a deer udder, after nicely removing its interior, he would fill with broth, to be used in raising the children. . . . (Haile 1932: 19)

The men appeared to do quite well during the separation, while the condition of the women gradually worsened. In some versions, the women taunt the men sexually by standing on the riverbank and exposing their genitalia. The condition of each, and the implications this has for different "ways of thinking," is described:

> And so some of those women were getting lonesome, this because of thinking of those with whom they had lived (their husbands). Here on this side, although they were in the same condition, they had simply made up their minds here on the men's side. (Haile 1932: 20)

Gradually, the women began to plead but, supposedly, not the men. Some women even ran into the stream and drowned:

> Sexual desires also tormented them. With a so-called oblong stone they attempted intercourse. They attempted intercourse

[141]

with feather quills. They had intercourse with leg muscles of animals. They had intercourse with hooked spine cactus. They attempted intercourse with "sitting cactus," they say. Yellow foxes had become their husbands. While badger had held excessive intercourse with them. After awhile his penis had simply turned to stone. . . .

Here on the men's side too, it was learnt that they attempted intercourse with mud. Some that went out hunting had used the does in the same manner for sexual intercourse. After heating the liver they had also used this for sexual intercourse. (Haile 1932: 22)

Nayéé' were, of course, born of these acts on the women's side. This is, as already noted, one of the references that Coyote has in mind when he refers to the ugliness that goes with the "beauty" of sexual desire and reproductive potential. Finally, a hunter who is about to use the liver of a deer to masturbate is visited by owl, who warns him against it and who speaks to him about what is taking place:

"It is now four years hence that you have moved across (leaving) the women behind that is well known to you" he said. "Now although this took place in consequence of her own act, which really brought this upon them (the women), though this be the real state of affairs, no good can come of it, my grandchild, therefore I am speaking to you" he said. "At present only a few women remain" he said . . . "Here on the side of the remnant of women, they are abusing themselves any old way he said. . . .

"Now these conditions are familiar to me for your (sake)" he told them. "If in this manner the woman disappear, how will the race get a new start?" he said. "If you men only (continue) living, why! the end (of things) would be reached" he said . . . "you must bring them across" he said. "If you do not bring them across again bad conditions will prevail. The earth (as it is) will vanish and the sky as well" he said. "If you bring them across again the course ahead will go on indefinitely" he said. (Haile 1932: 24–25)

This is a rather concise statement about what this story is all about: the necessity for the sexes to continue together, despite the difficulties that are inherent in their relating. This again is what noot'iił is all about. Owl goes on to say that when they do go back together, to wait four days before resuming sexual relationships with the females. This ceremonial restriction is, of course, observed today. The hunter returns to tell First Man what owl has said. The men attempt to convince him that they should go back together. After listening, he asks the opinion of nádlee who also advocates going back together, and in so doing describes his own incompleteness:

> "Look here I am seated as you are looking at me! A new start cannot be made through me!" he said. "I am pleased with this. In the past I was worried about it, my children" he said. "You have spoken to me as being master of that. Let it now be the bringing across" he said. (Haile 1932: 32)

The new start on one level, of course, refers to birth. But, it may refer more immediately to the "end" that is to come soon after this—when the nayéé' kill off most of the diyinii, or, in First Man's opinion "The ones that didn't keep things diyin." So, in part, the "monsters" that are a direct result of the separation, are an important reason for re-uniting.

They then came back together. In the version of the story I am quoting, Woman Chief and her daughter apologize to First Man and say that he is, in fact, a very great chief. They are all warned again not to have intercourse for four days. At this time, First Man devises a test; after both sides are bathed and dried:

> . . . They stood facing each other. On the south side women only were lined up while on the north side the men only filed in line. "Which side will go around marrying? Which side will desire (the other) most?" In this manner First Man spoke. For the purpose of learning this he placed them naked facing each other on either side. But it happened that the men's side proved the weaker. Accordingly it is so to this day. And as time goes on it is usually the man (by whom) marriage (is sought). (Haile 1932: 35–36)

So, lest we get the impression from the earlier statements that the men are relatively "cool" compared with the women, this final incident corrects that view. Both sides desire each other; the men were simply able to control themselves better.

This story ties things together very well. To assure noot'iił, there must be birth and there must be death. To use Coyote's words, "This in itself shows a difference." In addition, to assure birth, there must be another difference, that between males and females. But, gender both subsumes other differences and assures (through future creation) that differentiation will continue. The necessity for males and females continuing together is, of course, the essence of First Man's plan for the future, as well as the basis for Navajo and all other society. This is first of all encoded rationally or intellectually. The story just recounted (as well as other stories) is a part of this, as is the commentary that people make on the stories, as is, in a way, this monograph. All share the characteristic of attempting to "make sense" out of what appear to be the "givens" of human existence.

But, this rationalism or attempt at sensibleness, albeit necessary and even useful in certain contexts, has its limitations. First Man realized the limitations, and he realized that if he wanted to create something of relative permanence he would need solutions or encodings that were more than rational. For when it comes to the things that matter to human beings, reasonable solutions to emotional imperatives do not really work. Thus, in order to keep people together, First Man put sexual desire into all beings. This is the real guarantee that things will continue, the mechanism for and assurances of noot'iił and the basis for society. Perhaps it is not as profound a basis as social philosophers would have us believe, but a basis that most of us can understand more readily.

There is, of course, the other side to all of this as well—the jealousy, the worry, the adultery. But, if sexuality is necessary, and it is, then these go with it. That which assures that people will come together and continue together also drives them apart. The basis for alliance and for conflict are one and the same.

ETHICS

The story of the separation of the sexes gives us a starting point for the understanding of Navajo ethics and of ethical instruction. The statements offered are particularly elegant, even more so when they are contrasted with our own ethical traditions. Western philosophy has offered two seemingly opposite but really not too different "solutions" to the problem of ethics. Neither one works, or for that matter can work, except within very narrowly defined bounds.

The first of these is the authoritarian, prescriptive approach most conspicuous in Judaism and Christianity but also implicit in any system that sets up a "sacred" level and contrasts it with the profane. Such is the case, for example, when someone sets up "The Law" and contrasts it with "what people really do," or when a normal statement (what people really do) is elevated to the sacred level (as "most people smoke marijuana, so what is wrong with it?"). At any rate, the basis of the prescriptive approach is some authority above, or at least outside of, man. It can be anything; common examples are statistics, science, nature, and God. Right behavior is reduced to a set of "thou shalts" and, more importantly, "thou shalt nots."

These fail for a variety of reasons. First, because many of these prescriptive statements do not make sense; they seem arbitrary, illogical, or irrational. A second reason derives from this: many of these ethical directives go against "givens" of human existence, those things that some social scientists call "drives" or needs.

A final reason (obviously circular) for why this type of ethical system has difficulty working today is that it must exist within a context of belief, and very few have such belief anymore. Further, belief here is usually thought of as being attained through faith, and both faith and belief require a rather large, quite difficult step.

The second general type of approach to ethics, and the one that is quite popular today, is that of rationalism. This again is authoritarian in that Western tradition generally places reason outside of man, especially in its "pure" or most reasonable form. Right behavior is here discovered or understood strictly through logic and reason.

In this view a corollary imperative is that the issues upon which ethical decisions are to be made should be arrived at through reason. This has two different forms. One can either start with the assumption that everything is potentially an ethical question until reason eliminates it, or, conversely, one can assume that nothing is ethically important until reason shows otherwise. The first strategy makes the world too meaningful; the second makes it meaningless. In the first case everything that one thinks, feels, and does matters. Nothing is unimportant. Current examples include hair style, clothing, facial hair, the type of food one eats, and the use of aerosals. Anything and everything is meaningful and a statement of social and ethical import. The net result can be a partial or a total paralysis: totally not acting, because any action is too meaningful and because nothing can be rationally demonstrated as "correct."

The problem with all of this is, of course, that some things do matter more than others even though their importance is not easily demonstrated rationally. And the things that do matter are known (with certainty) viscerally. The rational approach reduces to the statement that unless something can be shown to be reasonable one should not feel it or do it. Jealousy is a good example. Frequently, I run into the following type of reasoning: Jealousy is an emotion that makes no sense, it does not do anything positive, somebody I care about also caring about another is in no way a reflection on me, etc.; therefore, why feel it? The trouble is that people do feel it.

Since most emotional states are unreasonable* or, at least, cannot be demonstrated to be reasonable, this approach again denies some very basic human things. There is another aspect of rationalism that I will mention in passing. Rationalism is an irrational basis for ethics. This is first of all true at the level of self-reference (if all statements must be based on reason, how can one reasonably demonstrate that statement?). But, even if we ignore this objection, the reasonable man knows that the ultimate rational statement is that there is no statement that can be demonstrated to be ultimately rational.

The subjective net result of relying on authority systems outside oneself is a feeling of anxiety and of helplessness. This state is exacerbated when the particular authority, and authority in general, is called into question at the level of the society. Ethics or right behavior presents an insoluble dilemma in such a context.

Navajo, in contrast, bounds the problem in such a way that it is potentially soluble. The system is, first of all, non-authoritarian,

---

*This despite the fact that one can accept or justify the need for emotional states or the need to express these states rationally.

or, at a minimum, not based on external authority. Diyinii do not tell earth-surface dwellers what to do; neither do they punish "wrong doers." This is not to say that they do not harm human beings; they do, but not for reasons of misbehavior. In the realm of "right behavior" (and the story of the separation of the sexes is an excellent example), diyinii bound the realm of the possible. The stories are about those things that are important to human beings; at the same time, they point up the potential problems in these areas. They then point up and emphasize what the givens are, the things that cannot be changed, by demonstrating attempts at solutions to these problems that deny these givens.

Thus, in the story of the separation, the fact of sexual desire and its effects are the theme. Sexuality is necessary for all the reasons previously given, and it is especially necessary to the Navajo. But, as we have seen, the package of which it is a part includes jealousy, worry, and adultery. This particular set, while providing the basis of the society and the culture, is also the cause of most, if not all, social problems. Further, these problems demand solution. The initial attempt at solution by diyinii was to live with the worry and the jealousy; the effort did not last very long. The second attempt was to deny sexual desire in particular and men's and women's need for each other in general. This was a disaster. So, the givens are sexual desire, gender, and other difference, birth, joy, beauty, and increase on the one hand, and, jealousy, worry, grief, death, and ugliness on the other. These givens combine to form a whole, a package which although quite necessary, also produces great difficulties. To have any chance at solving these problems, one must begin by accepting these givens.

The stories stop here. Diyinii never did finally solve these problems, nor can most human beings. It is at this point that we can insert the standard Navajo response to this kind of question: "What should one do in situation X?" Invariably, the answer comes back, "It is up to him." And, this is, of course, what diyinii are saying to us through the stories. It is at this point that one can insert rationalism or pragmatism or whatever to deal with these questions. It is only within this bounded context that solutions are possible.

This is why attempts at describing normal or even normative Navajo behavior are so futile. What is normal and normative is the degree of difference, even the idiosyncracy, that characterizes solutions. This, of course, is another part of the creation of difference already discussed.

In summary, then, let me reiterate the two essential points. First, the "authority" upon which the system is based is subjective, although it is more correct to say that the subject/object distinction is not very strong in Navajo. The things that are objectified in the stories as ałkéé naa'aashii exist, on one level, as emotional states within all of us. In fact, each of us is ałkéé naa'aashii, and we each contain all of the oppositions thus far discussed.

Second, by both pointing out the important problems and showing the solutions that are impossible, ethics becomes finite and manageable. One need not justify everything but only a limited number of things. All solutions are not possible, simply because they are reasonable, but the potential for solution exists only within limited bounds. Further, this bounding, as noted, takes those things that seem to be basic to human beings as given. Thought and reason now have a chance. This is further enhanced by the fact that one is seeking not the single right answer, but only the one that is workable.

CONCLUDING REMARKS

Harken: I begin with nothingness. Nothingness is the same as fullness. In infinity full is no better than empty. Nothingness is both empty and full. As well might ye say anything else of nothingness, as for instance, white is it, or black, or again, it is not, or it is. A thing that is infinite and eternal hath no qualities, since it hath all qualities.

This nothingness or fullness we name the PLEROMA. . . .

CREATURA is not in the pleroma, but in itself. The pleroma is both beginning and end of created beings. It pervadeth them, as the light of the sun everywhere pervadeth the air. Although the pleroma pervadeth altogether, yet has created being no share thereof, just as a wholly transparent body becometh neither light nor dark through the light which pervadeth it. We are, however, the pleroma itself, for we are a part of the eternal and infinite. But we have no share thereof, as we are from the pleroma infinitely removed; not spiritually or temporally, but essentially, since we are distinguished from the pleroma in our essence as creatura, which is confirmed within time and space.

C. G. JUNG
Septem Sermones ad Mortuos

It should by now seem rather odd that dualists (both Anglo and Navajo) take ałkéé naa'aashii to be a master symbol for evil. In so doing, a concept, the essence of which is process, is converted into something static. The more general problem may be in looking at the world view of others in terms of "sets of symbols." For, the concept "symbol" connotes thingness, while "set" connotes a kind of meta-thingness.

Interestingly, the concept of "witchcraft" is nothing more than a conversion of process into quiescence. The "evilway" rests on the maintenance, in the sense of perpetuation, of self or ego. The "goodway," its supposed opposite, rests on the same general premise—a pursuit of entity to the denial of process. The essence of ałkéé naa'aashii is that it is without essence. It is process and continuation. The component beings making up this process (and the labels that can be used to violate continuation by glorifying a point in it) are quite unimportant.

Since ałkéé naa'aashii subsumes all else, it is "correct" to say that it is evil or that it is good insofar as these (and all other attributes) have to be contained within such a major abstraction. But by emphasizing one to the exclusion of its opposite, we, conceptually, become witches ourselves. For, "witchlike" behavior, rather paradoxically, is oriented toward the pursuit of an ideal. And, by pursuing good or evil or any other ideal, the "witch" or the "Christian" is denying that all things are both (or neither); he further denies that there is merely continuation, not fixity. Jung comments on this with some eloquence:

> When we strive after the good or the beautiful we thereby forget our own nature, which is distinctiveness, and we are delivered over to the qualities of the pleroma, which are pairs of opposites. We labor to attain to the good and the beautiful, yet at the same

[149]

time we also lay hold of the evil and the ugly, since in the pleroma these are one with the good and the beautiful. When, however, we remain true to our own nature, which is distinctiveness, we distinguish ourselves from the good and the beautiful, and, therefore, at the same time from the evil and the ugly. And thus we fall not into the pleroma, namely into nothingness and dissolution. (Jung 1916: 381)

Pleroma, however, bounds creatura, that is, the beginning and the end of creatura is pleroma. The movement is from indistinctness to distinctness to indistinctness. The qualities that are balanced and void in the pleroma are "distinct and separate in us. . . ; therefore they are . . . effective" and,

The qualities belong to the pleroma, and only in the name and sign of distinctiveness can and must we possess or live them. We must distinguish ourselves from qualities. In the pleroma they are balanced and void; in us not. Being distinguished from them delivereth us. (Jung 1916: 381)

We are distinct, and our pursuit is distinctiveness. The pursuit of either good or evil transforms us into a fool or a witch. A part of this distinctiveness is the acceptance of "different ways of thinking"—the creation of a culture that shares the knowledge that little except this allowance for difference is shared.

But, as noted, "pleroma is both the beginning and end of created beings." Our distinctiveness is temporary. A part of man's distinctiveness, however, lies in his ability to observe and be aware of this process, see it as inevitable, and accept it with relative indifference.*

Thus, older "wise" Navajos both predict and accept the end of their world. Before the beginning was indistinctness and sameness, then progressive differentiation, then a "maximal" differentiation, then a progressive nondifferentiation or movement toward sameness. The life cycle, in fact the cycle of all "systems," is viewed in the same way. Before birth the child is not strongly differentiated

---

*Indifference is here used in a Zen Buddhist sense.

from his mother. The series of "birthing" rites move toward a greater and greater differentiation. "Individuality" increases until, and probably becomes maximal at, adolescence. Some, in fact, say that this is when ch'įįdii comes into the person. After death one becomes undifferentiated again. But, through knowledge, through the observance of a process that is inevitable, one can gradually "give up" creatura or give up distinctiveness.

The process here is, however, not the "pursuit of ideals" as Jung describes it. In fact, it is distinguished by not seeking. One cannot pursue dissolution—nothingness or allness—one merely accepts that "state" as inevitable. When one finally accepts that he is all, he accepts that he is nothing; when one realizes that the pleroma or the universe is within, it is tantamount to the realization of non-existence. If within and without are identical, then there is of course no boundary.

The concept emphasizes the pleroma. The most common means of definition is in terms of opposites, the definition always being incomplete. Thus, we have boundlessness, universality, and process. But the other side of this is entitivity and fixity: a marking (or creation) of islands of relative sameness or stillness. To this we now turn, to an emphasis on creatura, with the concept sạ'a naghái bik'e hózhǫ́.

CHAPTER 5

SĄ'A NAGHÁI
BIK'E HÓZHǪ

SĄ'A NAGHÁI BIK'E HÓZHǪ is *the* key concept in Navajo philosophy, the vital requisite for understanding the whole. The primary goal of this monograph is to arrive at and communicate the beginnings of such an understanding. Most of the groundwork has been laid; what remains is to tie the seemingly disparate pieces, some of them already discussed and some from elsewhere, together into an explanation of this single concept.

EARLIER INTERPRETATIONS

Western researchers have been studying są'a naghái bik'e hózhǫ at least since the time of Matthews, who had this to say about the concept:

> The expressions Sana nagai and Bike hozoni appear in many songs and prayers, and are always thus united.* Their literal translation is given above,† but they are equivalent to saying, "long life and

---

*In fact, they are not.
† "In old age walking" and "his trail beautiful."

happiness"; as part of a prayer they are a supplication for a long and happy life. Hozoni means, primarily, terrestrially beautiful; but it means also happy, happily, or, in a certain sense, good. (Matthews 1897: 266)

What is most remarkable is that subsequent accounts really differ very little from this initial attempt at definition. In general, there are only three basic ways in which researchers have attempted to discover and convey the meaning of the concept.

One basic strategy is etymological—the reduction of the concept to its supposed linguistic components. All previous analyses have, to some degree, used this approach, but Witherspoon's (1974) article, to be discussed below, is by far the best such attempt. A second general strategy is to attempt, rather directly, an abstract definition. Most researchers have made this attempt but Reichard's definition is the best. Finally, the third and most common strategy is objectification, most usually in the form of personification. Haile offers the best description of this method.

Here I will briefly summarize the best examples of each of these strategies. At the outset note that this review is non-exhaustive. An exhaustive review would run to several volumes and still be incomplete. An abstract concept cannot be understood by an inventory of examples, simply because, by definition, the inventory must be incomplete if the concept to be understood is truly abstract. Tł'aáh explained this to Reichard in a very succinct and accurate manner:

Since sǫ'a naaghái according to Tł'aáh and others of my informants, includes everything, we may expect to find it expressed by various symbols. (Reichard 1970: 48)

Unfortunately no one, including Reichard, listened to Tł'aáh's warning.

Reichard's Abstraction

Reichard had some very good teachers in Tł'aáh and the man she refers to as "Rain Singer." They described to her very clearly the beginnings of, and the outlines for, what could have been an understanding of both sạ'a naghái bik'e hózhǫ and, through such an understanding, a synthetic knowledge of Navajo religion. Such a synthesis was, of course, Reichard's ultimate goal. She instead chose to attempt it differently and failed. But, she was given the beginnings:

> The synthesis of all the beliefs detailed above [death and after life] and of those concerning the attitudes and experiences of man is expressed by sạ'a naaghái usually followed by bik'e hójóón. Various explanations are given for these phrases, which constitute the benediction (climax) of many prayers and songs. Xójóóní means "perfection so far as it is attainable by man," the end toward which not only man but also supernaturals and time and motion, institutions and behavior strive. Perhaps it is the utmost achievement in order. (Reichard 1970: 45)

This remarkably insightful statement takes us in many directions. The association of hózhóní with "perfection" and order is quite correct and much more accurate than the dualist's gloss of "good." As Matthews noted above, it is "good" only in a very limited sense, and it is in the sense of quality rather than morality. The second point in the above quote is that sạ'a naghái bik'e hózhǫ refers to many classes of things—not just to diyinii and earth-surface people but to more abstract, less tangible, concepts as well.

This leads into a third feature, which is the non-egocentric or nonpersonal nature of the notion. Reichard regards sạ'a naghái as part of, or an aspect of, "the physical hereafter," and in this sense man, and every other thing, become sạ'a naghái and necessarily lose their corporeal and "spiritual" individuality (Reichard 1970: 45). But in this view it is also associated with living to old age; or, of putting old age off or entering it gracefully. In this, Reichard's teachers were again Tł'aáh and "The singer of the Rain Ceremony." In their words:

> Sạ'a . . . (was) . . . "harmonious or desirable destiny" or even "restoration-to-youth." The singer of the Rain Ceremony said, "sạ'a naaghái is from the bottom of the earth. Sunrise and Sunset have it. It is the power of renewal for everything six months through Sun." (Reichard 1970: 47)

She therefore glosses the term "according to the ideal may restoration be achieved."

This rather brief translation label comes close to capturing są'a naghái bik'e hózhǫ́. I do not agree with the gloss, because I am of the opinion that brief translations of highly synthetic and central concepts are largely meaningless. But Reichard's and Rain Singer's comments point up the two critical features of the idea. First, są'a naghái is from the bottom of the Earth. In order to understand it, then, we must go back into the underworlds. This was made explicit by First Man when he left his medicine bundle behind. The second point is that są'a naghái bik'e hózhǫ́ is associated with rejuvenation, reanimation, and temporal punctuation.

In fact, these two features of temporality point up a much more inclusive atemporality. The incident of First Man leaving behind the medicine bundle again instructs us. It was left behind and then retrieved. Today the process is repeated, both in the sense of the curing achieved through the ceremonials, of which this journey is a necessary part, and, more generally, through knowledge acquisition, where all of us necessarily return to the source or the beginning. We can describe this process as historical; but it is really ahistorical in the sense that what happened is continually happening. That is, the ritual is not a re-enactment; it is a cyclical repetition or continuation. One could say, then, that the process exists across time, which is simply another way of saying that it exists outside of time.

The Etymological Reductions (*Witherspoon*)

In attempting to translate* this idea, Haile and, following him, Witherspoon reduce primarily to etymology, the supposed meaning of the component words, just as Matthews before them did.

---

*I use translate in a very general way. A teacher translates ideas so that a pupil may understand; an anthropologist translates exotic ideas into American, English, and so on.

A quandary presents itself here. Witherspoon and Haile have said important, if not totally accurate, things about Navajo world view. In general, many (if not most) of their statements have been created in the context of translation labels. But if their insights are important, their reduction (particularly of sạ'a naghái bik'e hózhǫ́) to etymology misses the mark completely. Navajo thinkers when asked "meaning" questions about certain things will sometimes spontaneously divide the words into parts and explain them historically. If you press, you can almost always get people to do this. The question of meaning, however, must involve more than this. The problem that is more central is to hit on the appropriate questions rather than to force answers. I asked general meaning questions about sạ'a naghái bik'e hózhǫ́ for two years and an etymological answer was never offered. Also, in the native texts on the concept, I have never seen such a reduction. The fact that Western researchers have sought the meaning of this concept primarily at this level is rather instructive of how anthropologists view the quality of Navajo (and, implicitly, their own) thought.

At any rate, such a reduction is an inappropriate strategy. Sạ'a naghái bik'e hózhǫ́ can exist at a level so general as to subsume all else in the universe. In some sense (as pointed out by Tł'aáh) all symbols are sạ'a naghái bik'e hózhǫ́ symbols. Related to this is the probability that one can rationalize any theory of meaning etymologically. But the ability to do this does not imply the meaningfulness of such an endeavor.

The material I include here is taken primarily from Witherspoon (1974), who takes his material largely from Haile (1943). In their view, sạ'ah is taken to be a derivative of the past tense form of the verb to grow or to mature. It is commonly used to denote someone or something that is "mature, ripe, experienced, or aged." It is associated with "death of old age" or, more precisely, reaching old age, a strong desire in Navajo life, the "natural" culmination of the life cycle, as it were. According to Witherspoon, "In the term sạ'ah, therefore, we have contained the Navajo concern for and emphasis upon life, their attitude toward birth and death and particularly toward death of old age as the goal of life" (Witherspoon 1974: 47–49).

A problem with this view is that the tone is wrong. Sǫ́ is high tone, and sǫ'ah is clearly low tone. No one really adequately explains this.[1] Another possibility is that the original form is not sǫ́ at all, but as'ah (or as'áh). This term is rather difficult to interpret, but it seems to refer more to life span, or to continuity of life culminating in old age. In short, it seems more to have to do with process than a particular moment. It may (and this is pure guess) also have some reference to generational continuance and old-age generations. An additional point is that the Jicarillas use as'áh naagháa da doo in song and claim that the Navajo pronounce it sǫ'a naaghái (Haile 1947: 22). The tone is "explained" by this, and the nasalization may come from assimilating the "n" on naghái.

Naghái is a form of the verb to go. The naa prefix emphasizes the repetitiveness and continuance of an act. In some sense, it also may be associated with an event "which is considered a restoration of a former state or condition." Thus, for sǫ'a naghái Witherspoon (1974: 52) states, "Sǫ'ah refers to the completion of the life cycle through death of old age, and naghái refers to the continued reoccurrence of the completion of the life cycle."

Bik'eh glosses "according to it" or by its decree. The bi "it" refers back to what precedes it. What follows bik'eh then is the product of or exists in conjunction with sǫ'a naghái. The by-product of sǫ'a naghái is hózhǫ́, a concept we have already discussed. The term is often translated as "beauty," as in hozhónee, "beauty way." Alternately, it is translated blessing, as in hózhǫ́ǫ́jí, "blessing-way." Often, too, the Navajo bilingual will translate hózhǫ́ǫ́jí as "the good way."

The dualists, of course, use the stem -zhǫ́ to describe their notion of goodness as opposed to evil. Thus, Wyman (1970: 7) states:

> The Navajo term includes everything that a Navajo thinks as good—that is, good as opposed to evil, favorable to man as opposed to unfavorable or doubtful. It expresses for the Navajo such concepts as the words beauty, perfection, harmony, goodness, normality, success, well-being, blessedness, order, ideal, do for us.

Kluckhohn (1968: 686) makes a similar statement regarding hózhǫ́:

This is probably the central idea in Navajo religious thinking. It occurs in the names of two important ceremonials (Blessing Way and Beauty Way) and is frequently repeated in almost all prayers and songs. In various contexts it is best translated as "beautiful," "harmonious," "good," "blessed," "pleasant," and "satisfying."

The prefix hó- in hózhǫ́ refers to "environment" as a whole. As a pronomial prefix, hó- refers to the "(1) general as opposed to the specific, (2) the whole as opposed to the part, (3) the abstract as opposed to the concrete, (4) the indefinite as opposed to the definite, and (5) the infinite as opposed to the finite"* (Witherspoon 1974: 53).

Hózhǫ́, then "refers to the positive or ideal environment. It is beauty, harmony, good, happiness, and everything that is positive, and it refers to an environment which is all-inclusive" (Witherspoon 1974: 53).

In conclusion, Witherspoon (1974: 53) describes sạ'a naghái bik'e hózhǫ́ thusly:

> The goal of Navajo life in this world is to live to maturity in the conditions described as hózhǫ́, and to die of old age, at which time one becomes incorporated in the universal beauty, harmony, and happiness described as sạ'a naghái bik'e hózhǫ́.

From the dualists' point of view sạ'a naghái bik'e hózhǫ́ is strongly associated with the good, in part because sạ'a naghái and bik'e hózhǫ́ are the source of that "goodness":

> Sạ'a naghái and bik'e hózhǫ́ are the central animating powers of the universe, and, as such, they produce a world described as hózhǫ́, the ideal environment of beauty, harmony, and happiness. All living beings, which include the earth, the sacred mountains and so on, have inner and outer forms, and to achieve well being these inner forms must harmonize and unify with sạ'a naghái and all outer forms just harmonize and unify with bik'e hózhǫ́. (Witherspoon 1974: 56)

---

*O. Werner (personal communication) takes exception to Witherspoon's analysis.

Witherspoon goes on to liken sa'a naghái bik'e hózhǫ́ to a generator or power source which produces hózhǫ́ for the inner forms of all living beings. Diyinii then are supernaturals because of their proximity to this source and because of their knowledge of the rituals which enable them to tap into it. Similarly, a curing ceremony identifies the patient first to various deities' inner forms, and then to sa'a naghái bik'e hózhǫ́, "as though each deity provided a separate channel to the same central generator" (Witherspoon 1974: 56–58).

He then combines his own view with that of Wyman in the following summary:

> Wyman explains that all Navajos should identify with sa'a naghái bik'e hózhǫ́, and that this should be their goal in life. All ceremonials have as their prime purpose the restoration of the ideal environment symbolized by the phrase sa'a naghái bik'e hózhǫ́ (1970: 30). To connect up with this universal harmony, happiness and beauty is the Navajo task in life. It is this that gives his personality meaning, his behavior direction, and his soul contentment. (Witherspoon 1974: 58)

As noted above, the contrastive element or the opposition for these thinkers is ánít'ịịjí sa'a naghái bik'e hózhǫ́, the source of hóchxǫ́, just as (supposedly) sa'a naghái bik'e hózhǫ́ is the source of hózhǫ́. Hóchxǫ́ is produced on the earth's surface by witchcraft and by contact with things that are báhádzid. Hóchxǫ́ is further associated with nature, chaos, ignorance, and evil, as contrasted with the culture, order, knowledge and good which are hózhǫ́ (Witherspoon n.d.: 19; Witherspoon 1974: 56).

I have critiqued Witherspoon's position throughout this work, and I see no need to repeat these ideas here. The most important point is that Haile and Witherspoon understood belief. In studying and coming to understand the Navajo, they both found a justification for and altered their own way of seeing the world. That legitimizes the native philosophy as no purely analytical statement could. To understand belief presupposes that one is able to experience it.

Personification

The third general way that Westerners have attempted to understand sǫ'a naghái bik'e hózhǫ́ is by objectification, specifically by means of personification. The most popular of these ideas is that the two, sǫ'a naghái ashkii and bik'e hózhǫ́ at'ééd, are nahasdzą́ą́ bii'gistíín—the life force, inner form, or in-laying one of the Earth. It is the view that Father Berard accepted, and it is currently voiced by Wyman and Witherspoon (in somewhat modified form).

A cautionary note is in order here. All the associations of sǫ'a naghái bik'e hózhǫ́ with particular beings are, in a sense to be explained below, correct. What is incorrect is the assumption that a particular objectification and sǫ'a naghái bik'e hózhǫ́ are identical; also incorrect is the further implied assumption that this identification process "defines" the concept. If, for example, a Western reader is told that sǫ'a naghái bik'e hózhǫ́ is in some sense equivalent to the "inner form of the Earth" he will very likely still not have a very clear idea of meaning other than perhaps a vague notion that "primitives" believe in earth gods.

At any rate, Slim Curley revealed this association to Father Berard, who believed that it was the final answer to the question of the meaning of the concept. I recounted a portion of that text earlier in the chapter on the medicine bundle. Let me repeat it here. The time is when First Man was revealing the contents of the bundle to other diyinii.

> When he had covered them four times as described, a young man and a woman arose from them. Absolutely without their equals in beauty, both had long hair reaching to their thighs. *The two happened to be those various things which he had carried about tied up in that bundle.* To fix your gaze on them was impossible, the glare from them was surprisingly bright. "This is the only time any of you have seen them, from now on none of you will see them again. Although they are right around you, even they are taking care of your means of living (subsistence) to the end of your days right around you, none of you will ever see them again." (Wyman 1970: 111–12; emphasis added)

To reiterate: in some (as yet undefined) sense the two young beauties are equated with all that is in the bundle. The contents, as previously stated, include jeweled corn (jewel prototypes), jewel wraps, the twelve-person group, and other things. In fact, the contents of the bundle are differently described at different times. What remains constant is that the items contained make life possible and worthwhile for the Navajos. We also know that these two (sǫ'a naghái ashkii and bik'e hózhǫ́ at'ééd) are not obvious or apparent, and they are seldom, if ever, seen. Only the various prototypical wealthy things are conspicuous. Thus: (1) Sǫ'a naghái and bik'e hózhǫ́ are in the bundle always. (2) They are equivalent to but in some sense separable from the contents of the bundle. (3) They cannot normally be seen. Further, the two represent, or are, some sort of a distillate or essence. They are prerequisite to all things in Navajo life, and they in a sense *are* life. Remember that all things that are living derive from this bundle and are sǫ'a naghái bik'e hózhǫ́.

In line with this reasoning, McNeley has made the point, supported by numerous textual materials, that sǫ'a naghái bik'e hózhǫ́ is, in some sense, equivalent to the various níłch'i that animate all beings.

> It would appear, therefore, that what have been thought of by ethnologists as earth's and perhaps sky's "inner forms" or "holy spirits," sǫ'ah naagháii and bik'e hózhǫ́ǫn, are conceived by the Navajos to have come to exist on earth's surface as aspects or components of "wind" which, in turn, exist within man and are essential to his life and well being. The inference may be made that it is primarily through the effects of these particular "winds" derived from earth and sky that hózhǫ́ conditions, those of "beauty" and of "well being," exist for the individual. (McNeley 1973: 201)

To continue with Slim Curley's story, one of the most important creations on the earth's surface was Changing Woman. This text has also been quoted earlier in this work, but it needs to be reiterated in this context. The story picks up at the time diyinii were at Gobernador Knob and when the monsters had slain most of them:

---

*A common view is that sǫ'a naghái is "sky's inner form" and bik'e hózhǫ́ is "earth's inner form."

Such were conditions when First Man, First Woman again discussed matters. Now this Earth's inner form which as said, he had made from his medicine corn bundle, he would repeatedly hold up in the direction of Gobernador Knob. (Wyman 1970: 140)

Soon after this, Changing Woman was found in or on the mountain. Slim Curley goes on to state:

You can see now that this (Changing Woman) is the child of the young woman and young man of exceeding beauty who, as mentioned earlier, had arisen from the medicine bundle which he had never laid aside to become the inner form of earth. It is clear too that she originated here at Gobernador Knob when he held the same medicine bundle up in that direction as they say. (Wyman 1970: 143)

In this version then, Changing Woman is the daughter of są'a naghái ashkii and bik'e hózhǫ́ at'ééd, as well as in some sense being the daughter of the Earth and the daughter of First Man. Later, after the twins[2] are born and the monsters slain, Changing Woman prepares to move to the West and at that time she makes a request of First Man:

Then there was that medicine bundle which First Man always carried with him. "I have in mind to take this with me, my father, my mother, more people are to come into being, I think. That is its purpose, since the sun has instructed me how it is to be done," she said. "Very well, my daughter," said both First Man and First Woman. (Wyman 1970: 199)

So the bundle and, by implication, the two "beautiful ones" come into the hands of Changing Woman. She needs it to carry on the creation process, previously in the hands of First Man.

Later Changing Woman takes the bundle with her to the West. Wyman (1970: 126 n. 111; 143 n. 125) and Father Berard say that są'a naghái ashkii and bik'e hózhǫ́ at'ééd with the bundle were then placed in the interior of the earth where they become nahasdzą́ą́ bii'gistíín. At the close of hózhǫ́ǫ́jí bahane', the bundle is in Changing Woman's house, the Rock Crystal Baskets having been obtained to keep it:

> Then at the rear of the room, she sat those (five) rock crystal bas-
> kets (obtained at the children's birth) one above the other inside of
> which she placed the medicine bundle of First Man. "Now this
> will remain in them, that was the purpose in acquiring them."
> (Wyman 1970: 283)

The five baskets arranged in this way of course represent the
placement in the Earth and the previous placements in the underworlds. There are four underworlds in which creation occurred by
means of the bundle and this fifth world where creation is still oc-
curring through the bundle. The nesting indicates that each higher
world, although separate, is a creation of the previous one. Thus the
continuity, the separateness, and the continuous creation are all
expressed.

These are by no means all the personifications of sạ'a naghái
bik'e hózhǫ́, but they are the most important ones. In addition, they
are all, in some sense, correct. The key point to reiterate and reem-
phasize here is that Father Berard, after what was literally a lifetime of
study, came to accept sạ'a naghái bik'e hózhǫ́ as being identical to
"the inner form of the Earth" and as the source of "goodness" in the
universe.

SẠ'A NAGHÁI BIK'E HÓZHǪ́ AS ENTITIVITY

So far we have several examples of the use of sạ'a naghái bik'e
hózhǫ́. The term can, first, be used as a name for the medicine
bundle of First Man and/or for its contents or for part of the bundle's contents. Second, it can refer to the inner form of the Earth or
the inner forms of the Earth and the Sky combined. Third, it is a
name for both the níłch'i bii'sizíinii and bii'gistíín of various phenomena. Thus, all things mentioned as created or placed in
hózhǫ́ǫ́jí can be labeled sạ'a naghái bịk'e hózhǫ́. But perhaps it is
more accurate to say that their animating quality is sạ'a naghái bik'e
hózhǫ́. What are often taken as the primary referents of this concept
are often just specific instances of this more general usage.

But, these examples do not seem to be of immediate help in arriving at a more general understanding of the concept. A reason for this failure is in the Western analyst's emphasis on the esoteric contexts of usage. For, although the term is esoteric and the "true meaning" is in some ways hidden, są'a naghái bik'e hózhǫ́ is used quite frequently in the stories, songs, and prayers and is therefore in daily and very frequent use. Another place to look, then, is where the native begins in these common usages.

One can, first of all, examine the pattern of the chantway prayers. These minimally describe the alliance of the patient with particular diyinii who both fight off the dangerous beings that are troubling him, and protect him from further contact with these (and other) dangerous ones. At this point the patient is described as being restored, reanimated, or renewed. He is transformed from a state of illness, or defective completeness, to a state of completeness. The prayers describe this process in fairly great detail, recounting the journeys of various diyinii on the patient's behalf and listing exhaustively the effect that the ceremony is having on the patient. At the culmination of (as well as at other places in) the prayer, the following or something very similar very often appears:

Sa'ą naaghái bik'e hǫ́zhóón násísdlį́į́'go, ádíshní
sa'ą naaghái bik'e hǫ́zhóón,
dootídilnééhii
díí násísdlį́į́' (repeat four times)
hǫ́zhǫ́ náhásdlį́į́' (repeat four times)

(Reichard 1944: 92–93;
with some modification in transcription)

The prayer is saying something like this: są'a naghái bik'e hózhǫ́, I have become; są'a naghái bik'e hózhǫ́, perfection (or without fault) I have become again as I have (and do) repeatedly become. Things all around or my total environment are "beautiful" (or they appear beautiful to me) again.

After one becomes są'a naghái bik'e hózhǫ́ again, it can be said that the world is hózhǫ́ again. As noted before, it is one's state, particularly one's perception, that changes, not necessarily the physical world. At one level then, the ceremony is aimed at bringing about a gestalt shift.

It is implicit in the above that when one is ill or, for whatever reason, in need of a ceremony,[3] one is not s̨a'a naghái bik'e hózhǫ́. This is made clearer in anaa'jí. One of the songs of the Hard Flint Boys begins with the identification of the patient with these beings, going on to say that because of this alliance he cannot be harmed by nayéé'. The culmination is "Now because I am (sa'a naghái) and one who causes fear I am the Flint Boys" (Haile 1938: 307). Haile (1938: 320 n. 112) suggests (and I concur) that bik'e hózhǫ́ is not mentioned here because the process of restoration is incomplete. The patient is therefore identified with one who "spends a long life spreading fear." This also occurs in the blackening songs of anaa'jí. The process here is basically one of attaining power to attract and kill enemies. At verse 23 the following is described:

> eneeya I live a long life, so I do, a long life, a long life I live, so I do, I live a long life, I live a long life, so I do, a long life, a long life, a long life I live, so I do.

> Because I am Milky Way Boy,[4] because I am long life boy, I live a long life. . .

> Because I am rainbow boy, because I am long life boy, I live a long life. . .

> Because I am Monster Slayer boy, because I am long life boy, I live a long life. . .

> Because I am Gazer on Enemy boy, because I am long life boy, I live a long life.
>
> (Haile 1938: 279)

Note that the identification here is with the very powerful or very dangerous diyinii. The preceding quote made this explicit for the Hard Flint Boys. Similarly, nayéé' neezghą́ní and his twin are the ones who undertake the dangerous journeys into the underworld in hóchxǫ́ǫ́jí prayers. Verse 30 of these songs continues with the same theme:

> So then, step into the shoes of Monster Slayer, do so! Step into the shoes of him whose lure is the extended bowstring, do so! Step now into the shoes of long life . . . step into them, that's all! And then, step into the shoes of the Gazer on the Enemy, do so! Step

into the shoes of him who lures the enemy to death, do so! Step
now into the shoes of long life . . . step into them . . . step into
them, that's all! (Haile 1938: 282)

Again, the alliance is with the two who are powerful and the
two who are dangerous. The purpose is to bring about the death of
the enemy, or the death of his ghost, or the death of his memory,
depending on the context and on one's point of view.

When the blackening is finished and the prayer recited, at the
conclusion of each verse we find (as in Reichard's text quoted
above), "sǫ'a nagháí bik'e hózhǫ́ nshłį́įdoo hózhǫ́ náhásdłį́į' (four
times)" (Haile 1938: 208).

Sa'a nagháí bik'e hózhǫ́ I have become or I have become again.
The world is hózhǫ́ again. (repeated four times)

Father Berard quotes Slim Curley in re-emphasizing this incompleteness versus completeness: "Happiness (bik'e hózhǫ́) is
mentioned with long life (sǫ'a nagháí) because the process of restoration, a liberation from the ghost, is considered complete. In the
blackening which precedes the ceremony of placing the shoulder
bands, happiness (bik'e hózhǫ́) is not mentioned, because restoration is in process only" (Haile 1938: 256 n. 127).

Two questions are raised here. The first is the one that Haile
directs his attention to, namely, why sǫ'a nagháí without bik'e
hózhǫ́? The answer suggested is that restoration is incomplete and,
by implication, the patient is somehow "incomplete." But the second difficulty is in why this incompleteness or unfinished restoration makes the patient "feared." There are two possibilities; the first
one was suggested in the above quote. It may be that when the
"ghost" is in the patient, it is this ghost that is being labeled "the
most feared one." If one accepts the dualistic premise of the nature
of the universe, this seems plausible.

The second possibility, and the one I favor, is that incompleteness is in itself dangerous, or, stated slightly differently,
the fact of incompleteness or imbalance, of being only sǫ'a nagháí,
makes the patient one who is dangerous or feared. Goddard's (1933)
texts of "bear songs" from the story segment entitled "Wanderings

of the Navajo" support this view. It is the bear, who started out as the pet of the People, that is singing these songs. The first one goes:

My hogan, I being a whirlwind,
My hogan, I being a gray bear,
Lightning strikes from my hogan,
There is danger from my hogan
All are afraid of my hogan.
I am of long life of whom they are afraid.
Hihini hi'
I blow my breath out

(Goddard 1933: 171)

Later there are other songs of a similar nature to nayéé' neezgháni and Big black bear:

Consider me.
I am nayéé' neezgháni.
Consider me, my mocassins being of black obsidian.
Consider me, my leggings being of black obsidian.
Consider me, black obsidian hangs down from my sides at four
  places.
Lightning strokes shoot out from me four times.
Where they go very bad talk kills you.
Over there the heads are bound in death.
Long life, I am the one they are afraid of.
Consider me.

(Goddard 1933: 176)

This song was sung immediately prior to an attack. What follows is something of an aside to the primary discourse. It is of interest because it rather well describes álílee naghái,[5] a phrase which one of McNeley's informants would quite consistently use instead of the usual sǫ'a naghái. As they were attacking then, they sang eight "travel" songs. Typical is the following:

I have become the heat mirage.
Towards the east I have become the black mirage with points
  projecting upward.

(Goddard 1933: 176)

With the aid of the song, "They crossed the prairie without being seen, due to the darkness caused by heat mirage." Back to the main thread, the bear now sang:

Big black bear.
My mocassins are black obsidian.
My leggings are black obsidian.
My shirt is black obsidian.
I am girdled with a gray arrowsnake.
Black snakes project from my head.
With zigzag lightning projecting from the ends of my feet I step
With zigzag lightning streaming out from my knees I step.
With zigzag lightning streaming out from the tips of my fingers
   I work my hands.
With zigzag lightning streaming out from the tip of my tongue I
   speak.
Now a disc of pollen rests on the crown of my head.
Gray arrow snakes and rattlesnakes eat it.
Black obsidian and zigzag lightning streams out from me in four
   ways.
Where they strike the earth, bad things bad talk does not like it.
It causes the missiles to spread out.
Long life, something frightful I am.
Now I am

                                        (Goddard 1933: 176).

This presents a marvelous picture of the way one would want to appear going into battle. I quote only excerpts from the remaining songs:

I am nayéé' neezghání.
Where I walk is dangerous
Long life being the one that causes fear I walk.
Where I walk is dangerous.

and:

Nayéé, neezghání.
Long life and one to be feared.
Now I am.

                                        (Goddard 1933: 176)

It is rather clear in these songs that the one who spreads fear here is the patient, the one who is long life, not the "ghost" of the enemy. This relates to a second, seemingly ambiguous feature of the uses of są'a naghái in anaa'jí and in the bear songs. In general, as Haile points out, the process in anaa'jí is one of transforming the patient from a state of incompleteness and sickness, to one of completeness. Very generally, sąʼa naghái describes the former state and sąʼa naghái bikʼe hózhǫ́ the latter. But it is not quite so simple, for, at least in a limited sense, sąʼa naghái, or the state of incompleteness, is also being sought. Thus, in the case of warfare, to be sąʼa naghái, to be the one that is feared and invulnerable, is desired. Further, in anaaʼjí, it seems as if this state of invulnerability or extreme strength must of necessity be entered into to again defeat the enemy, this time in the form of his "ghost" or his memory. In brief, then, it is a state of incompleteness that is desired or sought in certain contexts but that is given up or cast off in most situations. That is, in anaaʼjí the individual does not remain sąʼa naghái but exists temporarily in that state and goes on to become sąʼa naghái bikʼe hózhǫ́.

This all begins to make sense if we recall that sąʼa naghái is equated with sąʼa naghái ashkii, the male component within all of us (bikʼe hózhǫ́ being the female). Further, anaaʼjí restricts the involvement of women. This ceremony was created, according to No Hat, as a "solution" to the problem of spilling an enemy's blood. When Navajos first went to war, he said, and killed enemies, it was an incredibly dangerous, incredibly frightening thing. Anaaʼjí was developed to reduce this danger.

But, as has been pointed out, the danger to society is not just from the enemy's ghost or memory, it is also, and even primarily, from the warrior. There is a fairly obvious paradox here. A society needs its warriors. To become a warrior is to become invulnerable, feared, strong, and dangerous. But to become these (for society) is to place oneself outside society. To be sąʼa naghái is to be in the state of maleness unmediated by bikʼe hózhǫ́, femaleness, or self unmediated by society. In a way it is incompleteness; in another sense, it is a super-completeness. Anaaʼjí in this sense, then, is a re-entry process, a bringing back of the dangerous one to society.

There is a story of a great Ute warrior* and war chief who was wounded in a battle with the Navajos. His fellows began to sing over him to cure him. But then they looked at each other and went

---

*Allen Manning (personal communication).

to one side to talk about it. This warrior was very great, and in exhibiting his greatness it seems he brought many raids of reprisal against these people. These men were tired of war, and they knew that this man was, and could only be, a warrior. They then poisoned him and sang over him to kill him. His "greatness" offered no alter native save his death. The Navajo who told this story was asked whether or not, if this warrior had been Navajo, he would have had to be killed. The man said, "Of course not, we would have had anaaʼjí for him."

We can then offer a temporizing definition of sąʼa naghái bikʼe hózhǫ́ as that which is whole or complete. Sąʼa naghái bikʼe hózhǫ́ bounds "living" entities. In the following Frank Mitchell provides a more complete definition of the concept. He is describing, specifically, the inner forms of the mountains, which, as we know, are themselves sąʼa naghái bikʼe hózhǫ́:

> And a means which enables them (the inner forms of the mountains) to breathe, which enables them to speak to one another, and their power of speech which is distributed, their languages that are, the things they hold in their hands, their property that lies about them, and things that appear on them (their apparel) and that by means of which they are sąʼa naghái and bikʼe hózhǫ́, things which make it blessed* before them, blessed behind them, blessed below them, blessed above them, and which makes all their surroundings blessed, which makes their speech blessed by means of pollen, each one of these they possess, we found that each one of these persons who had been made possesses all of them, not one of them was missing on them. Thereby everyone of them is really alive, and all of them are really able to speak, and each one has something by which they can be useful. Furthermore, there is an offering for each one, and on this account they have their songs and prayers for that purpose, they have their names for that purpose, thereby they differ from one another and thereby they are known. (Wyman 1970: 464)

They are alive, they breathe, they have language, and they are useful. As noted previously, the Navajo creation is concerned with providing all of these—of animating beings. In the sense that they

---

*Hózhǫ́.

are alive, they are alike. But, they are also differentiated by means of their names, their offerings, and their prayers.

All diyinii can be individually labeled sǫ'a naghái bik'e hózhǫ́. Examples of other beings commonly labeled in this way include a human being, an animal, a plant, a "jewel,"[6] a "fabric" a cloud, and a hogan. But, there is another use common in the stories that emphasizes the relationship between beings rather than the bounding of discrete individuals. That is, one apparently complete entity labeled sǫ'a naghái is paired with another labeled bik'e hózhǫ́. We have already encountered at least two examples of this—one being sǫ'a naghái ashkii and bik'e hózhǫ́ at'ééd, the other being the "inner form of the Sky" (sǫ'a naghái) paired with "the inner form of the Earth" (bik'e hózhǫ́). In the Chief Hogan Songs" of Slim Curley we find another context for this relational use:

> Of Water Woman's origin I have full knowledge
> Of collected water's origin I have full knowledge
> Now of long life's, now of happiness's origin I have full
>   knowledge.
>
> (Wyman 1970: 113)

This type of statement can be used to describe a vast number of beings. Here, I will limit myself to a discussion of the more important (and more common) ones. The first set is the "twelve-person group,"* who existed (as described in Chapter 3) in some sort of prototypical form in First Man's medicine bundle. The following pairs are related as (sǫ'a naghái) (bik'e hózhǫ́):

> Darkness—Dawn
> Evening Twilight—Sun
> Talking God—Calling God
> Boy-who-returns-with-a-single-corn (kernel)—Girl-who-
>   returns-with-a-single-turquoise
> White Corn Boy—Yellow Corn Girl
> Pollen Boy—Corn Beetle Girl

Some of these pairs have already been described as ałkéé naa'aashii; in fact, all of them are. A song to the twelve very nicely describes the spatial aspect of that (ałkéé naa'aashii) concept:

---

*Wyman (1970: 167) in a footnote suggests that sǫ'a naghái ashkii and bik'e hózhǫ́ at'ééd created these twelve..

Now Darkness one is ahead in coming along. . .
Behind him long life goes along. . .
Behind him happiness goes along. . .
Then behind him Dawn comes along.
Behind him long life. . .
Behind him happiness. . .

(Wyman 1970: 166)

The other ten are then sung to in about the same way. But, at the end of each stanza "before-behind" is used for the first of each pair and "behind-before" for the second.

The various cardinal phenomena diyinii, most of whom are members of the twelve-person group, are also variously related as (sạ'a naghái) (bik'e hózhǫ́). To reiterate something of what was said in the previous chapter, a reference to the cardinal phenomena by name or by reference to various dine'é, or to the mountains, or to those named as the inner forms of the mountains, or to the direction is not necessarily a reference to mutually exclusive beings. Similarly, depending on context, each pair of inner forms is related in a Calling God/Talking God way, as yé'ii, as ałkéé naa'aashii, as well as being related as (sạ'a naghái) (bik'e hózhǫ́).

But, an additional aspect of the sạ'a naghái bik'e hózhǫ́ relationship that has already been briefly alluded to is that it is hierarchical. Thus, on one level, Blanca and Hesperus Peaks are paired as (sạ'a naghái) (bik'e hózhǫ́); on a second level, the beings that are associated with these peaks stand within them as a (sạ'a naghái bik'e hózhǫ́) pair. Thus, for Blanca and Hesperus we have the following structure:

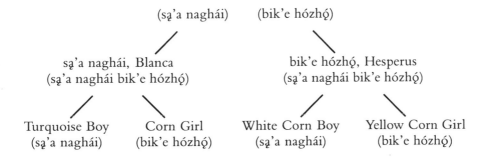

Blanca Peak then combines with Hesperus to form a są'a naghái bik'e hózhǫ́ entity, while at the same time they are each themselves są'a naghái bik'e hózhǫ́. Finally, they contain within them a pair related as (są'a naghái) (bik'e hózhǫ́).

Thus far, then, są'a naghái bik'e hózhǫ́ seems very analogous to our concept "system." It bounds entities which may contain within them other entities, as well as themselves being contained by larger entities. We thus have an analytical device which enables us to begin to see how the Navajo universe is divided and bounded. In this regard, the two questions of the extremes present themselves: the first being, "What is the largest entity that is są'a naghái bik'e hózhǫ́?"; and, the second, "What is the smallest?" That is, at what point does one have only components, a są'a naghái and a bik'e hózhǫ́ "part" that are themselves not są'a naghái bik'e hózhǫ́? There is, of course, no absolute answer to either question, especially in the case of the former. All paradigms leave the question of the largest system open.

At the other extreme more can be said. We have already considered a temporally limited example of a male being only są'a naghái. A more general exception is the case of twins. Here, the first born is są'a naghái and the second bik'e hózhǫ́; neither are themselves są'a naghái bik'e hózhǫ́. The expected traditional behavior toward twins reflects this—they are not to be separated but should live together throughout their life. Additionally, they are treated as a single patient in a ceremony.

A married couple is also są'a naghái bik'e hózhǫ́ (as here is, of course, each partner) and there seems to be a feeling that a couple represents a stronger entity than does a single person. Men often tell stories relating to this. One common theme is how they were married off at a fairly young age to an older woman who got them to settle down. A second theme concerns the death of a wife and how her widower "went wild" and felt helpless. The stories about jealousy also reflect this general idea. For acute jealousy to occur, a strong dyadic boundary must co-exist with a relatively weak ego boundary.

In general, the more inseparable a pair is, the more likely they are to be regarded as a single entity by Navajo theoreticians. An extreme example is the case of White Shell Woman and Changing

Woman. The most common school of thought is that they are two names for a single person. But Grey Mustache, for one, says that they are two; also, in some songs (Wyman 1970: 447, for example) the two are paired in a (sǫ'a naghái) (bik'e hózhǫ́) relationship.

The pair Nayéé' Neezghání and Tóbájíshchíní, already discussed in the previous chapter, offer a related example. They are twins and therefore inseparable; they are a single entity composed of two parts. Within the dyad, Nayéé' Neezghání takes the part of leader, hero, male. Tóbájíshchíní takes the role of female, stay-at-home, protector of his brother from afar. Nayéé' Neezghání goes out to kill the monsters, while Tóbájíshchíní remains in the hogan watching a prayerstick to see if his brother is in trouble (at which time presumably he makes some sort of ritualistic, or more physically direct, intervention). Most of the "inner forms" are inseparable pairs, but again, there is debate on this. Also, dyadic entivity is greatly contingent on context.

It has been pointed out elsewhere that the key problem in ethnographic discovery is in hitting the right slice, or in finding the correct bounding of the universe. Sǫ'a naghái bik'e hózhǫ́ minimally is a device which enables us to do this. It allows us to see and to create wholes as Navajos see and create them. Often these boundings are noncongruent with those that we have been taught are important or "real." In general, our culture stresses monads as the basic and strongest unit of, say, society. The larger units are built on this, and boundaries (or entitivity) become progressively weaker as one moves upward. A moment's reflection on this "fact" points up that it is perhaps not so obviously "correct." Humans exist as monads only in very unusual situations; hermits are one example (although as Molière has pointed out, they carry their society with them), "feral children" are perhaps another example; but if the literature (or the creation of the children in the literature) is correct, these children are not very "humanlike." In short, the larger units that human beings compose (especially "families," however we define that unit) seem to have stronger boundaries than the units that compose them.

At one level, then, we have a device that enables us to discover a part of the Navajo world view. This alone is rather important, as most "emic" or "ethno" oriented ethnographers begin their analyses

with the assumption that theirs and the native's worlds are basically the same. (On this point, see Farella 1976.) But, beyond this
we can begin to study entitivity, wholes, or bounding in general.
We can begin to ask what there is about something such that we
perceive it as a whole rather than as a part or as incomplete. The
task is made simpler and more attainable by the fact that Navajo
theoreticians often disagree on boundariness. It is through these disagreements that we can perhaps begin to understand what entitivity
is all about. Stated slightly differently, it is through the disagreements that one can begin to discern the paradigm (in Kuhn's sense).
The paradigm is simply that which the debaters accept as given (or
phrase their disagreement in terms of).[7]

One final point. On whatever basis Navajos bound an entity, it
is not in terms of homogeneity. Wholes seem to be composed of
two parts which are in a sense complementary and in another sense
opposed. We now turn to a more detailed examination of the criteria
for wholeness, only to discover that we already know most of them.

SẠ'A NAGHÁI BIK'E HÓZHǪ́: A SYNTHESIS

Thus far in this work, I have attempted several things. This monograph is first an attempt to explain certain concepts in Navajo philosophy which are both important in their own right and are essential parts in the understanding of the whole that is associated with
sạ'a naghái bik'e hózhǫ́. A second thing I have attempted is something of a simulation. When one starts to learn anything Navajo (or
I suppose anything else for that matter) one begins with a large
number of seemingly unrelated pieces, with no notion of how they
fit together. In the Navajo case the discovery of the integration is
made quite a bit more difficult by the number of previous writings
that are, with notable exceptions, misleading. I have in part attempted to replicate this feeling of unrelatedness and to withhold
the synthesis which I think puts the pieces together. I have done this
in large part because it was the way the learning experience was
structured by and for me.

The following story segment was given to me by Grey Mustache. It was related at the end of two years of talking to him, and it
was, unfortunately, the last discussion I had with him. He presented
it as something very important, and he presented it as the story that
would put things together for me:

First Man thought about what would be the most important
thing in peoples' lives, very much like people do today. He
thought about possessions, especially livestock and the various
means of making a living, and he thought about ideas and about
plans people make for the future. He realized his medicine, the
ánít'į was necessary for all these things. Further, the medicine was
necessary to make possible all the benefits of hózhǫ́ǫ́jí. But, although what he did brought all those things into being that benefit mankind, the reason he did these things was for himself, for his
own benefit. Thus, the ones that know hózhǫ́ǫ́jí nowdays don't
say that First Man said "Let it (the ánít'į) set there." That instead is
the kind of thing that Coyote would say. The reason that First
Man left it behind was to provide the potential for things in the
fourth world.

Most people who tell this story start on top, on the earth's surface, but it started down below in the First World when the medicine that was left behind, the ánít'į, was created.

It began with First Man's thought, and he was thinking again
about generations of growth, how animate beings would continually increase. And having thought about this he set to work on
his wife, that is, he had intercourse with her. After he did that, she
started out having children. He had achieved what he had thought
about, he had assured continuous birth in the future.

It is by means of sạ'a naghái bik'e hózhǫ́ that this is assured.
You see the semen of First Man is called sạ'a naghái, and the reproductive fluid of First Woman is bik'e hózhǫ́. That's what sạ'a
naghái bik'e hózhǫ́ is all about, it is by means of these that we
increase to this day.

But it not only animates beings, it is also what causes males and
females to become sexually excited. If these had not been created,
there would have been no separation of the sexes in the underworld. If there had been no separation, there would have been no
generational increase. From there sạ'a naghái bik'e hózhǫ́ was
placed into us and into all animate beings.

The first children they had were twins. He immediately killed
them. He ripped off their skin and their fingernails and everything
else. He used their skin for medicine and carried it with him and

[177]

with this he remade them as a whole. From this moment, from this act, ałkéé naa'aashii were spoken of. From the time that they were reanimated. His medicine became of use to people today according to that. This is when dził łeezh was given to us; this is what was called ánít'ị.

From these beginnings, breath was placed into the prototype cardinal light phenomena. And from there inner forms were placed into the mountains, the sky, and the earth. These were the first vehicles of bii'gistíín.

When First Man placed the ánít'ị, he placed the responsibility for generational increase into his children sạ'a naghái and bik'e hózhǫ́. Then they were sacrificed in a diyin manner. In exactly that way dził łeezh was given.

And along these lines these things will be asked about from child to father to grandfather. And the questions about these things and all else will ultimately be questions about kinship, how we are related to the beginnings.

This story made a whole out of what had seemed to me to be many disparate pieces. It further points out the unifying principle in everything. As the last paragraph states, there is only one type of question to ask about important matters, and that is the question of kinship, or relatedness.

Without this story there would only have been beginnings and no one later on to ask about or be related to that time.

Without sạ'a naghái bik'e hózhǫ́ there would have been neither the assurance of (in the form of sexual desire) nor the mechanism for animation; there would have been no continuity of generations, no death, no wealth, no ceremonials. In short, nothing of any importance.

In a previous section we noted that sạ'a naghái bik'e hózhǫ́ was in some sense wholeness or entitivity. As Westerners we are inclined, I think, to relate that to ego, to the performance of the individual. Here, with sạ'a naghái bik'e hózhǫ́, the importance is placed on, and the wholeness is derived from, one's relationship to the beginning, to the past, to one's father, one's grandfather, to First Man and First Woman, to Changing Woman. A current metaphor in our society is that of one's roots, one's beginnings, and interestingly enough the same metaphor is used in Navajo. An animate being, one who is sạ'a naghái bik'e hózhǫ́, is rooted to the Earth, and this anchor extends downward into Her. By means of it one is sustained and nurtured. By saying that one is sạ'a naghái bik'e hózhǫ́ makes emphatic one's direct relationship to the beginning of life in the universe.* And, by going back to these beginnings one's direct relationship to current life, all who are "my brothers" or "my sisters," is emphasized.

Looking ahead, by being sạ'a naghái bik'e hózhǫ́ my direct relationship to and responsibility to future generations is accentuated. An important part of this is the sexual desire in me, a part of my being sạ'a naghái bik'e hózhǫ́, which assures that I will have children and that they will have children. Further, a part of my relatedness to and knowledge of the beginnings is that I will practice and pass on to my offspring these teachings.

Finally, and perhaps most importantly, as a part of this I will die, my life force (sạ'a naghái bik'e hózhǫ́) will return to the Dawn and become part of the "undifferentiated pool of nílch'i" that will animate future living things. That is the "biological" part of things, as it were. But there is, additionally, a related cultural imperative. From an evolutionary perspective, as soon as we "decide" to pass on our programs genetically and culturally we become, at best, redundant. But, if a part of the teaching (the transmission of the cultural program) is that "It's up to you" to decide for yourself, as it is especially in the case of the Navajo, the death of the parent/grandparent/teacher is culturally mandated. The Navajo imperative on not giving up certain knowledge until one is ready to die is then more than mere "belief" or "superstition", it is an essential part of the cultural programs that are transmitted.

The gradual relinquishing of boundary and of ego as one grows older in the ideal case is again a part of this process, as is the absence of ch'ı̨́ı̨́dii (or a part of one's spirit that holds on to life). On the other side, the "witch" does exactly the opposite. He not only holds on to ego and boundary at the expense of his progeny, but he refuses to pass on his cultural programs. He refuses to transmit his knowledge. A witch could then be defined as one who passes on his programs neither genetically nor culturally. In the ánít'ı̨́ báhoghan he reuses the life force and life stuff of his offspring to perpetuate him-

---

*Certain stars, the sky, other "non-earthly" phenomena are included; hence, the use of the word "universe."

self. Further, he refuses to (and cannot) pass on what he knows. He becomes an island. In a way he is like diyinii before the creation of sąʼa nagháí bikʼe nózhǫ́. At that time, there were no births and no deaths.

There are two aspects of this view that should be mentioned. One is the negative feelings that Navajos have for someone who lives too long. A second point was alluded to earlier. With ignorance come accusations of witchcraft, which encourage a refusal to transmit knowledge, which breeds more ignorance, and so on. By not allowing (or by not making it appropriate for) older people to teach, we do not allow them to complete their lives and we do not allow them to attain the relative egolessness that is a part of the "ideal" death. Another way of seeing this is that the society, by means of witchcraft accusations, increases witchcraft types of behavior.

Overall then, the entitivity that we alluded to earlier as characteristic of sąʼa nagháí bikʼe hózhǫ́ is characterized by a de-emphasis of the egoistic boundary. Sąʼa nagháí bikʼe hózhǫ́ bounds animate beings, but by reference to the beginning, the future, and one's relatedness to other beings, rather than by rigidification of the skin that appears to enclose us.

The relatively clear form that most animate beings have today was not always so. The "In the beginning time" was inhabited by "mist" or "haze" people. Physical descriptions of diyinii by people today are universally quite vague.* Additionally, indefiniteness of form is recalled and replicated at several points in the ceremonial system. "Mirage stone" and "Haze stone" are an essential part of most medicine bundles; the "talking prayersticks" to ałkééʼ naaʼaashii are made from them, for example. "Talking" and "Calling" gods are often described in a haze or mist way (as "White Mist Talking God"); Changing Woman was conceived after mist or haze covered the mountain, and so on.

With the solidification or, perhaps more accurately, the completeness of form, went a corresponding absence of increase. This is

---

*People say "We're not really sure how they (diyin dineʼé) looked; they were probably half-animal and half-human."

the time when there were "no births and no deaths." When First Man and First Woman created sexual desire this all changed again. It is as if the completeness of form is counter-balanced by an incompleteness of affect. Another way of looking at this is that with completeness of the individual, there was no process. For, as we already noted in the chapter on ałkéé naa'aashii, the teleological imperative of generational continuance is responsible for all process and change in the universe.

The one who is both complete of form and of affect is, of course, the hermaphrodite. But, with the completeness is the incompleteness or lack of need for future generations, and therefore the lack of society. It is, I think, no accident that the First Death Person who is now chief of the underworld is most commonly referred to as a hermaphrodite. This is, of course, what nádlee told First Man during the separation of the sexes. "Through me there will be no continuance, no future generations." In short, no process.[8]

Są'a naghái bik'e hózhǫ́ then is completeness, but its source is the lack of completeness of the individual. As Westerners we often view the complete person as the man apart, the one who can go it alone. In the Navajo context the emphasis is on being a part of the past, the future, and of the world around us. The phenomenon of being a part of something is most immediately affectually based. The feelings that matter to human beings, as for example those based on sexuality, have są'a naghái bik'e hózhǫ́ as their source; other emotions that matter are derivatives of these. But, all affect of any consequence to human beings is associated with incompleteness. Navajos know that the rigidification of form is something of an illusion. As McNeley has pointed out and as we alluded to earlier, our skin is a very permeable interface, especially at the whorls of our feet, our hands, our fingertips, and the top of our head. By means of nítch'i we are connected to all beings around us, and by this means our feelings and thought are aspects of connectedness, rather than attributes of an illusory self.

Są'a naghái bik'e hózhǫ́, then, is continuous generational animation. McNeley is correct in equating it with nítch'i, the "wind" or "air" that animates all beings. And Witherspoon is also correct in

[181]

describing sạ'a naghái and bik'e hózhǫ́ as "the central animating powers of the universe."

The sources of this power on the earth's surface are the cardinal light phenomena—Dawn, Daylight, Twilight, and Darkness; the mountains; the Sun and Moon; and the Sky and the Earth. From these the sheep, the hogan, the plants, different animals, the waters, and all other living things were, and continually are being, animated. From these primary beings we ourselves were, and continually are being, given life.

Ultimately, however, there is only one source of sạ'a naghái bik'e hózhǫ́, and that is ánít'į́. It has two manifestations, the one being reproductive fluid, the other being the flesh and life force of another living being. Utlimately the only source of life can be life stuff. It is that simple.

Today when we talk about these things, however, we are most immediately and importantly talking about dził łeezh and hózhǫ́ǫ́jí. Dził łeezh is a single symbol that captures all that we have discussed. Literally it is, of course, the mountain soil, the medicine bundle of hózhǫ́ǫ́jí, First Man's magic bundle. Earlier we described its make-up and some of its components.

It contains within it soil from the mountains of the cardinal directions, the mountains which are today the immediate source of life and breath on the earth's surface. The soil is also the earth's flesh. Relative to this, Frank Mitchell emphasized earlier that it was wetted by the dew. The soil is contained within "unwounded buck-skin," by which is meant the skin of a deer not killed in the conventional manner. Traditionally, it is said, the deer was run down and, when it lay exhausted, a bag filled with corn pollen was placed over its snout, thus suffocating the animal.

The bundle is, of course, sạ'a naghái bik'e hózhǫ́, the immediate source of all animation on the earth's surface. All the components are themselves sạ'a naghái bik'e hózhǫ́, from a limited temporal perspective, and ałkéé naa'aashii from an extended one. In fact, we primarily have a highly redundant ałkéé naa'aashii encoding. The cardinal phenomena, as already noted, are the primary referents of ałkéé naa'aashii, and the source of sạ'a naghái bik'e hózhǫ́ on the earth's surface. The killing of the deer is a replication of the ritual slaughter of the twins in the underworld, the life force not being allowed to leave either the twins or the deer. The bundle is then multiply alive, and alive through re-animation as its sources of life are all ałkéé naa'aashii.

Further, the primary function of the bundle and the rite, as previously noted, is reanimation. Three conspicuous usages of hózhǫ́ǫ́jí are at birth, at the girl's puberty ceremony ("kinaaldá") and for "renewal" of medicine bundles. All other ceremonies, each in themselves passages of a sort, have their báhózhǫ́ǫ́jí part. And, as previously noted, the story itself is primarily concerned with the re-animation of beings that existed from the beginning, not creation from nothing, but re-animation—the hogan, the mountains, the other cardinal phenomena, and the various "deities" are but a few examples.

As a part of this, hózhǫ́ǫ́jí is equated with the whole we label "Navajo culture." Especially in the sense that the continuation of the one is identical to the continuance of the other. "One day the practitioners of hózhǫ́ǫ́jí will wake up, and their minds will be blank; they will totally have forgotten the songs, the prayers, the story. It will be as if it never existed." And this loss is exactly coterminus with the end of the Navajo way of life. The two, hózhǫ́ǫ́jí and "Navajo culture," are regarded as a single entity. Another part of this is that the practice of hózhǫ́ǫ́jí is thought to make the Navajo people and the Navajo culture strong. When hózhǫ́ǫ́jí is practiced it benefits all, not, as with the other ceremonies, just the participants.

So, for the native, the bundle and the rite are multiply and highly redundantly symbolic of re-animation—in terms of origins, rites of passage, curing, social relationships, and Navajo culture. But there is an additional aspect that is supplied by an outsider.

In a monograph entitled "Navajo Pottery and Ethnohistory," David Brugge (1963) argues that hózhǫ́ǫ́jí is a nativistic or revitalization movement that began to emerge around two hundred years ago. He uses several types of evidence: primarily his material is archaeological, but he also includes historical and ethnographic materials, the latter based on the content and use of the ritual.

The basic idea is that hózhǫ́ǫ́jí developed as part of a movement away from Pueblo influence on Navajo culture. Archaeologically the two types of evidence are in the areas of pottery styles and architecture. Ethnographically, Brugge makes the following comment, which he labels "speculation":

> Blessingway holds a central position in Navajo religion and the Navajo way of life, giving both a unity in spite of a complex diversity. It is the impression of the author that most tribal religions lack this sort of association with a single basic ceremony which influences all the other ceremonies. Such a ceremony would seem to be one that the people acquired to fill a very great and basic need, such as would be the case with a nativistic movement. (Brugge 1963: 25)

The fact, already alluded to, that hózhǫ́ǫ́jí presupposes a non-zero-sum universe is very supportive of Brugge's hypothesis. Thus, it emphasizes and brings about growth, while costing no one. Further, the fact that the ritual hózhǫ́ǫ́jí benefits everyone on the Reservation, not just the patient, heavily supports it as, in some sense, an ethnic identifier.

Thus, the external observer and the "native" both see it the same way. For the Navajo it is, primarily, the ritual of reanimation. For Brugge it was a revitalization movement.

Brugge goes on to suggest that the nativisim of Navajo religion may still retain its power to adapt* to changing modern conditions. I tend to agree. But, what is to me so very striking is the redundancy of this "adaptation" encoding. If one bothers to listen to hózhǫ́ǫ́jí, it is strikingly apparent that that is what the story is about—a series of ecological, social, and economic adaptations on the earth's surface. Also, use of the ritual is a re-creation of the adaptation process described in the story, as applied to the individual (or other patient). That is, the ritual is used for the relatively major adaptations to life; it is invoked to aid in, define, and create major personal growth experiences. Further, in the above we have pointed to some key Navajo symbols, and here again their redun-

---

*Specifically in reference to Peyote.

dantly obvious message is growth, adaptation, and re-animation. Finally, an "objective" archaeological observer sees the same theme from an external perspective.

One final note. Navajos know very well about all levels of adaptation—ecological, social, and personal. In addition, they see it as basically the same process, and regard themselves as a part of, not separate from, it. They also happen to be very good at adaptation. But, most importantly, they know it is a risky business. On the level of a society, an old way can disappear; at the level of the individual, personal growth can lead to one's literal or symbolic death. Navajos certainly feel sadness for and mourn such happenings, but they are not very surprised by them. The risk, the danger, the uncertainty are inevitably a part of the process. Hózhǫ́ǫ́jí recalls and marks these deaths and rebirths of the individual. For him there will additionally be a relatively final death. The ritual also will mark the death of a culture. When hózhǫ́ǫ́jí is suddenly forgotten, that which we call Navajo will be permanently and irrevocably lost. That death is to be mourned certainly, but, if we accept process, it too must be accepted.

CONCLUDING REMARKS

"The first one (sa'a naghái) will own what is called repeated increase, the second one will own without decrease (bik'e hózhǫ́)" (Frank Mitchell to Father Berard Haile 1949: 206).

The Navajo term used for "repeated increase" is k'e'ąąńdílzhish; doo ńdínę́ę́sh is the term glossed "without decrease." Father Berard has this to say about them linguistically:

> K'e'ąąńdílzhish—a literative and a hieratic term interpreted to mean increase (endure) always or time and again, and doo ńdínę́ę́sh to mean without fault. The feeling is that the first term equates with continuance in time, the second with perfect contentment. . . . The two personify the most desirable goals in man's life. As a matter of course the two terms are not colloquial

but are very common in Blessingway songs and prayers. (Haile
1949: 207–8, n. 254).

The Frank Mitchell text continues with the common refrain:

Behind them it will be hózhǫ, below them it will be hózhǫ, above
them it will be hózhǫ, all their surroundings will be hózhǫ, their
speech will extend out in (a hózhǫ way). . . . (Haile 1949: 205–6)

And later:

You will be found among everything (especially ceremonial affairs) without exception exactly all will be sǫ'a naghái by means of
you two, and exactly all will be bik'e hózhǫ by means of you
two. . . . (Haile 1949: 207)

With the equation of sǫ'a naghái bik'e hózhǫ with ałkéé naa'aashii
we describe the process of continuous birth and continuous death.
Ałkéé naa'aashii describes, and is, the process. Sǫ'a naghái bik'e
hózhǫ is the vehicle for increase, reproduction, and sexuality.

At the time ałkéé naa'aashii were spoken of, dził łeezh and
hózhǫǫjí were given. So, we have hózhǫǫjí, ałkéé naa'aashii, generations of birth, and dził łeezh all equated. At a more immediate and
more concrete level, the source of sǫ'a naghái bik'e hózhǫ is the
cardinal phenomena, both the lights and the mountains (more concrete yet—the dził łeezh). Within each of the mountains and between the mountains are ałkéé naa'aashii.

Hózhǫǫjí re-creates the entire process. It first describes the history of life and recalls this animation for beings on the earth's surface. It reminds us of the birth/death opposition constantly, but
especially in the descriptions of the animation of the Sun, the
Moon, the mountains, and, with these, when it describes temporal
punctuation.

The medicine bundle is the symbol for and source of all of this.
The living soil is inside unwounded buckskin; within the skin of a
deer that was killed without allowing his life force to escape. It is
thus multiply alive. It further captures and replicates in the gathering of the soil for the bundle, the ałkéé naa'aashii in and between the
mountains. The ritual slaughter of the deer repeats the process in
the underworlds that began death and continued life.

And this bundle made from the skin of the animal that dies, but whose life force continues, is repeatedly used to animate and to re-animate beings on the earth's surface. Just as it was always used.

These beginnings, the history of animate beings, and the life within this bundle are all placed into us as diyinii, as sąʼa naghái bikʼe hózhǫ́. Thus, birth and sexuality are very "holy" or "sacred" things. The gods that matter then are not "on high"; they are within us. That which is the most "sacred" and revered is the profane.

CHAPTER 6

AND TIME TURNS
BACK AROUND

BLESSINGWAY AND NAVAJO CULTURE are, from the native perspective, identical. In addition, both describe not a fixed point in time, but an ongoing process of adaptation. In a sense then, this view is in agreement with those that view culture as adaptation. In another crucial sense, however, it is quite different, for adaptation from the Navajo perspective is rather different than it is from our own.

To oversimplify, adaptive or problem-solving strategies can be either technological or epistemological. The emphasis in the former is on altering the world, the emphasis in the latter is on altering one's perception of, or way of looking at, the world. As Westerners, we generally emphasize technological solutions. Navajos tend to emphasize the epistemological. The example most often cited in this monograph is ritual, which is as much oriented toward bringing about a gestalt shift on the part of the participants as it is in producing "objective" change.

This is all fairly obvious, but less obvious are the types of errors that are potentially produced if the two types of modalities are confused.

Acculturation studies done on the Navajo have, I think, mistakenly emphasized the "things" of acculturation. Specifically, they have stressed the behavior and the material world. They have looked at the technological and not at the epistemological, and they have seen the Navajo as becoming highly acculturated. This is a mistake. In what remains of this monograph I will argue that these technological changes are, in fact, an attempt to maintain a traditional epistemology. I further want to argue that the specific epistemological strategy employed is paradoxical—a labeling of the new as old and of change as an attempt to stay the same.

Thus, I am arguing that the Navajos are not change oriented but rather that they are changing in order to remain "traditional." Specifically, they are altering their technology to maintain their epistemology.

THE CONTEXT

First Man created the context that we, as Westerners, label Navajo. The story of the creation is a metalogue, in that the way in which First Man went about his creation is the way in which his children are "supposed" to behave today. In the last chapter, we quoted Grey Mustache's comments on First Man's motives:

> . . . First Man thought about what would be the most important thing in peoples' lives, very much like people today. He thought about possessions, especially livestock and the various means of making a living and he thought about ideas and about plans people make for the future. He realized his medicine, the ánít'į, was necessary for all these things. Further, the medicine was necessary to make possible all the benefits of hózhǫǫ́jí. *But, although what he did brought all these things into being that benefit mankind, the reason he did these things was for himself, for his own benefit. . . ."*

With this statement we should juxtapose Grey Mustache's reminder, at the end of the above story, that all questions are ultimately questions about kinship and relatedness. In short, we have the pairing of the social (kinship) and the selfish as givens. And, when First Man created sǎ'a naghái bik'e hózhǫ́, and with it sexuality and reproduction, he laid the foundation for both as two sides of the same thing: reproduction being the basis for kinship (the social); and sexual desire being both the assurance that mating and, with it, births would occur and that there would be competition for mates (the selfish).

First Man took a rather more realistic view than most social theorists, in that he accepted (and was instrumental in creating) both the social essence of man and his selfish nature. Taking both of these as givens, there are two general solutions for the social theorist and architect. The first is the one most commonly attempted by Westerners. It consists of attempting to alter the basic "selfish" nature of the individual. Thus, the proper content of socialization is defined as having a person alter this basic nature and be moved in the direction of humanism. The child is viewed as being born selfish, bad, animal, or whatever, and it is society's job, in the guise of his parents, to alter that and to make him into a good citizen, an important part of which has him giving to others.

Thus, by means of socialization, the attempt is made to subsume ego to society (a part of the more general process of subsuming nature to culture). But socialization (in the Western sense) is always very tentative at best. Unbalanced or uncontrolled ego is covertly waiting to spring viciously at society. Since socialization is in fact so tentative, it cannot be relied upon. Instead, society must ultimately be defended and propped up by authority, whether it be the army, the police, parents, or educators. The task is to defend the fragile society against the powerful and dangerous ego. So, from the Western perspective, there is no resolution, only a constant battle. Society has never won, but it manages to subsume or hold in abeyance most egos most of the time. When individuals rebel or act out, the solution is, of course, more society in the form of more authority, specifically more power.

The Navajo way of looking at things is in my opinion, rather more elegant if clearly paradoxical. The basic statement is: The social imperative is that you should be selfish; or, To be social, you must be selfish.

First Man's task, then, was to create society as a context where selfish or egoistic action would necessarily be socially positive. "Pure" capitalism would be an example of one such, rather unsuccessful, attempt at constructing such a context, and it might be noted in passing that revitalization movements in general (and very likely by definition) have the characteristic of redefining selfish as social, specifically of defining personal gain as being beneficial to all.

At any rate, First Man set about creating Navajo society so that, if man behaved selfishly, it would, at worst, harm no one, and, at best, benefit everyone. Further, his own actions are the model. Remember what Grey Mustache said, ". . . What he did brought all these things into being that benefit mankind, the reason he did these things was for himself, for his own benefit. . . ."

The essential foundation block in this endeavor was to assure that the process would be non-zero sum. Or in terms of the Navajo gloss, "ever increasing, never decreasing." As we have already pointed out, the mechanism for that is gender, sexuality, and reproduction. The way the system was "designed" was to ensure that growth could occur and that anyone's gain would not be contingent on another's loss. In fact, First Man did even better. He arranged it so that anyone's gain would, within limits, be of social benefit.

The sexual reproductive process is, of necessity, accompanied by a structure of relatedness, of k'é, of kinship. A fundamental part of this relatedness is the sharing of property and general sharing of gain. It goes further, however. As we pointed out above, the practice of hózhǫ́ǫ́jí and its accoutrements benefit everyone. And since gain or growth is hózhǫ́ǫ́jí, the gain of one should result, in some ways, in the gain of, if not all, many.

As has been pointed out above, the economic basis for this growth was (from the Navajo perspective), the sheep. If one did what was correct with them, the herd would increase. To refer back to anaa'jí and hózhǫ́ǫ́jí, "Some would be rich and some would be poor." And, as pointed out above, with the economic differences would go other differences. Also, one person's ·gain (being rich) would not be another's loss. The "real" economic base was, of course, not the sheep but an unrestricted supply of grazing land. This was the parameter that made possible the non-zero summation of the context.

In ethics and social interaction we see the same dynamic. As we have noted, the question of "proper behavior" is such that the significant parameters are defined very broadly. Within these bounds it is left up to the individual. Such a system is workable only if there is a minimum of required social interaction. It would not, for example, work in an apartment house. It would have a better chance of working in an environment where one's nearest neighbor was spatially very distant. When your primary ethical maxim is "It's up to him," then what "he" does better have very little to do with you.

To summarize, there is a paradoxical imperative at the base of Navajo society—"To be social, one must be selfish." The above discussion points to a second underlying maxim or basic premise, namely, "don't compete." Obviously the two can co-exist only in the non-zero sum or "increase with no decrease" context.

To understand these maxims and to more fully understand the "socially correct" we have to look at the opposite, at witchcraft. Whereas appropriate behavior is selfish and noncompetitive, witchcraft is selfish but competitive. It is the direct pursuit of distinctiveness or of ego.

To reiterate part of what was described previously, the most common (if not the only) theme of witchcraft stories is grave robbing and/or incest. They are both theft at the source, in that they take ánít'į́ from the non-differentiated generational context and use it in a personal and therefore antigenerational manner.

The body, put into the Earth, continuously animates Her. This occurs both through the release of the person's life force and through the body's decomposition, which also animates the Mother and the beings on the Earth who are Her children. As we have constantly stressed throughout this work, this is the essential process. There must be death and a release of life stuff and life force to be recycled. If there is not, it will be as it was in the underworlds with no births and no deaths. Grave robbing is theft at the source, in that it interrupts this cycle; by doing so, it is theft from everyone.

The second feature of the stories is incest. This again is "theft" from everyone. One's kinswomen are, in fact, described as "belonging" to the rest of society and not being "owned" by their families and clansmen. Sexuality is the mechanism for generational increase, just as, combined with marrying out, it is the basis of kinship and therefore the basis of society. Incest is a denial of generational increase and continuance because it is quite literally a denial of generations (e.g., my parent = my spouse). Again it strikes at the basis of and the heart of the system.

Not only does the "witch" deny the process through his actions, but he denies it by his thoughts and his world view. When a Navajo is labeled a "witch," it is seldom because of clear evidence of grave robbing or of incest. It instead usually describes someone who is making basic epistemological errors. During the life of an individual, ego intensifies from birth to (and is probably maximal at) adolescence. The movement into old age is characterized by a gradual relinquishing of ego.

Both of these extremes are essential to the generational process. Thus, the time of sexual maturity is the time when ego and selfishness are most intense. And it is through this intensification that reproduction and, with it, generations are assured. With maturation and movement into old age goes the teaching of one's children and grandchildren. This is a part of the relinquishing of self and of ego, a movement from being "apart" to being "a part." The generations or future one has created genetically, one also educates. The transmission of genetic programs is assured by the intensification of self (sexual desire). The transmission of cultural programs is a part of the process of de-emphasizing self, of relinquishing one's boundary, which in turn is a movement toward what is perhaps the final dissolution of boundary at death.

As we have emphasized throughout this work, these programs are not just passively transmitted. In the process, the complexity of the system increases. From the Navajo perspective we have talked about difference increasing. In terms of biological programs this is accomplished by mating with someone who is different genetically (marrying out) and reproducing. In terms of cultural programs, this is achieved by teaching and by being taught, by discussion and by argument—by bringing in what is new and giving out the old. It is through generations that it all happens, and it is in accepting generational or non-egoistic continuance that one can relinquish his boundary and accept dissolution.

The witch uses sexuality to perpetuate ego. He uses life stuff ánít'į (both corpse "medicine" and sexual fluid) to continually reanimate himself, rather than future generations. Similarly, he does not teach. He does not transmit cultural programs. In short, his goal is personal immortality as opposed to generational continuance.

We thus have a brief overview of the system as it is supposed to work as seen from the inside. The two social maxims are "behave selfishly" and "don't compete"; the context is non-zero sum. If one behaves selfishly but is competitive, one is a witch,[1] and the witch in stealing from the source can alter the context so that it moves in the direction of zero summation.

To be Navajo one must "obey" these two maxims. I propose that the acculturation process for the Navajo has been a series of attempts to do this. Externally then, the Navajos have appeared to become more like Anglos, but I believe that this external change has been made in order to remain traditional. That is, I am proposing that in order for the Navajos to remain "traditional" they have come to appear more and more Western.

I now want to look at two conspicuous attempts at adaptation in terms of these general parameters—hózhǫ́ǫ́jí and peyote.

TWO CONSPICUOUS ADAPTATIONS

Navajo culture allows for difference rather than insisting on sameness. It goes further than that, however, in that on several levels it relabels phenomena that are different as "the same." Navajo ethics provides us with a brief, already familiar example. The primary ethical imperative, if one could describe it that way, is, "It's up to him." To overstate slightly, anything anyone does can be subsumed under the heading "Navajo ethics." A whole variety (or a potential variety) of behavior (the things that are different) is relabeled as "the same," in this case as a part of the same culture or, more specifically, as a part of the same ethical system.

What is described as "traditional" today by Navajos are those ideas and things that are a part of Blessingway. The meta-statement contained within Blessingway is "the only permanence is change." So to be traditional is to believe in change.

In looking at hózhǫ́ǫ́jí from outside we see the "traditional" as being "new." For, as Brugge has argued and as we noted in the preceding chapter, hózhǫ́ǫ́jí is very likely a part of a nativistic movement. Let me again quote Brugge here, as he very nicely describes the specifics of what I consider to be the key element to such a movement.

> It is very probable that Blessingway . . . was the core of a nativistic reassertion of the Athabaskan way of life *with mechanisms for the integration of foreign elements* that were compatible with it. The "ceremonial break,"* a concept that pervades many aspects of Navajo life, was probably one of the mechanisms to Navajo-ize non-Navajo traits. . . . It was through the development of simple *mechanisms of this sort to allow for the symbolic Navajo-ization of foreign traits* that gives Navajo culture its incorporativeness, so that entire technologies can be integrated into the culture without causing basic changes, and the culture can be adapted relatively easily to changing conditions. *The flexibility* of Navajo material culture *seems to be in part due to the fact that permissive and restrictive injunctions* relating to material culture *are considered to be largely a private matter* for the individual to observe according to his own beliefs. . . . The relative isolation of the individual in dispersed family groups allows greater freedom than in an urbanized society and actions may be dictated to a greater degree by economic need and personal desire than by social pressure. (Brugge 1963: 22–23; emphasis added)

Aside from the conceptual error (the implication that Navajo society is opposed to the personal rather than the selfish being defined as social), this is a very remarkable statement. It, first of all, re-emphasizes a point made above: the context we label "Navajo" allows for a great deal of individual difference. A second point follows from this. Nativistic movements (at least for the Navajo) are not so much concerned with excluding what is foreign (purifying) as they are with incorporation by relabeling "theirs" as "mine" or

---

*The "ceremonial break" is, at the material level, an interruption or "imperfection" in a design. Two examples are the contrasting thread going out to the side of a rug and the interruption in the design around the rim of a pot. As Brugge states, these are very simple devices to relabel the things that are theirs as mine.

what is "new" as "traditional." Specifically we have the meta-statement "Whatever is contained within the rite/story hózhǫ́ǫ́jí is defined as essentially Navajo."

Then very simply by definition, by calling things that had been viewed as different "the same," one created "a society" or a culture or whatever you want to label it. Within "Navajo culture" there are ideas that are Pueblo, Spanish, Mexican, European, American, Ute, Paiute, and Havasupai, to name but a few. The People themselves include Anglos, Mexicans, and members of other tribes.

As an important part of this inclusiveness hózhǫ́ǫ́jí incorporated wealth acquisition as important. It further associated wealth with "living the good life," and it made the "selfish pursuit of wealth" an appropriate or even desirable life strategy.

We shall return to this in a moment, but for now let me contrast this strategy of inclusiveness with other peoples' seemingly quite conservative adaptations. Some groups (Pueblo peoples being one well-known example) have become very secretive about their cultural teachings. In general, they pursue distinctiveness by means of exclusiveness rather than by adopting a strategy of inclusiveness and relabeling as do the Navajo. At this point I recall something that I read or was told (unfortunately I cannot recall the source). An anthropologist (or linguist) was arguing that Native Americans really want to pursue tradition and the anecdotal evidence for this was that in the Pueblo he had worked, the most requested book was E. C. Parson's (1939) work on Pueblo religion.

As mentioned earlier, LaBarre (1972) makes a similar point in his more recent editions of *The Peyote Cult*. He states that his book had been much in demand among practitioners who wanted to be sure that "they'd gotten it right." This reliance on non-native, written sources in a native, non-literate context is very strange indeed.

So then, hózhǫ́ǫ́jí can, in part, be seen as an adaptation to a changing context. It, in turn, altered this context; or, to state it slightly differently, it was so successful as "short-term" adaptation that it was a long-term failure. Hózhǫ́ǫ́jí, especially the sheep, was a non-zero-sum strategy in a non-zero-sum context. The success of the adaptation (especially the large sheep herds) transformed the context to one that is clearly zero sum. As an indication we can look at the Navajo population on the reservation. On returning from Fort Sumner it was estimated to be 5,000–7,500.* Today it is 140,000–175,000, and the area of the reservation has decreased. The vast majority of these people are raised with non-zero-sum ethic (hózhóójí) and the associated cultural meta-maxims: "To be social is to be selfish," a part of this being "Attain wealth" combined with the statement "Don't compete."

My suggestion here is that the Native American Church provides a "solution" to the conflicting demands of the current situation. More specifically, it is an attempt to maintain the traditional maxims in an environment that is no longer appropriate to them.

Given the two basic rules and given the zero–sum ecology on the reservation today, there is no way to maintain the details of a traditional existence. If, for example, one is to be successful with sheep, one needs to compete with neighbors. Some people, in fact, do this especially by seeking remedy to grazing–permit violations in the tribal courts and in the local chapter. They are obviously not well liked. If one does not compete, one will remain poor.

This mention of grazing permits brings up a related point that has been alluded to rather indirectly. Much (if not all) of the difference described in hózhǫǫjí is quantitatively based. For example, individual difference seems contingent upon two things: large families and a difference in the quantity of one's possessions (especially the sheep) that was both a part of such difference and instrumental in creating other differences. Grazing permits are a very effective way of making everyone very nearly "the same" or, to state the converse, of eliminating difference that is quantitative.

The schools provide another example of difference diminishing. It is no accident that English is seen (by older Navajos) as the "one" language and ideology (in process terms analogous to the "one" language of the first world) that will replace their own.

There is, given this context, an adaptation that will enable a person to remain "traditional" in terms of noncompetitive wealth acquisition. But it necessitates certain transforms that require one to

---

*This could very easily be somewhat low.

be nontraditional in detail. It involves working for wages, most generally off the reservation but not uncommonly (although less elegant as a "solution") on reservation. If one works for wages off reservation, one very clearly is not competing with his neighbors. If it is on reservation or in border towns, it is less clear but still "acceptable." Certain other connecting threads are a part of this adaptation, however.

The "details" of the traditional Navajo existence has two primary features. The one is the sheep, and the other is the large, extended family. The wage-earning adaptation that satisfies the metarules "necessitates" that these details be altered.

The sheep are labor intensive, and this labor was until very recently provided by the children. With the herding, of course, went the taking and learning of responsibility, and, in turn, the acquiring of sheep (property) of one's own at an early age. Additionally, in a setting where there were no limits on grazing, the more children one had, the more sheep one could own. For those that do not know the reservation very well, note that the school, usually a residential or boarding school is now a "given" in that setting. Only very recently and in fairly isolated instances are the pupils taken by bus from their homes to school. The traditional labor force involved in herding is no longer available. Additionally, note that the upwardly mobile Navajo wants his children in school and often strongly encourages him to be monolingual in English.

Thus, one needs to be nontraditional (competitive) if he is to raise sheep. Even if this were not the case, the traditional labor force (who, in turn, were traditionally educated by this herding) is no longer available.

In a setting where there is no labor for herding and where herd size is limited, cattle are a better investment than are sheep. They are, first of all, more valuable.* Secondly, they require very little in the way of attention. They can be, and are, left for weeks at a time to fend for themselves.

---

*One sheep is a grazing unit. A cow is worth, I believe, five units. The value of a slaughter cow is, of course, much more than five times the value of a slaughter sheep.

Another function in all of this is that the advantages of geographic mobility in looking for wage labor makes certain related transforms advantageous. A nuclear family or a limited extended family is more mobile than the rather large, typical reservation residential unit. Given this limiting of family size, the boarding school and the shift to cattle make additional sense.

The Native American Church[2] enables one to make these adaptations and still remain "traditional." The changes inherent in the religion are defined as a return to an older, more conservative or "truly traditional" way of life, rather than as something new. The transformations which the Native American Church is instrumental in bringing about are, in fact, quite conservative in that they are the same transforms we have identified for hózhǫ́ǫ́jí.

The first of these is the selfish/social relabel. Peyote modifies the Blessingway definition of social in two related ways: first, by defining society in terms of a smaller or more restricted unit and, second (and perhaps as a part of the limiting), by redefining gender roles.

The first of these is exemplified by the changes that have taken place in witchcraft behavior and accusations. In brief, witchcraft is most effective (and most probable) between "relatives." More precisely, between "extended family" members. Characteristically, a witchcraft interaction is fairly long term and part of a social interaction that is more generalized qualitatively.

As a speculative hypothesis let me suggest that "witchcraft" accusations define or bound the periphery of one's society, relatives, or extended family. As resources are perceived to be scarce or more limited, the distance between relatives engaged in ongoing witchcraft relationships should diminish. That is, closer and closer relatives should become involved.

The fact of witchcraft behavior and/or accusations is not *per se* a reflection of anything "wrong" in the society. But if an essential characteristic of the society is kinship, or kindred relationships that are extensive, a sign of the breakdown of that society will be a change in the distance of witchcraft accusations toward closer and closer relatives. Further, an essential part of the ongoing nature of such interactions is that the "witchcraft" be returned in kind. A curing ceremony not only makes it better for the patient, it returns the "medicine" to the person who "originally" sent it.*

An interesting thing seems to be happening among certain Peyote practitioners to whom I talked. When someone is affected by "evil" sent by another, they do the traditional type of curing, but they deny sending the medicine back to the originator. Rather, they exorcise and then protect the patient with a "wall of good." More accurately, they surround the patient and his nuclear family with this wall. Thus, they cannot be affected by the thoughts or activities of anyone outside this boundary. This is simply another way of saying that the effective social network is made smaller.

Related to this is a reframing or relabeling of gender and generational roles. Characteristically, it was the female who brought stability to the family. Until males reached a fairly advanced age, there was not much for them to do and they were looked at as fairly dependent, fragile, and out-of-control types of beings. As previously noted, it was not uncommon for young men to marry somewhat older women, and the explicit purpose was to keep the male in control or to provide some sort of mothering for the recalcitrant youth.

Peyote superficially reverses this practice, while symbolically maintaining constancy. Men are the important members of the Church and it is the young to middle-aged men that are most active—in other words, just those individuals who had no status in recent tradition but who are most likely to be important as wage laborers. In addition, in these families the wife and children behave with almost a caricature of respect toward the husband/father who in turn is expected to work and to acquire and maintain wealth for his nuclear family.

Superficially then, there are two general types of behavioral transforms which make peyote adaptive to the larger American context. They are, first, the restriction of the active social unit in the direction of the nuclear family and, second, the labeling of the male as the key family member.

---

*The one who "started it" or originally sent it is obviously a matter of dispute.

At the same time, peyote keeps things the same symbolically. In general, I am arguing that ritual (or symbol systems) label or define things as remaining "the same" while permitting or allowing behavior to change in the direction of being more adaptive. Further (and I suppose this is obvious), this homeostasis maintained by ritual is at the level of the labeling of the relationship between the elements in the system. With peyote, this symbolic constancy can be seen with regard to gender. As previously noted, peyote is the only Navajo medicine which is solely female. Symbolically, peyote and the Native American Church are almost ultra-female. Combined with this is a Navajo basic premise which goes something like this: Stability (or the appearance of stability) can be maintained only with a strong female element. This has been described for marriage. Also note that Blessingway, itself a revitalization movement, stresses female symbols, especially the Earth and Changing Woman. Peyote, then, allows the male to behave differently by keeping or, in fact, strengthening his relationship with a female symbol, a relationship that is, in fact, required by "tradition."

One final thing that the Native American Church does is shift the resource focus from sheep to money, especially wages. While the herding has very clearly become zero sum, money is defined (just as pure capitalists think of it) as "ever increasing, never decreasing." The sheep have become dollar bills.*

The argument I am making is very simple and very general: Apparent change often (if not always) is conservative or an attempt to remain "the same." As Westerners we very often make the fundamental mistake of thinking in terms of the primacy of materialism and its associated technology. Thus, when we see a "native" working for wages and driving a pickup truck, we assume that he has, in some sense, become less of a native and more "Americanized." The converse error is also very often made. That is, when a Navajo goes to court on a grazing-permit violation or a Pueblo people exclude "foreigners" from a rite, we assume that they are trying to hold onto tradition.

---

*This should be taken very literally. In the Native American Church hogans I visited, large (roughly 2′ by 3′ or 4′) replicas of $100 bills were on the wall.

It seems to be that we are most often mistaken. When we talk about change we are usually talking about the things most important to us—the material. The Navajos have never been very good materialistically (any archaeologist can tell you this). They have, however, been good with ideas and, very likely as an extension of this skill, good at adaptation. From First Man (and especially First Woman) onward they have known how to use paradox.

This continues. An interesting and perhaps important question is, "For how long?" or, to state it slightly differently, "When will there no longer be Navajos?" In part, this is answered by the People themselves. In the stories, the Navajos predict the demise of their culture. But this may simply be another paradox. If a teaching includes within it the statement that the teaching will, at some future date, no longer be accepted, that teaching will always be valid.

NOTES TO CHAPTERS

Chapter 1. Navajo Religion

1. The Native American Church is an example of ethnography becoming a part of the philosophy described. LaBarre (1972; published first in 1938) notes that his book is used by members to assure "the correctness" of their ritual.

2. "Entirely different sort of thing" seems to be the presumption of those in the French structuralist tradition (e.g., Lévi-Strauss, Lévi-Bruhl). "On a different level" is more of a description of those in the British structural functional tradition (e.g., Bateson, V. Turner).

3. See Reichard (1944), *Prayer: The Compulsive Word.*

Chapter 2. Diyin Dine'é: Gods and Men

1. In this section and in most of this chapter, I discuss diyin and argue that it is unlike our concept "holy." In addition, the term dine'é does not properly translate as "people." It can refer to groups of people, as in its application to clans, but such a use is far too limited. One can talk about various "animal" dine'é, "plant" dine'é, and "natural phenomena" dine'é. It refers to a grouping or a set of entities that are in a way animate or, more precisely, capable of growing reproductively but that are not at all identical to that class of things we label "living." In the case of diyin dine'é, the gloss "people" does not readily describe their form, partly because it is not known, partly because the form of diyinii was (and perhaps still is) changeable and changing.

2. Allen Manning quite correctly, in my opinion, states that the -zhǫ́ stem is used in Navajo to describe that which Pirsig (1974) describes by the term "quality" in *Zen and the Art of Motorcycle Maintenance.*

3. Father Berard includes a note to the translation: "Coyote is the agent of First Man's witchery. First Man seems to pose as the savior of the holy people but, with the aid of Coyote, as a rule deprives them of some power that they happen to possess" (Haile 1932: 94 n. 22). I do not think this is quite the way to look at it and will elaborate my viewpoint later in the text.

4. A third quite important example of this is reserved for Chapter 3. It is the incident of First Man's "forgetting and leaving behind in the underworlds his medicine bundle."

5. Goddard (1933: 133–34) provides almost exactly the same account. First Man says "That they were discussing what should be in the world. They wanted to know how to live until old age. They had also discussed the Sun, the Moon, the mountains, the months, the trees and what should be on the earth."

6. In some contexts, there are four "brothers." In addition to nayéé' neezghání and tóbájishchiní, there are łeeyaanee' yání and tsói nádleehé. These last two may be alternate names for the first two.

7. The use of terms of ownership or possession to refer to knowledge is quite intentional and quite accurate. As Haile (1968: 29–38) points out, knowledge can be viewed as "intangible property."

8. McNeley (1973) is the work to consult on níłch'i.

9. Interestingly, breathing is emphasized in a very analogous way by Zen Buddhists.

Chapter 3. Creation

1. Almost the identical statement is found in Goddard (1933: 127).

2. There are several points, some anomalous to be made about bii'gistíín, on the one hand, and níłch'i bii'siziinii, on the other. Haile (and others) say that bii'gistíín describes the relationship between the "sacred" "natural phenomena" and the beings that inhabit and animate them. Níłch'i, he says, animates diné and dine'é-type beings, those that are like people and animals. This includes, but is not limited to, human beings. McNeley says that bii'gistíín and níłch'i are identical. I am quite certain that they are not; but I also am quite certain that the categories that Haile posits are too exclusive. At a minimum bii'gistíín is more tangible than níłch'i, but both exist within others to animate them. I suggest that the tangible beings that animate natural phenomena, like yé'ii and/or Talking and Calling Gods, are related as bii'gistíín to that phenomenon. But in addition, they (the ones who are bii'gistíín) are in turn animated by níłch'i. Also, in certain contexts, níłch'i may be regarded rather tangibly and in this limited sense be the same as bii'gistíín.

One further point. People who are not particularly knowledgeable will say that bii'gistíín is exclusively a witchcraft term. This derives from the fact that the term's most common usage today (and the only one that most people know) is in reference to yeenaaldłoshii—the skinwalker or werewolf. It refers to and describes the one lying inside and using the skin.

3. Depending on context, the same beings may be generically labeled yé'ii, on the one hand, or "Talking" and "Calling" Gods, on the other. The former use is found primarily in hózhǫǫjí, the latter in nine-night ceremonials.

4. Probably ntł'iz is the word he translated as "hard goods." I think a more appropriate gloss is "unmanufactured or natural valuables"; thus, turquoise is ntł'iz in its natural state but not after being cut and polished and put into a piece of jewelry.

5. Woman Chief or First Death Woman is a really interesting figure. In some stories she is First Man's mother-in-law; in Frank Michell's hózhǫǫjí she is the wife of the Sun. She is involved rather importantly in the separation of the sexes.

Today, she is in charge of the dead in the underworld, as she was the first to die. Some stories have her as a woman, some as a couple, and some as a hermaphrodite. See Chapter 4 for more on this.

6. Witherspoon (1974 especially) is in agreement with Haile on this point and most others. He sees są'a naghái bik'e hózhǫ́ as the source of hózhǫ́ in the universe and są'a naghái bik'e hózhǫ́ ánít'įįjí as the source of hóchxǫ́.

7. In a footnote Wyman (1970: 111) (following Haile) says that there were two bundles. The one was for hózhǫ́ǫ́jí and was later given by First Man to Changing Woman. The second was for witchcraft purposes and was kept by First Man and consulted by him concerning any plans he had in mind.

8. As in all creation, the knowledge of what is to be created, that is the knowledge of form, precedes the creation. There is no scientific or religious theory that does not have this "flaw"; it is just the way it is. If one rereads the above quote, it will be apparent that Changing Woman is here functioning in a way very similar to the way our scientists perceive or suggest that chromosomes, genes, DNA, RNA, or whatever, work. That is, she is at the same time the repository of the knowledge of form and the one who determines it; in short, the form of corn is encoded in her.

9. Dził leezh is literally mountain soil or mountain dust; but the most common reference, and the one automatically associated with the term, is to the hózhǫ́ǫ́jí medicine bundle. Thus, it is identical to hózhǫ́ǫ́jí bájish—the hózhǫ́ǫ́jí bundle. It is also hózhǫ́ǫ́jí bee azee'—the medicine of hózhǫ́ǫ́jí, although the label medicine is obviously a poor translation of azee' in this context.

Chapter 4. Ałkéé Naa'aashii: Universal Process Through Opposition

1. Wyman (1970: 484 n. 369) notes, "Thus Blessingway predicts that when ceremonials are discontinued for want of knowledgeable practitioners the end of the Navajo way of life will have come."

2. The emergence stories that do not make the cardinal phenomena primal make First Man and First Woman primal. Thus, in either case, gender is primal; this quality has always existed and will continue to exist.

3. English translations of the names of the mountains are really not translations at all, but Anglo place names of where the mountains are located. These facts differ with different writers and in different periods of ethnography, and quoting the English place names has become confusing. Sisnajinii, Wyman identifies as Blanca Peak; what Father Berard labels Perrin's Peak here, Wyman identifies as Pelado Peak. The others are the same.

4. "Use name" is a term that I made up. It is a not very happy alternative to "true name," which I want to avoid. There are no true names, although I suppose one could say that each entity has several true names. There are instead a variety of names that appear in particular contexts and that, when employed, aid one in getting the being to listen in a particular way. The way that tádidiin ashkii is addressed in hózhǫ́ǫ́jí is not the way that you address him in tł'ééjí, the aspect of him that you want to emphasize and utilize being quite different in each case. All beings are complex and multifaceted. To say that there is one "true name," just as in saying that gods are the embodiment of abstract moral or qualitative essences, totally denies this.

5. One of my teachers had a discussion with an Apache on the cardinal phenomena which was recounted to my research assistant some weeks later. In a certain prayer, the cardinal sequence was mentioned beginning with Darkness. The Apache said that they began the sequence in that prayer with Dawn. My research assistant and teacher agreed that this is unimportant as the phenomena are ałkéé naa'aashii. This nicely demonstrates how a synthetic statement or concept works.

6. In the literature, one finds a tripartite division of Sun and Moon entities. There is, first, an inanimate disc or set of discs that are the Sun and the Moon that we see. There is, secondly, an inner form for each of these. And finally, there are the ones that carry the discs across the sky—Jóhoonaa'éí and Tł'éhonaa'éí. This set of distinctions does not seem to work very well, or to be employed by the native with any obvious consistency. At any rate, I refer to the latter pair and I use the glosses Sun, Sun Carrier, on the one hand, and Moon, Moon carrier, on the other, interchangeably to refer to them.

7. Haile and Wyman interpret this paragraph as referring to the "main objectives of Blessingway." This is certainly true but quite incomplete and, in a way, trivial. Hózhǫ́ǫ́jí represents the whole; it is the main stalk. But the task is to understand it and the whole that it represents, not to reduce one thing that is not understood to something else you cannot possibly understand.

8. The seasons are associated with the other temporal phenomena and are themselves ałkéé naa'aashii. This is interpreted in various ways. Frank Mitchell (Wyman 1970: 380–383) associates the three winter months with Dawn; the three spring months with Horizontal Blue; the three summer months with Twilight; and, the autumn months with Darkness. The same sequence is maintained in the discussion of Changing Woman's transformations. In Slim Curley's (Wyman 1970: 234–38) version of hózhǫ́ǫ́jí the "two who were picked up" see her first as a woman greatly advanced in age. She then went to the east side of her dwelling, picked up a white shell cane, and approached and addressed the Grand Corn Stalk; after this, she sat down as a middle-aged woman. She then went to the south, where the same was repeated except that a turquoise cane was used; she then sat down as a woman about to be middle-aged. Then to the west with an abalone cane, and she became a young woman just about to mature. Finally, she went to the north and picked up a jet cane and became a young girl just about to become a young woman.

From my point of view, this sequence does not work very well. There is another way of looking at it which is perhaps more accurate. Some, Wyman and Haile included, argue that the four-season year is an adaptation from the Anglo calendar. They believe that the two-season, winter-summer year is "traditional." It is difficult to argue historically the merits of either position, but it is the case that the two-season year works better synthetically and hierarchically, that is, as a part of or extension of the other temporal divisions.

Thus, Changing Woman can be described as the one who has a change come upon her every six months. The summer is associated with the day and the winter with the night; they are ałkéé naa'aashii. Activity cycles are a part of this division. In the winter, the Earth and most of the beings that live on her surface rest (hibernate) or die; in the summer, they come back alive again, things grow, the hibernating creatures become active again. The Earth (Changing Woman) rejuvenates, becomes young again, and lives on continuously. Witches can do this on an egocentric basis as well. Similarly, *generations* of humans and other living things are a part of this process.

9. This is, of course, the same theme as that of the "shoe" or "moccasin" game, where the day and the night dine'é compete to see whether there should be only day or only night. Coyote, of course, runs back and forth between the two sides. The result is a draw; neither side wins the game, so that today there is half day and half night.

10. As an aside, it is interesting to note that translations, at least between quite different languages, always seem to be at a very concrete level. This leads anthropologists and others into some fairly interesting, if very likely totally inaccurate, conclusions on native thought. This is not to say that the conclusions are wrong—only that the target is wrongly identified.

11. This and a subsequent quote are actually from Haile's version III of hózhǫ́ǫ́ji by River Junction Curley. It is most commonly a part of anaa'jí; however, Haile in fact thought this version wrong (not hózhǫ́ǫ́jí, that is) because it included the story of nayéé'.

12. Wyman and Haile say that this is a reference to the seasons, primarily to the warm and cold weather, but also to the hunger associated with or "being inside" the cold, and the plenty that is "inside of" the warm weather.

13. There are other "aspects" to or stories about death as well, some of which I can fit into my schema, but some of which I cannot. The most difficult of these for me to understand is the story of First Death Woman or, alternatively, the First Death Couple or the First Death Hermaphrodite. She (he or they) was the one that first died immediately after the divination described above. Two were sent to look for her and saw her combing her hair down in the place they had just emerged from. The two are called ałkéé naa'aashii, and in most of the versions of the story they die shortly after they find her. When they saw her, she said, "All who die in the future will come back to me." Her place is usually described in quite oppressive terms, very like the Christian hell, on the one hand, and the ánít'į́ báhoghan, on the other. I do not know how she fits into things, and my ignorance was in no way alleviated by the fact that people refuse to talk about her, or are ignorant, or claim to be, about who she is and how she fits. Frank Mitchell, in his version of hózhǫ́ǫ́jí, attempts a synthesis by making the wives of the Sun and the Moon carriers into "twin" First Death Women, as the carriers already have a clear and established relationship to death. But I don't think that it worked. In the Haile (1932) text "Where People Moved Opposite" she is, at the outset, the mother-in-law of First Man, and largely responsible for the separation of the sexes. I can make some very tentative suggestions about her, but I strongly reiterate that I do not think she fits very well into any synthesis that I can think of.

She may be a source and a locus of egocentric eternal life. As explained later, this is essential "witchcraft" and directly contrary to the synthesis of world view offered here. Support for this point of view is in the reluctance of people to talk about the subject, and in the similarity of First Death Woman's home with descriptions of the ánít'į́ báhoghan. In addition, the ánít'į́ báhoghan is always described as being underground, although not necessarily in the underworlds. I myself dislike this view because it simply sets up another deity as the personification of evil.

There is another possibility that is more synthetic but potentially even less accurate. Bodies or corpses can be said to return to and to animate nahasdzą́ą́ shimá, "Mother Earth." Corpses also return to First Death Woman; there may be partial identity here, or perhaps some other relationship between the two. But, this is a long shot, and one that I do not adhere to.

The point of view I would most strongly (although not very strongly) support is that First Death Woman is a later addition to Navajo religion, having one of two sources. She may, on the one hand, be Christian or derive from Christian ideas of the devil and of hell. On the other hand, she may fall out of a revitalization movement. Brugge suggests, and I think he is correct, that hózhǫ́ǫ́jí is a part of such a movement. As previously noted, the Earth and Changing Woman are the source of wealth, and, as such, they are primarily nurturers, and only weakly báhádzid or dangerous. It may be that before hózhǫ́ǫ́jí, the Earth was viewed as a more balanced being, as almost all other Navajo deities are. If so, it would not be unusual to divide the Earth into two beings, one personifying the positive, the other the negative. This would be preliminary to elimination of the negative side altogether; that is, it would be a temporizing solution. Today, in fact, the character of First Death Woman is being forgotten, and the danger in the Earth is not very primary to her character.

One final note, First Death "Woman" is sometimes spoken of as an hermaphrodite. Stories of the hermaphrodite are extremely difficult to elicit; they are without a doubt the most valuable knowledge available to the Navajo. At the same time, they are very likely some of the most synthetic. The stories of First Death Woman may, in fact, be identical to the stories of the hermaphrodite. In ways to be explained later, the "witchcraft" association would tend to support this view. I strongly feel, although I have little evidence to support it, that this view is correct and that, if one wanted to do research on Navajo world view directed at a synthesis, this should be a primary target, ignoring for the moment the practical difficulties of getting anyone to talk about it.

Ch'įįdii, which is usually glossed "ghost" or "evil spirit of the dead," relates to this. A person who dies without adequate knowledge leaves ch'įįdii behind. But, what that is is difficult to identify precisely. Hóchxǫ́ǫ́jí-type ceremonies are involved with eliminating the ch'įįdii of various native beings; anaa'jí is concerned with foreign ghosts. This may be simply the memory of the dead one; some medicine men will, in fact, argue that the memory is its sole referent and that there is no tangible ghost. In general, however, there is a strong association between ch'įįdii and the corpse, but exactly what part of a being this is, I cannot say. It is also associated with First Death Woman; her location in the underworld can be called ch'įįdiitah.

Finally, there are the stories of the Sun and Moon carriers. They are paid in deaths, that is by receiving the life force and perhaps the ánít'į of certain beings who have died. There are various explanations for how this occurs; some say that they receive a certain set of life forces; as, for example, some say the Moon is paid in the deaths of Anglos. Remember here, as well, that the deaths being talked about are not just the deaths of human beings but of all animate beings. So, an alternative view is that some of the life force that goes to hayoołkááł dine'é and is "washed clean" goes, after that, to the Sun and the Moon. This is the view that I would accept; a corollary to it is that life force is redistributed to animate other "natural phenomena" as well.

14. McNeley was the first to find that one's nítch'i bii'sizíinii was, in some sense, ałkéé naa'aashii.

15. A way of describing this is in terms of the concept shimá or the shimá-shiyáázh relationship. Witherspoon (n.d.: 15) defines shimá at its most abstract as "any being or entity which gives or sustains life." Examples are the Corn, the Earth, the sheep. If his definition is correct and if my argument is valid, then death and the corpse would also be shimá. There is also a less abstract usage (n.d.: 6) to apply to "females of my own clan." Again the essential characteristic has to do with nurturing and/or giving and sharing food. It may be that all "witchcraft" is a violation of this shimá relationship. Basically, one can be shimá and give food, or be one who potentially can give you children; the two are obviously mutually exclusive. The "witch" uses the females of his clan sexually and thus steals from the ones who have a potential sexual claim on her. In using the Earth one steals from and denies her nurture to everyone. In short, the essence of k'é seems to be in the shimá concept and in the notion of nurturing. The essence of bąhági, or of "witchcraft," seems to be in both the taking of that nurturing from others and the sexual use of one who should be a nurturer. Also, interestingly enough, O. Werner has found no stories among Navajos concerning mother-son incest (although he finds examples of all other "types"). It may be that all witchcraft is a form of symbolic incestuousness in the shimá-shiyáázh relationship.

16. Zero sum and non-zero sum are terms used in game theory. Zero sum refers to a wager where one person wins an amount and another loses an equal amount; hence, $(+\$1) + (-\$1) = 0$. Non-zero sum refers to a context where a gain (or a loss) is not balanced some place else in the context. "Pure" capitalism has often been thought of as a non-zero-sum game. "Increase with no decrease" is clearly a non-zero-sum concept.

17. Menstruation is, quite obviously, part of an ongoing cycle and therefore has no "real" beginning or end. One can punctuate his description of it anyway that one wants. In our culture such descriptions begin with the "death" or the shedding of the lining of the uterus; the bleeding is "caused" by this. Navajos, on the other hand, take the blood as a signal for, the beginning of, or the "cause" of fertility. As such, its primary association is beauty (in fact, kinaaldá is a celebration of the first period) and not ugliness.

18. I will use maleness and femaleness to refer to these fairly abstract gender qualities and will use male and female to refer more to external or superficial appearance. But, essence-type words are rather stilted and artificial in English, and I would like to use Navajo terms. There are such words, but they present problems—very likely, more in my knowledge of them than anything else. Ba'áád ("female") and bik'ą ("male") would, on first glance, seem to be the abstract terms I want. One can divide, for example, stories and chants into a ba'áádjí and bik'ąjí. Further, in the stories diyinii sometimes use these as terms of address toward their mates, as, for example, shik'ą ("my husband"). But, people say that the term should not be used to apply to human beings as it has a gross, insulting connotation, implying strongly the notion of animal sexuality. But, in its abstract usages, it does not seem to have this connotation. Perhaps, this is my problem; it may be that the very abstract can be reduced to or derived from the very mundane, like the "animal sexuality." In fact, in the next chapter we shall see that this may not be too far off the mark.

19. This is one of the few texts that Haile wrote down only in English; this is really unfortunate. It is a very important story and, I am sure, is more subtle than the translation conveys.

20. Ursula LeGuin (1975: 85) has this to say about the third person pronoun in English: "Many feminists have been grieved or aggrieved by *The Left Hand of Darkness* because the androgynes in it are called 'he' throughout. In the third person singular, the English generic pronoun is the same as the masculine pronoun. A fact worth reflecting upon. And it's a trap, with no way out, because the exclusion of the feminine (she) and the neuter (it) from the generic/masculine (he) makes the use of either of them more specific, more unjust, as it were, than the use of 'he'."

Chapter 5. Sǫ̀'a Naghái Bik'e Hózhǫ́

1. Haile (1943: 90–91) makes a rather feeble attempt suggesting that the "knowledgeable" people "transposed" the central term so as to hide the meaning from lay people.

2. A related personification in a fragmentary text on star lore elicited by Haile (1947: 50) is of some interest. It concerns what are for us the constellations Orion and Pleiades; they gave birth to twin(?) girls, the daughter of Orion being called sǫ̀'a naghái and the daughter of Pleiades bik'e hózhǫ́. By intercourse with the Sun, both of these girls, in turn, gave birth to boys. The child of sǫ̀'a naghái was called yé'iitso. Bik'e hózhǫ́, the sister of sǫ̀'a naghái, gave birth to twin boys called "monster slayer" and "born for water." What is of particular interest here is the balance or opposition alluded to earlier. On the one hand the most fearsome of nayéé', on the other the most heroic and useful of diyinii—opposed, but in this case, "brothers."

3. Ceremonies are by no means exclusively for curing. Things can be wrong and a ceremony needed even when there is no illness. Similarly, a man may have a ceremony (often as a celebration) when things are going really well. Any reason (or none at all) is adequate.

4. Father Berard explains (p. 318, notes 67 and 68) that "The Milky Way Boy is identified with the Hard Flint Boys in the form of the constellation Pleiades, who travelled by means of the milky way and rainbow."

5. Navajo-English dictionaries translate álílee as "supernatural" which helps very little. It refers, I think, primarily to sensory or physical excellence. To see great distances, to move very quickly, to sense or perform in a superhuman way is álílee. To become invisible, as in what follows, is an example.

6. Ńtł'iz is usually glossed "jewel" or "hard goods," yódí, "fabric" or "soft goods." But, "raw material" versus "manufactured goods" seems to better describe the distinction. For example, turquoise is ńtł'iz until it is put into a bracelet, ring, necklace, or whatever; at that time it becomes yódí. Interestingly enough, the presentation given to a singer for or as part of the ceremony is referred to as yódí.

7. See also Werner, Manning, and Begishe (1979).

8. Interestingly and predictably, the Navajo relabel the hermaphrodite as a social phenomenon, as bringing growth and wealth to the family he is born to. Alone he can do nothing, but in a context that is already decidedly social, he

possesses complete (both male and female) knowledge, and he transmits it to his kin.

Chapter 6. And Time Turns Back Around

1. There are two other possibilities. They are non-competitive and not selfish which would be "like Coyote" and competitive and unselfish which would, I suppose, be like a Christian missionary.

2. Brugge (1963: 25–26) has made a somewhat similar suggestion: ". . . it may well be that the nativism of Navajo religion still retains the power to adapt to changing modern conditions. The author suggests that a likely test of this hypothesis would be found in the future developments of the Peyote ceremony among the Navajo. If it should become another truly Navajo ceremony, Peyote way, so to speak, consecrated by Blessingway, this would be substantial evidence that Blessingway has not lost its unifying force in Navajo culture." In the areas where I lived, this seemed to be happening. It was not totally clear that "Peyoteway" was seen as "consecrated by Blessingway," but that was the direction things were taking.

BIBLIOGRAPHY

BATESON, GREGORY
1972 *Steps to an Ecology of Mind*. New York: Chandler Publishing Company.

BOHANNAN, P.
1957 *Justice and Judgment among the Tiv*. London: Oxford University Press for the International African Institute.

BRUGGE, DAVID M.
1963 *Navajo Pottery and Ethnohistory*. Window Rock, Ariz.: Navajoland Publications, Navajo Tribal Museum.

DYK, WALTER
1938 *Son of Old Man Hat*. New York: Harcourt, Brace and Company.

EVANS-PRITCHARD, E. E.
1951 *Social Anthropology*. London: Oxford University Press.

FARELLA, JOHN
1976 *"Limitations of Ethno-Scientific Methodology."* Paper presented at Southwestern Anthropological Association Annual Meeting, San Francisco, Calif.

FRANCISCAN FATHERS
1910 *An Ethnologic Dictionary of the Navajo Language*. St. Michaels, Ariz.: St. Michael's Press.

FRANK, JEROME D.
1961 *Persuasion and Healing*. Baltimore, Md.: Johns Hopkins University Press.

GEERTZ, CLIFFORD
1973 *The Interpretation of Cultures*. New York: Basic Books.

GODDARD, PLINY EARLE
1933 *Navajo Texts. Anthropological Papers of the American Museum of Natural History*, vol. 34.

HAILE, FATHER BERARD
1932 "Where People Moved Opposite." Unpublished manuscript.
1938 *Origin Legend of the Navaho Enemyway.* Yale University Publications in Anthropology, no. 17.
1943 "Soul Concepts of the Navajo." *Annali Lateranensi* 7: 59–94.
1947 *Head and Face Masks in Navaho Ceremonialism.* Saint Michaels, Ariz.: St. Michael's Press.
1947b *Starlore Among the Navaho.* Santa Fe, N. Mex.: Museum of Navajo Ceremonial Art.
1949 "Blessingway, Version II." A manuscript of a text elicited from Frank Mitchell.
1968 *Property Concepts of the Navajo Indians.* The Catholic University of America Anthropological Series No. 17. St. Michaels, Ariz.: St. Michael's Press.

JUNG, C. G.
1916 "Septem Sermones ad Mortuos." In *Memories, Dreams, Reflections.* New York: Vintage Books (1961).

KLAH, HASTEEN
1942 *Navajo Creation Myth, the Story of the Emergence.* Santa Fe, N. Mex.: Museum of Navajo Ceremonial Art.

KLUCKHOHN, CLYDE
1944 *Navajo Witchcraft. Papers of the Peabody Museum,* vol. 22. Cambridge, Mass.: Harvard University.
1968 "The Philosophy of the Navajo Indians." In *Readings in Anthropology.* Ed. Morton H. Fried. 2d ed. New York: Crowell.

KLUCKHOHN, CLYDE, AND DOROTHEA LEIGHTON
1962 *The Navaho.* Rev. ed. Cambridge, Mass.: Harvard University Press.

LA BARRE, WESTON
1972 *The Peyote Cult.* New York: Schocken Books.

MATTHEWS, WASHINGTON
1883 A Part of the Navajo's Mythology. *American Antiquarian* 5: 207–24.
1888 The Prayer of a Navajo Shaman. *American Anthropologist* (o.s.) 1: 149–70.
1897 *Navajo Legends. Memoirs of the American Folk Lore Society,* vol. 5.
1902 *The Night Chant. Memoirs of the American Museum of Natural History,* vol. 6.

McNELEY, JAMES KALE
1973 "The Navajo 'Wind' Theory of Life and Behavior." Ph.D. diss. University of Hawaii.
1981 *Holy Wind in Navajo Philosophy.* Tucson: University of Arizona Press.

MEAD, MARGARET
1952 *The Changing Culture of an Indian Tribe.* New York: Columbia University Press.

MORGAN, WILLIAM
1936 *Human Wolves Among the Navaho.* Yale University Publications in Anthropology, no. 11.

NEWCOMB, FRANC J.
1940 *Navajo Omens and Taboos.* Santa Fe, N. Mex.: The Rydal Press.

O'BRYAN, AILEEN
1956 *The Diné: Origin Myths of the Navajo Indians.* Bureau of American Ethnology, Bulletin 163.

ORTNER, SHERRY B.
1970 "Food for Thought: A Key Symbol in Sherpa Culture." Ph.D. diss., University of Chicago.

PARSONS, ELSIE CLEWS
1939 *Pueblo Indian Religion.* Chicago: University of Chicago Press.

PIRSIG, ROBERT M.
1974 *Zen and the Art of Motorcycle Maintenance.* New York: Bantam Books.

REICHARD, GLADYS A.
1944 *Prayer: The Compulsive Word.* New York: J. J. Augustin.
1970 *Navaho Religion: A Study of Symbolism.* Princeton, N.J.: Princeton University Press.

SCHNEIDER, D.M.
1968 *American Kinship: A Cultural Account.* Englewood Cliffs, N.J.: Prentice-Hall.

STEPHEN, ALEXANDER M.
1930 "Navajo Origin Legend," *Journal of American Folk-Lore* 43: 88–104.

TURNER, VICTOR
1967 *The Forest of Symbols.* Ithaca, N.Y.: Cornell University Press.

VON FOERSTER, H.
1970 "Thought and Notes on Cognition." In *Cognition: A Multiple View.* Ed. P. Garvin. Rochelle, N.J.: Spartan Books.

WERNER, O., ALLEN MANNING, AND KENNETH BEGISHI
1979 "A Taxonomic View of the Traditional Navajo Universe." Unpublished paper.

WERNER, OSWALD, AND KENNETH BEGISHI
1968 "Styles of Learning: The Evidence from the Navajo." Unpublished working paper.

WHEELWRIGHT, MARY C.
1949 *Emergence Myth According to the Hanelthnayhe or Upward-Reaching Rite.* Santa Fe, N. Mex.: Museum of Navajo Ceremonial Art.

WITHERSPOON, GARY
n.d. "The Central Concepts of Navajo World View (II)." Unpublished Paper.

WITHERSPOON, GARY (*continued*)

1974 "The Central Concepts in Navajo World View (I)." *Linguistics: An International Review*

1975 *Navajo Kinship and Marriage.* Chicago and London: University of Chicago Press.

1977 *Language and Art in the Navajo Universe.* Ann Arbor: University of Michigan Press.

WYMAN, LELAND C.

1970 *Blessingway.* Tucson: University of Arizona Press.

1973 *The Red Antway of the Navajo.* Sante Fe, New Mexico: Museum of Navajo Ceremonial Art.

INDEX

Acculturation, 189
Aesthetics, 35–36
Afterlife, 127
Ałkéé naa'aashii: and affect, 121–23; and cardinal phenomena, 102, 107; and gender, 112; and Jung, 148–51; and reanimation, 96–97; and Sun and Moon, 111; and witchcraft, 128–32
Ánít'íí, 33, 40, 79, 81

Báhádzid, 37, 160; and Changing Woman, 63
Bigáásh, 73, 76–77; as ánít'íí, 77–78
Bii'gistíín, 72, 105–6, 206 n.2
Blessingway. *See* Hózhóójí
Brugge, David, 183–84

Capitalism, 191–92
Cardinal phenomena, 40, 103–11; in creation, 98; inner forms of, 105–7; as wrappers for medicine bundle, 84
Changing Woman, 32; birth of, 55–56; characteristics of, 62–68; creates the Navajo, 86–91; relationship to First Man, 56–62; and reproduction, 100; as Sun's consort, 57

Coyote, 42–45, 58; and ałkéé naa'aashii, 123; on daily activity cycle, 109–11; on death, 126–27; on difference, 117; on marriage, 61
Creation: and ałkéé' naa'aashii, 126; as cyclical, 95; and death, 126; as differentiation, 119–20; and entropy, 95; and increased complexity, 95, 119–20; and information, 95; placement of inner forms, 72–74; sexual nature of, 75–76; of sheep, 91–92
Cultural change, 19, and epistemology, 189–90; and technology, 189–90
Culture, 18

Danger. *See* Báhádzid
Darkness. *See* Cardinal phenomena
Dawn. *See* Cardinal phenomena
Death, 45–46; and knowledge, 30, 179
Diyin, 64–69; as represented by First Man, 50
Diyin dine'é, 113, 172; characteristics of, 23–30; and context, 38; and earth-surface people, 25; and form, 70–71; and knowledge, 25–26, 37; as natural phenomena, 23, 30; rela-